The Message of the Psalms

THE MESSAGE

O F ▪ T H E

Psalms

A THEOLOGICAL COMMENTARY

WALTER BRUEGGEMANN

Augsburg ▪ Minneapolis

THE MESSAGE OF THE PSALMS
A Theological Commentary

Cover design: Pollock Design Group

Library of Congress Cataloging-in-Publication Data

Brueggemann, Walter
  The Message of the Psalms

  Bibliography: p.
  1. Bible. O.T. Psalms—Commentaries.   2. Bible.
O.T. Psalms—Theology.   I. Title
BS1430.3.B78   1984   223'.207   84-21734
ISBN 0-8066-2120-6 (pbk.)

Manufactured in the U.S.A.   APH 10-4370

To
Ernest F. Nolte
Whose heart is steady

Contents

Abbreviations

ATR	*Anglican Theological Review*
BAR	*Biblical Archaeology Reader*
BASOR	*Bulletin of the American Schools of Oriental Research*
CBQ	*Catholic Biblical Quarterly*
HTR	*Harvard Theological Review*
IDB	*The Interpreter's Dictionary of the Bible*
JSOT	*Journal for the Study of the Old Testament*
JBL	*Journal of Biblical Literature*
JNES	*Journal of Near Eastern Studies*
JSS	*Journal of Semitic Studies*
SJT	*Scottish Journal of Theology*
SVT	*Supplement: Vetus Testamentum*
USQR	*Union Seminary Quarterly Review*
VT	*Vetus Testamentum*
ZAW	*Zeitschrift für die alttestamentliche Wissenschaft*
ZTK	*Zeitschrift für Theologie und Kirche*

Preface

The Psalms are a strange literature to study. They appear to be straightforward and obvious. They are not obscure, technical, or complicated. Yet, when one leaves off study of them, one is aware that the unresolved fascination endures. Any comment upon them is inevitably partial and provisional. That is certainly true of such a limited manuscript as this. But the reason for the partial, provisional character of this study is not simply because of such limitations, but because of the nature of the material. There is simply more than can be touched and handled. So one finishes with a sense of inadequacy, of not probing enough. That, of course, is why the Psalms continue to nourish and nurture long after our interpretation has run its course. We are aware that the claims of the literature have not been exhausted.

1. I have assumed the great deposit of critical scholarship that is indispensable for study of the Psalms. I have not thought it useful or necessary to repeat all of that, or even to specify the sources of those learnings. But it will be evident that I am dependent on and do take seriously that fund of critical learning. Indeed, my basic plan of organization is derived from the form-critical consensus.

2. I have utilized a "scheme" of orientation—disorientation—new orientation. But I want to say, both to those who may critically assess the book and to those who may use the book as a door to psalmic spirituality, that I do not intend the proposed scheme to be a straitjacket. I do not imagine that the scheme is adequate to comprehend the Psalms, for we do not have such a "master key." I intend this principle of organization only to help us see things we might not have seen otherwise. The test of a good paradigm is whether it serves in a

heuristic way for future study. Most specifically I have used this device as a way of showing how the "psalms of negativity" may be understood in the life of faith.

3. In an attempt to be "postcritical," I have had in mind especially the pastoral use of the Psalms. By that I mean how the Psalms may function as voices of faith in the actual life of the believing community.[1] So I have sought to consider the interface between the flow of the Psalms and the dynamics of our common life. I am cautious, if not suspicious, about any neat grid of developmental stages or "passages." I am equally cautious about any neat grid of the Psalms, but it does seem clear that there are moves and seasons in the life of faith, even if we encounter them in various ways. I have sought for the interface between *those experiences common to us* and *the offer of faith* in the Psalms. I do not want to be rigid about this or reductionist. But I want to show that such a pastoral agenda can benefit from critical scholarship and need be neither excessively popular nor obscurantist.

Of the critical methods available, I have largely followed the form analysis of Gunkel, refined in important ways by Westermann. The threefold scheme I have used is centrally informed by the genre of the Psalms. Second, I have been surprised to find that Mowinckel's understanding of the creativity of the cult has been more helpful than I had expected. It has been mediated to me through Berger and Luckmann and their understanding that the "social construction of reality" is an active, creative task.[2] The cult (or wherever such social construction happens) is a setting for imaginative, creative speech that forms new worlds for us. And this is not remote from our experience. I have also tried to pay attention to the emerging methods of sociological[3] and rhetorical[4] analysis that are latent in Gunkel's work but only now coming to full attention. These methods suggest, as I intend to show, that what goes on in the Psalms is peculiarly in touch with what goes on in our life.

4. I have felt no obligation fully to cover all of the Psalms. If the scheme has viability, it may suggest how other psalms might also be placed and understood in relation to the whole. Specifically I have not paid attention to the royal psalms,[5] the songs of Zion,[6] or to the great historical recitals.[7] They did not strike me as the most useful for the present work. But that does not mean they are without value for pastoral concerns.

5. My main interest has been theological. I have concluded at the end of the study (and not as a presupposition) that the shape and dynamic of the Psalms can most usefully be understood according to the theological framework of crucifixion and resurrection. By that I do not want to turn the Psalms into a "Christian book," for I have repeatedly stressed the profoundly Jewish character of the material. Rather, I mean the following:

a) The moves of orientation–disorientation–new orientation are for Christians most clearly played out in the life of Jesus of Nazareth, but not exclusively there. I find Phil. 2:5-11 a helpful articulation of this movement. It can, without any forcing, be correlated:

> *Orientation*: "Though he was in the form of God...."
> *Disorientation*: "[He] emptied himself."
> *New Orientation*: "Therefore God has highly exalted him...."

I do not understand that in any ontological way and am not interested in Christological speculation. Rather, the life of Jesus, and especially the passion narrative, does portray his life in precisely that fashion, perhaps with special affinity to the liturgical destiny of the king.

    b) The liturgical form of this same matter is, for the life of the church, evidenced in Baptism. The same two moves that I have sketched in the Psalms are the key discernment of Baptism:

> We were buried therefore with him by baptism into death...that as Christ was raised from the dead...we too might walk in newness of life (Rom. 6:4).

We understand in Baptism that the loss of control of our lives (disorientation) is the necessary precondition of new life (new orientation).

    c) In the radical reflection of the Old Testament (in Jeremiah, Ezekiel, and Second Isaiah) these same moves are made around the destiny of Jerusalem.[8] It is a city that must be plucked up and broken down in order that it may be built and planted (Jer. 1:10). That same sense of deep cost and discontinuity has been important for Jews in trying to understand the Holocaust and the surprise of the state of Israel.

    d) All three dimensions of our tradition, the life of Jesus, the Baptism of Christian believers, and the destiny of Jewish fortunes around Jerusalem, attest to the reality that deep loss and amazing gift are held together in a powerful tension.

    The gain in this for the study of Psalms is that it shows how the psalms of negativity, the complaints of various kinds, the cries for vengeance and profound penitence are foundational to a life of faith in this particular God. Much Christian piety and spirituality is romantic and unreal in its positiveness. As children of the Enlightenment, we have censored and selected around the voice of darkness and disorientation, seeking to go from strength to strength, from victory to victory. But such a way not only ignores the Psalms; it is a lie in terms of our experience. Childs is no doubt right in seeing that the Psalms as a canonical book is finally an act of hope.[9] But the hope is rooted precisely in the midst of loss and darkness, where God is surprisingly present. The Jewish reality of exile, the Christian confession of crucifixion and cross, the honest recognition that there is an untamed darkness in our life that must be embraced—all of that is fundamental to the gift of new life.

e) The Psalms are profoundly subversive of the dominant culture, which wants to deny and cover over the darkness we are called to enter. Personally we shun negativity. Publicly we deny the failure of our attempts to exercise control. The last desperate effort at control through nuclear weapons is a stark admission of our failure to control. But through its propaganda and the ideology of consumerism, our society goes its way in pretense. Against all of this the Psalms issue a mighty protest and invite us into a more honest facing of the darkness. The reason the darkness may be faced and lived in is that even in the darkness, there is One to address. The One to address is in the darkness but is not simply a part of the darkness (cf. John 1:1-5).[10] Because this One has promised to be in the darkness with us, we find the darkness strangely transformed, not by the power of easy light, but by the power of relentless solidarity. Out of the "fear not" of that One spoken in the darkness, we are marvelously given new life, we know not how. The Psalms are a boundary (cf. Jer. 5:22) thrown up against self-deception. They do not permit us to ignore and deny the darkness, personally or publicly, for that is where new life is given, whether on the third day or by some other uncontrolled schedule at work among us.

6. My own thinking about the Psalms has taken place between the two quotes of Updike and Miranda that stand at the head of the book. Updike suggests that such religious language is "the words of the dead," the words that linger with power and authority after their speakers have gone.[11] Indeed perhaps because we are "speech creatures," the most enduring thing about us is our serious speech to each other. So I take these psalmic words as "the voice of the dead," who may turn out to be the most living, present, and powerful ones among us (cf. Heb. 12:1). Updike's marvelous characterization of Rabbit comes when Rabbit is face to face with these powerful words that he cannot mock or dismiss or trivialize, as he does almost everything else. That moment of candor is reenforced by Elie Wiesel's remarkable statement, "Poets exist so that the dead may vote."[12] They do vote in the Psalms. They vote for faith. But in voting for faith they vote for candor, for pain, for passion—and finally for joy. Their persistent voting gives us a word that turns out to be the word of life.

On the other hand, at the far extreme, Miranda speaks out of a very different context.[13] Whereas Updike speaks an artistic, literary reality, Miranda has almost no time for such aesthetics, but aims at the social reality. He brings to our work the hurt of the marginal and the critical tools of social analysis. I have not set out to do liberation theology, as Miranda might urge, for I have been committed to no goal but to hear the Psalms. But the psalm writers will not tolerate a faith in which human well-being is not honored. They are impatient with any God who thinks or acts otherwise. This Jewish insistence warns against any easy Christian spirituality. With force and regularity the questions of justice, righteousness, and equity are regularly brought to the throne, often to our surprise.

I am not sure that the offers of Updike and Miranda belong together. Updike's Rabbit would not think so, because passionate issues of justice are hardly in his purview. Too bad for Rabbit. Too bad for us, for Rabbit is a study about us and our affluent modernity. Perhaps that is why Rabbit at best is only at the very edge of this poetry. He cannot enter into it, claim it, affirm it, or be shaped by it. He cannot praise; he cannot cry out. And he is so much us. The Psalms are an invitation to Rabbit and all his clan to enter this world of dark discontinuity, for it is a world in which faithful address and answer make a transformative difference.[14] That is why "we shall all be changed." The Psalms will not quit. They have not quit. And they keep inviting people like Rabbit into the wholeness that comes in embraced brokenness.

Citations of scripture passages are either from the Revised Standard Version or are the author's own translations.

The dedication to Ernest F. Nolte is acknowledgment of a lifelong debt. He has been friend, teacher, mentor, colleague, pastor, model, and most of all, "believer-inner." He lives the pathos and delight of the Psalms. He is a man of the torah. He is like a tree planted by streams of water (Ps. 1:3). His heart is steady (Ps. 112:8). And we are better for it and blessed by it.

I add a special word of thanks to Professor Terence E. Fretheim, who has been a thoughtful and judicious editor, and to the director of book development at Augsburg Publishing House, who has supported me along the way toward publication.

"Laugh at ministers all you want, they have the words we need to hear, the ones the dead have spoken."
Rabbit in John Updike, *Rabbit Is Rich*

"It can surely be said that the Psalter presents a struggle of the just against the unjust."
Jose Miranda, *Communism in the Bible*

I

Introduction

The book of Psalms provides the most reliable theological, pastoral, and liturgical resource given us in the biblical tradition. In season and out of season, generation after generation, faithful women and men turn to the Psalms as a most helpful resource for conversation with God about things that matter most. The Psalms are helpful because they are a genuinely dialogical literature that expresses both sides of the conversation of faith. On the one hand, as von Rad has seen, Israel's faithful speech addressed to God is the substance of the Psalms.[1] The Psalms do this so fully and so well because they articulate the entire gamut of Israel's speech to God, from profound praise to the utterance of unspeakable anger and doubt. On the other hand, as Luther understood so passionately, the Psalms are not only addressed to God. They are a voice of the gospel, God's good word addressed to God's faithful people. In this literature the community of faith has heard and continues to hear the sovereign speech of God, who meets the community in its depths of need and in its heights of celebration. The Psalms draw our entire life under the rule of God, where everything may be submitted to the God of the gospel.

Psalm interpretation is at the present time beset by a curious reality. There is a devotional tradition of piety that finds the Psalms acutely attuned to the needs and possibilities of profound faith. (To be sure, some of that devotional literature is less than profound.) This tradition of Psalm usage tends to be precritical, and is relatively uncomplicated by any scholarly claims. There is also a well-established scholarly tradition of interpretation with a rather stable consensus. This tradition of interpretation tends to be critical, working beyond the naivete of the devotional tradition, but sometimes being more erudite than insightful. These two traditions of interpretation proceed without much knowledge of, attention to, or impact on the other. The devotional tradition of piety is surely weakened by disregarding the perspectives and insights of scholarship. Conversely, the scholarly tradition of interpretation is frequently arid, because it lingers excessively on formal questions, with inability or reluctance to bring its insights and methods to substantive matters of exposition. This cleavage, of course, must not be overstated, for there are some contacts and overlaps among interpreters, but that contact is limited, modest, and too restrained.

What seems to be needed (and is here attempted) is a *postcritical* interpretation that lets the devotional and scholarly traditions support, inform, and correct each other, so that the formal gains of scholarly methods may enhance and strengthen, as well as criticize, the substance of genuine piety in its handling of the Psalms.

1. There is a long, faithful history of Psalms interpretation in the service of the gospel that has been undisturbed even by the critical consensus.[2] Today this understanding is embodied in personal piety that focuses on a few well-known and well-beloved Psalms, especially 23, 46, and 121. Such popular piety tends to be highly selective in the psalms used and frequently quite romantic in its understanding of them, so that the Psalms serve to assure, affirm, and strengthen faithful people. This selective (and romantic) tendency is reenforced by much liturgical practice in the church, which makes use only of positive and "nice" psalms that support the polite hermeneutic of the church. (Even some Roman Catholic books, which are the most inclusive, omit Psalm 109 as "too much" for the worship life of the church.) The following discussion is quite critical of such selectivity. My argument will be that to value fully any psalm, it must be used in the context of all of them. The more narrow the selection, the more harsh should be our criticism, for every such deletion tends to block out some dimension of Israel's life with God. The result of such selectivity is that the range of interaction between God and Israel is seriously and cripplingly reduced.

My criticism, uncompromised as it is, is nevertheless restrained, because the Psalms permit the faithful to enter at whatever level they are able—in ways primitive or sophisticated, limited or comprehensive, candid or guarded. The faithful of all "sorts and conditions," with varying skills and sensitivities, here find "the bread of life" as abiding nourishment. Any critical scholarship must respect that gift that is given and received in this literature, even if we do not understand the manifold ways in which that communication occurs.

2. Behind and before this popular contemporary usage, which continues the practice of many generations, we must also take account of another precritical use. Not only simple believers, but the great teachers of evangelical faith have also found the Psalms a peculiar resource for faith. They did so without

the aid of much of our contemporary scholarship. Especially the great Reformers were driven in their evangelical passion and discernment precisely to the use and study of the Psalms. Even as Luther grounded his insights on reformation in the Epistle to the Romans, so he found his primal announcement of "the new righteousness" in the Psalms.[3] That theological tradition concluded that the Psalms articulate the whole gospel of God in a nutshell.[4] This is also true of Calvin, who was not a man of detached rationality (as he is frequently caricatured), but had a profound piety which sought an adequate and imaginative expression of faith. It is in the Psalms that he found the whole faith of the whole person articulated. He was able to say that the Psalms are an "anatomy of the soul," fully articulating every facet of the cost and joy of life with God.[5]

These understandings of the Psalms are not only precious to us; they are decisive. We must not permit any of the gains of later critical scholarship to detract us from these claims. This, however, is not to suggest that the great reformers were "precritical." They did indeed practice and advance the best critical modes of study available to them, as we must.

3. We are not precritical people. We are heirs of a scholarly consensus that must not only be taken into account, but must be embraced as our teacher. In what follows, I shall try to deal with the Psalms, fully informed by the scholarly consensus, which may be summarized rather simply.[6]

The main gains of Psalms scholarship have been made by the form-critical approach of Hermann Gunkel.[7] It was his great insight that the forms of expression and modes of articulation in the Psalms can for the most part be understood in a few recurring patterns.[8] (To be sure, not all Psalms can be thus subsumed, and we need feel no special pressure to do so.) Moreover, these few typical modes of speech expressed certain characteristic gestures of faith, and they presumably reflect certain recurring life situations and/or liturgical practices. Thus what Gunkel saw is the convergence of modes of speech, religious claims, and social settings.

This means that in a study of the Psalms, we cannot and need not, for our purposes, consider every single psalm on its own. And we need not treat each separate psalm as an isolated entity to be interpreted as though it stood by itself. We may rather take up certain representative psalms that serve as characteristic and typical examples of certain patterns of speech, articulating certain typical gestures and themes of faith, and reflecting certain typical situations of faith and unfaith. Thus a study of the Psalms may begin with attention to the typical, though details and specific developments in individual psalms must be noted. The detailed development demonstrates the remarkable openness of the typical to various developments in the hands of various speakers.

The second major advance in Psalms study was made by Sigmund Mowinckel, a student of Gunkel.[9] Mowinckel developed the hypothesis, which has attracted widespread and persistent scholarly attention, that these representative psalms are best understood in a single liturgical setting that dominated Israel's life. Mowinckel proposed that many of the psalms reflect the annual enthronement festival, enacted dramatically in the Jerusalem temple at New Year's time. In that festival Yahweh, the God of Israel, is dramatically and liturgically reenthroned for the new year, which is the renewal of creation and the guarantee of well-being. The Davidic king in Jerusalem plays a major role in that ceremony, and, of course, derives great political gain from the theological claims of the liturgy. Mowinckel found a way to comprehend many of the Psalms in his remarkable hypothesis.[10]

Scholarly reaction to his hypothesis is twofold. On the one hand, the hypothesis is much too comprehensive and totalitarian, making claims that are too broad and incorporating too many psalms of various kinds into a single action. And that action itself is premised on unsure comparisons, given the lack of clear Israelite evidence. Thus Psalms interpretation must be more pluralistic and diversified in order to allow the Psalms freedom to operate in many different aspects of Israel's life. On the other hand, for all its excessiveness, Mowinckel's hypothesis still occupies the center of the field and still provides the best governing hypothesis that we have. Thus we may permit it to inform our work as long as we treat it as provisional and are attentive to its imperial temptation. It must be treated as a proposal and not as a conclusion. But given renewed interest in the liturgical character of the Psalms,[11] Mowinckel's study offers a great many important insights for finding analogous uses in our own liturgical practice.

A third scholarly gain is the contribution of Claus Westermann.[12] (Westermann's work has not gained the "canonical status" among scholars held by Gunkel and Mowinckel, but his work appears to this writer to be of comparable importance.) Following the form analysis of Gunkel and ignoring the liturgical hypothesis of Mowinckel, Westermann has urged that the lament is the basic form of psalmic expression, and that most other psalm forms are derived from or responses to the lament. He has shown that the lament psalm expresses the basic moves of faith in God, ranging from deep alienation to profound trust, confidence, and gratitude. The major contribution of Westermann for our study is the discernment of a literary dynamic in the movement of the Psalms that corresponds to and gives voice to the dynamic of faith that we know in our experience with God.

4. This discussion will pursue a *postcritical* reading of the Psalms. That is, we shall try to take full account of the critical gains made by such scholars as Gunkel, Mowinckel, and Westermann, without betraying any of the precritical passion, naivete, and insight of believing exposition. Specifically there is a close correspondence between *the anatomy of the lament psalm* (which

Westermann as a critical scholar has shown to be structurally central for the entire collection) and *the anatomy of the soul* (which Calvin related to his discernment and presentation of biblical faith). To pursue that close correspondence, we shall propose a movement and dynamic among the Psalms that suggests an interrelatedness, without seeking to impose a rigid scheme upon the poems, which must be honored, each in its own distinctiveness. Above all, we intend our interpretation to be belief-full, that is, in the service of the church's best, most responsible faith. The point is to let the text have its evangelical say, to make its evangelical claim. Both critical learning and belief-full naivete may serve that intent.

The following discussion is organized around three quite general themes, poems of *orientation*, poems of *disorientation*, and poems of *new orientation*.[13] It is suggested that the Psalms can be roughly grouped this way, and the flow of human life characteristically is located either in the actual experience of one of these settings or is in movement from one to another.[14] By organizing our discussion in this way, we propose a correlation between the gains of critical study (especially Gunkel and Westermann) and the realities of human life (known to those who most use the Psalms in a life of prayer):

a) Human life consists in satisfied *seasons of well-being* that evoke gratitude for the constancy of blessing. Matching this we will consider "psalms of orientation," which in a variety of ways articulate the joy, delight, goodness, coherence, and reliability of God, God's creation, God's governing law.

b) Human life consists in anguished seasons of hurt, alienation, suffering, and death. These evoke rage, resentment, self-pity, and hatred. Matching this, we will consider "psalms of disorientation," poems and speech-forms that match the season in its ragged, painful disarray. This speech, the lament, has a recognizable shape that permits the extravagance, hyperbole, and abrasiveness needed for the experience.[15]

c) Human life consists in turns of surprise when we are overwhelmed with the new gifts of God, when joy breaks through the despair.[16] Where there has been only darkness, there is light. Corresponding to this surprise of the gospel, we will consider "psalms of new orientation," which speak boldly about a new gift from God, a fresh intrusion that makes all things new. These psalms affirm a sovereign God who puts humankind in a new situation. In this way, it is proposed that psalm forms correspond to seasons of human life and bring those seasons to speech. The move of the seasons is transformational and not developmental; that is, the move is never obvious, easy, or "natural." It is always in pain and surprise, and in each age it is thinkable that a different move might have been made.

But human life is not simply an articulation of a place in which we find ourselves. It is also a movement from one circumstance to another, changing and being changed, finding ourselves surprised by a new circumstance we did not expect, resistant to a new place, clinging desperately to the old circumstance.

So we will suggest that the life of faith expressed in the Psalms is focused on the *two decisive moves of faith* that are always underway, by which we are regularly surprised and which we regularly resist.[17]

One move we make is *out of a settled orientation into a season of disorientation*. This move is experienced partly as changed circumstance, but it is much more a personal awareness and acknowledgment of the changed circumstance. This may be an abrupt or a slowly dawning acknowledgment. It constitutes a dismantling of the old, known world and a relinquishment of safe, reliable confidence in God's good creation. The movement of dismantling includes a rush of negativities, including rage, resentment, guilt, shame, isolation, despair, hatred, and hostility.

It is that move which characterizes much of the Psalms in the form of complaint and lament. The lament psalm is a painful, anguished articulation of a move into disarray and dislocation.[18] The lament is a candid, even if unwilling, embrace of a new situation of chaos, now devoid of the coherence that marks God's good creation. The sphere of disorientation may be quite personal and intimate, or it may be massive and public. Either way, it is experienced as a personal end of the world, or it would not generate such passionate poetry.

That dismantling move is a characteristically Jewish move, one that evokes robust resistance and one that does not doubt that even the experience of disorientation has to do with God and must be vigorously addressed to God. For Christian faith that characteristically Jewish embrace of and articulation of disorientation is decisively embodied in the crucifixion of Jesus. That event and memory become the model for all "dying" that must be done in faith. That is why some interpreters have found it possible to say that the voice of lamentation in the book of Psalms is indeed the voice of the Crucified One. I do not go so far, and prefer to say that the Christian use of the Psalms is illuminated and required by the crucifixion, so that in the use of the Psalms we are moving back and forth among reference to Jesus, the voice of the psalm itself, and our own experiences of dislocation, suffering, and death. There are, of course, important distinctions among lament psalms. Thus *psalms of the innocent sufferer* more directly apply to Jesus than do the *psalms of penitence*. Nonetheless, taken as a whole, that dimension of the history of Jesus is a major point of contact for lament psalms.

The other move we make is a move *from a context of disorientation to a new orientation*, surprised by a new gift from God, a new coherence made present to us just when we thought all was lost. This move entails a departure from the "pit" of chaos just when we had suspected we would never escape. It is a departure inexplicable to us, to be credited only to the intervention of God. This move of departure to new life includes a rush of positive responses, including delight, amazement, wonder, awe, gratitude, and thanksgiving.

The second move also characterizes many of the Psalms, in the form of songs of thanksgiving and declarative hymns that tell a tale of a decisive time, an inversion, a reversal of fortune, a rescue, deliverance, saving, liberation, healing.[19] The hymnic psalm is a surprising, buoyant articulation of a move of the person or community into a new life-permitting and life-enhancing context where God's way and will surprisingly prevail. Such hymns are a joyous assertion that God's rule is known, visible, and effective just when we had lost hope.

That astonishing move is a characteristically Jewish move, one beyond reasonable expectation, one that evokes strident doxology because the new gift of life must be gladly and fully referred to God. For Christian faith that characteristic Jewish articulation and reception of new orientation is decisively embodied in the resurrection of Jesus. That is why the church has found it appropriate to use such hymns with particular reference to Easter. This means that the use of these hymns and songs of thanksgiving moves back and forth among references to Jesus' new life, to the voice of Israel's glad affirmation, and to our own experience of new life surprisingly granted.

We may chart our way of relating the form of the Psalms to the realities of human experience:[20]

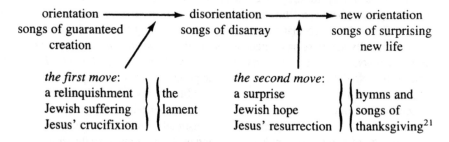

In ordering the Psalms in such a way, I hope to suggest a link between a critical study of forms and a precritical awareness of experiences of well-being and betrayal, of despair and surprise. By linking together such critical analysis and such precritical awareness, I hope to suggest a postcritical way of interpreting the Psalms that does full justice both to our personal dimension of experience and our most sophisticated analysis. Thus I hope it will become clear that our critical sensitivities can serve our religious experiences so that we may speak more knowingly and more faithfully out of our faith situation.

The theological dimension of this proposal is to provide a connection among *(a)* focal moments of Christian faith (crucifixion and resurrection), *(b)* decisive inclinations of Jewish piety (suffering and hope), *(c)* psalmic expressions that are most recurrent (lament and praise), and *(d)* seasons in our own life of dying and being raised. If the Psalms can be understood with these knowing sensitivities, our own use of them will have more depth and significance in the practice of both Jewish and Christian forms of biblical faith. In the last analysis, the Psalms have what power they have for us because we know life to be like that. In a society that engages in great denial and grows numb by avoidance and denial,[22] it is important to recover and use these Psalms that speak the truth about us—in terms of the governance of God.

5. Before moving to the Psalms themselves, three preliminary comments need to be made:

a) Clearly the move through this grid of orientation—disorientation—new orientation is not a once-for-all experience. In different ways, we frequently find ourselves in varying conditions in relation to God; but neither do I want to suggest any regularized movement of a cyclical kind. It is not difficult to see, however, that yesterday's new orientation becomes today's old orientation, which we take too much for granted and defend. Goldengay has made the shrewd point that we not only slide from new orientation to old orientation, but also may find the same psalm serving to express either, depending on the context and intention of the speaker. Thus, while I have offered a grid, I do not want it taken too precisely, for life is in fact more spontaneous than that. I offer it simply as a way to suggest connections between life and speech, or as Ricoeur puts it, between "limit experiences" and "limit expressions."

b) The experience that these psalms interface may be of various kinds. Conventionally scholars have made a distinction between *communal* and *personal laments*, and Westermann has correlated with that *songs of thanksgiving* and *hymns*. No doubt that is correct. But the point I make is that experientially, in terms of faith situation, the personal and public issues are all of a piece, and depending on our commitments, each may be experienced as the same threat or surprise of faith. I prefer to speak impressionistically, so that the actual experience may be of many different kinds, as long as it summons us to the same dynamics of faith.

c) Such a grid in two movements reveals an understanding of life that is fundamentally alien to our culture. The dominant ideology of our culture is committed to continuity and success and to the avoidance of pain, hurt, and loss. The dominant culture is also resistant to genuine newness and real surprise. It is curious but true, that *surprise* is as unwelcome as is *loss*. And our culture is organized to prevent the experience of both.

This means that when we practice either move—into *disorientation* or into *new orientation*—we engage in a countercultural activity, which by some will be perceived as subversive. Perhaps that is why the *lament psalms* have nearly dropped out of usage. Where the worshiping community seriously articulates these two moves, it affirms an understanding of reality that knows that if we try to keep our lives we will lose them, and that when lost for the gospel, we will be given life (Mark 8:35). Such a practice of the Psalms cannot be taken for granted in our culture, but will be done only if there is resolved intentionality to live life in a more excellent way.

As for me, I said in my prosperity,
 "I shall never be moved."
By thy favor, O Lord,
 Thou hadst established me as a strong mountain.

Psalm 30:6-7a

2

Psalms of Orientation

The *psalms of orientation* were created, transmitted, valued, and relied upon by a community of faithful people. To these people, their faith was both important and satisfying. A beginning theological point for the Psalms are those psalms that express a confident, serene settlement of faith issues. Some things are settled and beyond doubt, so that one does not live and believe in the midst of overwhelming anxiety. Such a happy settlement of life's issues occurs because God is known to be reliable and trustworthy. This community has decided to trust in this particular God. Many of the Psalms give expression to that happy settlement, to the reality that God is trustworthy and reliable, and to the decision to stake life on this particular God.

Here we will consider five representative types of psalms that reflect well-oriented faith in a mood of equilibrium. These various poems are not easily assigned to any standard form. They might best be treated as Westermann's *descriptive hymns*.[1] That is, they are statements that describe a happy, blessed state in which the speakers are grateful for and confident in the abiding, reliable gifts of life that are long-standing from time past and will endure for time to come. Life, as reflected in these psalms, is not troubled or threatened, but is seen as the well-ordered world intended by God. They approximate a "no-surprise world" and consequently a world of "no fear." They do not report on an event, a happening, or an intrusion. Rather, they describe how things are and indeed always are.[2] It will be clear that we are not following any strict form analysis, but are paying primary attention to the content and the mode of articulation.

These psalms in various ways are *expressions of creation faith*. They affirm that the world is a well-ordered, reliable, and life-giving system, because God has ordained it that way and continues to preside effectively over the process. At the same time, there is a profound trust in the daily working of that system and profound gratitude to God for making it so. Creation here is not a theory about how the world came to be. That is not how the Bible thinks about creation. It is rather an affirmation that God's faithfulness and goodness are experienced as generosity, continuity, and regularity. Life is experienced as protected space. Chaos is not present to us and is not permitted a hearing in this well-ordered world.

Elemental certitudes are known to be operative in the world. The *nomos* holds, and there is as yet no inkling of *anomie*.[3] Experientially, of course, such certitudes have behind them previous awareness of disorientation, for that belongs to human experience. The process is continually dialectic. But formally, these psalms tend to disregard such previous experience and begin anew.

The function of this kind of psalm is theological, i.e., to praise and thank God. But such a psalm also has *a social function* of importance. It is to articulate and maintain a "sacred canopy" under which the community of faith can live out its life with freedom from anxiety.[4] That is, life is not simply a task to be achieved, an endless construction of a viable world made by effort and human ingenuity. There is a givenness to be relied on, guaranteed by none other than God. That givenness is here before us, stands over us, endures beyond us, and surrounds us behind and before.[5] The poetic speech of the Psalms is our best language for such givenness, which is not initiated by us but waits for us. There is a coherence that provides a context for our best living. Whenever we use these psalms, they continue to assure us of such a canopy of certitude—despite all the incongruities of life.

Notice that the Psalms not only point to such a protective reality; they evoke it, present it, keep it in place. This is a major gain of Mowinckel's work on the creative power of public worship.[6] Such worship is indeed "world-making."[7] These psalms become a means whereby the creator is in fact creating the world. That perhaps is one meaning of the saying, "God creates by Word." That creative word is spoken in these psalms in the liturgical process, and it is in the world of worship that Israel "re-experiences" and "redescribes" the safe world over which God presides.[8]

Such high faith can be gladly affirmed, but it will also be better understood if we assess it critically. So it may be helpful to ask who experiences life this way and who wants most to make these kinds of assertions.

Such a satisfied and assured assertion of orderliness probably comes from the well-off, from the economically secure and the politically significant.[9] That is, such religious conviction comes from those who experience life as good, generous, and reliable. This does not make these poems suspect, but it permits us to read them knowingly, for not everyone experiences life this way and can speak so boldly about it. Life is well-oriented only for some, and that characteristically at the expense of others. In these psalms we enter into the religious sensitivity and life experience of those who know life to have congruity, symmetry, and proportion. They are those whose "lines have fallen for me in pleasant places" (Ps. 16:6). This means they have ended up with the best land, and so find it not difficult to live a life of gratitude.

With such a suspicious possibility, we dare to suggest that creation faith, a sure sense of God's orderliness, is not always high and noble faith. Sometimes it is void of such pure motive and serves only to celebrate the status quo, the happy but inequitable way life is presently arranged. In using these psalms, we must be alert to the slippery ways in which creation faith easily becomes social conservatism, which basks in our own well-offness:

> The theology which connected itself to given ordinances inevitably bound the belief in Creation to things that at times involved the worship of the creature...God's will in Creation comes to be identified with the power which proceeds from the collectivist group. If this group turns the belief in Creation into a political concept, adapting its terms to further its own objects, which may coincide with the objects of a particular party, the theology which stands in judgment of all this...inevitably comes to make the Church a political factor, indeed the foremost political factor.[10]

There are times when such psalms may be used freely. But there are times when such psalms must be used carefully or with a knowing qualification. For we know persons and communities whose experience of injustice and disorder deeply contradicts this faith. Then we must always ask whose interest is reflected and served by such psalms and by their use.

It follows that these psalms may not only serve as "sacred canopy" to permit communal life. They may also serve as *a form of social control*. Thus they may induct the young into a system of obedience and rewards, and so promote approved social conduct of a certain kind. They may also label the socially disapproved as the ones who violate God's creation. And they may be used to justify morally the view that those who do not prosper in the world are those who live outside the parameters and priorities of God's creation. Creation faith is most usually articulated by the powerful people in society. It is the royal apparatus that experiences life as well-ordered. Creation faith subtly serves to grant self-approval, to warn dissenters, and to admonish children. In using these psalms, it will be important to watch for such partisan applications, which arise when God's creation is easily and unambiguously identified with our social experience of well-being and moral effectiveness.

Having said that, we may make one affirmation in another direction. The religious power of these psalms is considerable *for all sorts and conditions of people*. These psalms have been articulated by the socially successful, but their religious seriousness extends beyond the ''successful.'' These same psalms provide a point of reference even for those who share in none of the present ''goodies,'' but who cling in hope to the conviction that God's good intention for creation will finally triumph and there will be an equity and a sabbath for all God's creatures. It is for that reason that these psalms can be taken with an eschatological note, acknowledging that the creation of God has not been fully completed, but this community waits with confidence. Such an eschatological note, I suggest, moves the psalm from its original social function of social *construction and maintenance* to this broader more widespread use concerning *transformation* and new creation.[11]

The Psalms bespeak a healthy, oriented life that is anticipated, even if not yet experienced. There moves in these psalms a deep conviction that God's purpose for the world is resilient. That purpose will not yield until creation is brought to fullness. The Psalms assert that the creation finally is committed to and will serve the Creator. The Psalms thus are anticipatory of what surely will be. Strangely enough, they may serve as a point of criticism against the status quo, to assert that when the Creator's way comes to fruition, the inadequate present arrangements will be overcome. Thus the very psalms that may serve as *social control* may also function as a *social anticipation*, which becomes *social criticism*. But that requires that we be aware and intentional in our usage and the orientation that we articulate through them.

Songs of Creation

The most foundational experience of orientation is the daily experience of *life's regularities*, which are experienced as reliable, equitable, and generous. The psalmic community readily affirmed that this experience is ordained and sustained by God. A proper response is one of gratitude. The world is God's way of bestowing blessing upon us. Our times are ordered by God according to the seasons of the year, according to the seasons of life, according to the needs of the day. In all of these processes, we find ourselves to be safe and free; we know that out of no great religious insight, but because that is the way life comes to us.

Psalm 145

This psalm is a representative statement of Israel's joyous and grateful confidence in the Creator. In the psalm there is no development of plot or building of intensity. Indeed, it is essentially static in form, articulating what is enduringly true of the world. What is true at the beginning of the psalm is still true at the end. What is true from beginning to end is that Yahweh securely governs, and that can be counted on. We are given a series of affirmations that could be rearranged without disrupting the intent. The present order is necessary, however, because the psalm is an *acrostic*. That is, each line begins with a letter of the alphabet in sequence. Thus the first line begins with א, the second with ב, and so on through the alphabet. Though this is inevitably lost in translation, we may appreciate its intent. It is to assert the fullness and comprehensiveness of creation, to praise God for a world well-arranged and oriented, from A to Z.[12] There is here no slippage, tension, or incongruity. This is Israel in its most trustful, innocent, childlike faith.

1. Verses 1-7 are an introduction. It is characteristic in Israel to do praise by telling about those who will do it. The range of praise is from the personal 'I" to the intergenerational community (v. 4). The God praised is as intimate as any God (v. 1), and as regal as the awesome king (v. 1), who does what is great, unsearchable, terrible, glorious, wondrous.[13] This is speech that is religiously sensitive, alive to the awesomeness of God articulated in the *order* of the world.[14] The alphabetic structure suggests this is a carefully crafted psalm, reflecting a disciplined learning community. Perhaps Prov. 25:2-3 on the theme of "search/unsearchable" indicates that the psalm belongs in a royal context, i.e., in a school where the children of the elite reflect on the mystery and mandate of creation. Notice in verse 3, God's greatness is "unsearchable."[15]

2. But if verses 1-7 reflect a royal, didactic setting, verses 8-9 are a different matter. They probably reflect Israel's oldest theological assertion about God, which is certainly older than royal reality in Israel (cf. Exod. 34:6-7).[16] Yahweh is here named twice. In these four phrases, Yahweh's main characteristics are asserted: gracious, merciful, slow to anger, abounding in steadfast love, good, compassionate. Fully to explore these terms would require extended exposition, but we may summarize by saying that they express God's free, passionate and limitless self-giving to the covenant partner, in this case, the whole created world. Perhaps the rest of the psalm is best understood as an extrapolation from these verses to see how God's characteristic self-giving is experienced in the daily blessings of creation.

The characteristics of God stated here are not those dealt with by popular theology.[17] Instead, these are dimensions of personal, relational, covenantal life. The creation holds together because of Yahweh's *faithfulness*. From that inexplicable but unwavering faithfulness, all of life is trusted to have coherence. Two points can be made about this celebration of faithfulness. First, this is not a conclusion reached through theological analysis and speculation. It is a judgment made out of experience of daily reliability, evidence from the simple facts of being nourished and having the necessities of life provided. Second, such a mode of trustfulness seems to have much in common with Erik Erikson's "basic trust," whereby a child learns to 1   in the reliability of life and of parents in quite concrete ways.[18] It is fair enough to speak of this psalm as "childlike" in its trust (cf. Matt. 18:3-4).

3. Verses 10-13a return to the theme announced in verse 1, namely, that this is the king, the undoubted sovereign. These verses grandly express the majesty of God's rule and the presence of God's glory. The vocabulary includes "kingdom" three times, "power" twice, and "glory" twice. The reliability of the world is not intrinsic to it, but is a gift given by this faithful governor.

4. But verses 13b-20a make a shift that surprises us and provides the main clue for the psalm. In a bold evangelical move the psalm asserts that Yahweh's great power is directed especially toward the weak and the needy. There is no further reflection on God's *regal* person, but only on God's *self-giving* attentiveness to God's creatures, the ones who have no claim but depend solely on God's inclination. The language of self-giving by God which enables transformed humanness is echoed by Mary: "He has put down the mighty from their thrones, and exalted those of low degree; he has filled the hungry with good things" (Luke 1:52-53). Psalm 145 celebrates the order of God's creation, which not only governs, but surprises and inverts and gives unwarranted gifts to unlikely creatures. God's regal power is mobilized to care for the otherwise uncared for.

The text is dominated by the word *all*.[19] But the generalizing tendency does not lose its concreteness. What is generalized is Yahweh's detailed attentiveness to those who lack power for life. The shift from *regal power* to *compassionate regard* is decisive and intentional. This one is not only "the king," but "my God." God's terrible acts are for the needy.

The verbal form expressing Yahweh's actions is characteristically participial; that is, this is not an intrusive eventfulness, but an assured ongoing process that Yahweh does regularly and everywhere. The psalm asserts that God is known fully in the reliable feeding processes. So there is embedded in this section the lovely and familiar "table prayer" of verses 15-16. That devotional habit is precisely to the point. There is a linkage between the great cosmic claim of creation and the daily gift of nourishment and sustenance. The intimacy of this trust in the nourishing God is well put in the Heidelberg Catechism:

...that he protects me so well that without the will of my Father in Heaven, not a hair can fall from my head (1).

Although the assurances are general, in verses 18-19 it is clear that this creation faith has a covenantal dimension. Although the gifts are not exclusive of others, the experience of such nourishing protection is granted precisely and especially to those who call and fear. The equilibrium of the world is experienced best by those who live contentedly with Yahweh's expectations.

5. We may pause with verse 20, which looks back to the old creedal formula of Exod. 34:6-7. God's relatedness is always two-sided: *to rescue* and *to judge*.[20] Up to this point, this psalm (and especially vv. 8-9) has offered only the positive side. But now we have an antithetical parallel stated in chiastic form. The verbs are *preserve* (שׁמר, in a participle; on *preserve* cf. Ps. 121) and *destroy* (שׁמד, an imperfect). The objects are *lovers* (אהב, "covenant keepers") and *wicked* (רשׁע, "covenant breakers"). This verse is a harsh and sobering qualification of the grand claims of the psalm. Perhaps this verse is the voice of realism; that is, creation does work within the boundaries of obedient responsibility. It may also be a form of social control, in which the managers of social order administer the blessings of God only in certain directions—among the *deserving*. The *gifts* of God become carefully administered *rewards*.

The verse is enough to see the subtle linkage of a free celebration of creation and a sober assertion of a particular social form and a social interest. That is how the orientation of social life is experienced. Whenever we celebrate God's goodness, we celebrate it as it is cast in "fleshly" form, which is never as free as the initial offer. To maintain a fully oriented life, one must accept the regnant boundaries.

We take Psalm 145 to be the fullest representative of those psalms that understand creation as a mode of equilibrium, coherence, and reliability. Such a presentation of life is an act of high faith, but it seems also to reflect the experience and interests of the "well-off." Indeed, such faith seems often to come with such social location, and we must take both seriously. We mention three other psalms that serve the same function.

Psalm 104

Psalm 104 is also an extended celebration of the goodness and awesome character of creation.

This psalm has a different tone from that of 145. Whereas Psalm 145 focuses on the compassion of the Creator, Psalm 104 has much more concern for the splendor of creation. In contrast to Psalm 145, it is striking that the name of God is nearly absent, occurring mostly in opening and closing conventions.[21] That absence may reflect that this psalm is borrowed from Egypt, that it is a hymn about creation rather than the Creator, that it is urbane and royal and not intended to be historically specific about Israel's memory. All of these evoke a poem celebrative of the order, symmetry, and majesty of creation. The scope of the claim is not unlike that of Second Isaiah (cf. Isa. 40:12-17) and especially the whirlwind speeches of God (Job 38–41).

Psalm 104 is again structured around a series of participles, which suggests a standard descriptive hymn of praise. The speaker catalogs noteworthy features in creation and assigns them all to Yahweh.

That grand and almost overwhelming recital is ended in verse 23. The end point in the recital is appropriately that the function of "man" is as worker in God's creation. That is his lot in life. It is not a curse or a special burden. Such work belongs to the proper life of humankind in the proper functions of creation. The remainder of the psalm includes three telling conclusions drawn from reflection on God's ordered world:

a) God is known to be confident, serene, and at ease. The metaphor for this is "the sea" (v. 25). Conventionally the sea is expression of dread and intense threat. Here the sea is God's plaything in which the great sea monster serves only for God's peculiar amusement (cf. Job 41 for a parallel taking of delight in what some might regard as a monster). Elsewhere the sea monster is an embodiment of evil. Here what some think is evil is seen as responsive to God and, in God's way, more tame than we suspected.

b) In verses 27-30 we are treated to a usage appropriate for a table prayer not unlike Ps. 145:15-16. But there is a difference. Here those who get food are all the creation. The whole world is daily dependent on God's sustenance, God's face, God's presence, God's breath. The world is impressive and to be celebrated. But it has no independent existence. It is genuinely creation, i.e., always referred to the Creator. The world is well-ordered and reliable. But on its own, it has no possibility of survival or well-being. All of that is daily gift.

c) That awareness leads the speaker in verses 31-34 to be moved to spontaneous wonder, gratitude, and praise. The psalm translates these very large claims to a personal delight in God's goodness. In these verses, more than anywhere in the psalm, Yahweh is called by his right name. Yahweh is named precisely by those capable of gratitude and spontaneous surrender. The speaker is made aware that God

> rules in such a way that leaves and grass, rain and drought, fruitful and unfruitful years, food and drink, death and sickness, riches and poverty and everything else come to us not by chance, but by his fatherly hand.[22]

The speaker of verses 31-34 is one for whom all chance is overridden in parental care. The psalm does not put forward a cosmology. It has a pastoral concern for giving assurance of the reliable orientation of the world. So Calvin can say:

> It is also intended to strengthen our confidence in regard to the future, that we may not live in the world in a state of constant fear and anxiety, as we

must have done had not God testified that he has given the earth for a habitation to men.[23]

While Calvin uses the masculine language of his time, he does see so helpfully that cosmic claims are here presented in parental metaphor:

> He bears the character of the best of fathers, who takes pleasure in tenderly cherishing his children and in bountifully nourishing them.[24]

Calvin might well have used maternal language. In any case, the world is well parented.

Even this psalm cannot resist the conclusion of verse 35. The world is a free gift from God, but with it comes an expectation and a cost. It cannot be otherwise. Every generation learns what the first humans in the garden learned (Genesis 2-3). The nourishing Lord has not abdicated sovereignty. In this kingdom of delight that parental will must indeed be honored. As in Ps. 145:20, this verse suggests the psalm does not express disinterested faith, but guards a certain arrangement of social life.

Psalm 33

Psalm 33 is *a new song* (v. 3) that sings about *a new world*. It is the world about which Israel always sings, the new world that Yahweh is now creating. It is a world ordered by God's justice over which God presides with faithfulness. To such a world the only appropriate response is confident and sure praise to the one who makes that world available to us.

1. Verses 1-5 announce the main themes of the psalm and provide a good example of the basic structure of Israel's hymnic expression. That structure consists in two clearly delineated elements. First, in verses 1-3 there is a series of five *imperatives* summoning Israel to praise: rejoice, praise, make melody, sing, play. The summons is itself an act of self-yielding praise.

Second, this is followed in verses 4-5 by giving *reasons for praise*, characteristically introduced by ''for'' (כי), stating acts or qualities of Yahweh that warrant and evoke doxology. The reasons offered here provide the material for a full confession of Israel's God: ''For the word of the Lord is upright; and all his work is done in faithfulness. He loves righteousness and justice; the earth is full of [his] steadfast love.'' Thus Israel's *praise in new song* (vv. 1-3) matches *Yahweh's new world* (vv. 4-5).

The appropriateness of *this speech* on the lips of *this people* is explicit. In verse 1, the ones summoned to praise are ''righteous and upright,'' i.e., they keep the torah and belong properly to Yahweh's well-oriented world. This is matched in verses 4-5 with the statement that Yahweh's word is upright (v. 4), that he loves righteousness (v. 5). Exactly the same adjectives are used for those who praise and that to be praised. This is a relation and a world without incongruity. Everything fits together in detail.

But the adjectives used for Yahweh are more extensive. In addition to the two repeated from verse 1, three others are used: *faithfulness* (אמונה), i.e., utterly reliable; *justice* (משפט) (with *righteousness* [צדק], a traditional word pair concerning Yahweh's covenantal commitments); and *steadfast love*, (חסד) which plays a crucial role in this psalm. (A like cluster of terms characterizing Yahweh is found in Hos. 2:19-20, and see the triad in Jer. 9:24.) The characterization is not unlike that of Ps. 145:8-9, derived as we have seen from Exod. 34:6-7.

Finally, note that verses 4-5 are nicely arranged so that the name Yahweh is placed at the beginning and end of this little credo, perhaps answering to the double use of the name in verses 1-3. In any case, the ground for the doxology is that the world in its steadfastness evidences Yahweh's own faithfulness. Creation is not confused with the Creator, but is an important witness to the Creator, for only such a Creator could have formed such a creation.

2. Verses 6-9 are a reflection on the power of Yahweh's word, already mentioned in verse 4. This section begins with a statement of creation by the word (v. 6) and concludes in verse 9 with the point reiterated. Creation by God's word is only one mode of creation, but it is the most awesome and majestic. It asserts the utter dependence of the world on Yahweh's speech, for the world is indeed "fresh from the word" (Rom. 4:17). But it is also a statement of discontinuity, for God is in no way enmeshed in or bound by the creation. The relationship is free, and the decisive move is toward the world from God, never from the world to God.

The details of verse 7 sound Job-like in their splendor. They articulate Yahweh's utter governance over the world. The image of waters in a bottle bespeaks the awesomeness of Yahweh over against the smallness of the world. Compare the same disproportion in Isa. 40:12-17. How great thou art, indeed!

The appropriate response to such majestic rule is "fear and trembling" (v. 8). As his subjects, creatures are aware of the deep inequity between Creator and creation, of the inability to achieve any parity. This is an advance beyond verses 1-5, where the match we have noted begins the hymn with a sense of congruity. Now the doxology moves radically to affirm that while some adjectives apply to both God and the worshiper, in fact the distance between them is not to be overcome. It is not *compatibility* but *incongruity* between Creator and creatures that evokes praise done in fear and trembling.

3. Verses 10-17 reflect on Yahweh's awesome and unquestioned *power*. This is a fairly standard doxology to Yahweh's power, reminiscent of Job 5:8-15; 9:5-10; and Isa. 44:24-28. Rhetorically the unit is governed by a series of verbs that describe Yahweh's characteristic actions, which are without par-

allel: brings to…nought, frustrates, looks down, fashions, observes. And these are followed, two times, by reflective extrapolations. First, in verse 12, a conclusion is drawn about being God's people. Second, in verses 16-17, human plans are futile in the face of God's overriding sovereignty (cf. Gen. 50:20).

The metaphor of God looking down from heaven (v. 13) is an important usage (cf. Ps. 2:4; Deut. 26:15). It asserts both that God is utterly free of the world and yet is utterly attentive to it. The entire unit of Psalm 33 expresses complete confidence. Israel need not be anxious, because God's rule is not in doubt and will not be challenged. It is this kind of confidence about God's governance of the creation that permits freedom from anxiety in Matt. 6:25-33.

4. As usual, Israel's creation faith is not much interested in ontological questions. So in verses 8-22, the implications of creation faith—all the awe, power, majesty which soar—are drawn toward the faith and needs of the worshiping congregation. Even such a cosmic claim is handled with an eye on the pastoral concerns of the community that sings this song.

The climax is introduced with "Behold" (הנה) (v.18). A verdict is to follow. It is a verdict given about Yahweh, but it is also a verdict drawn about the world. The two verdicts come together. The metaphor is tightened. In verse 13, it was general: "Yahweh looks down." Now it is specific: "the eye of Yahweh." It is not a general looking down on the whole world. Now it is upon the faithful who fear and hope (cf. Deut. 11:22). Israel lives under Yahweh's watchful care. But that care is peculiarly attentive on behalf of the obedient. The psalm is evidence of how *creation faith* is drawn into the claims of *torah religion*.

Notice with what delicacy this new song is wrought. The fear motif calls us back to verse 8, but that general term has now been made specific (v. 18). The ante is now upped, because the ones who *fear* are the ones who *hope* (v. 18). All people may *fear*; Israel *hopes*. Israel's hope is not general or vague. It is focused on the steadfast love of Yahweh (v. 18, already asserted in v. 5). The whole earth is full of that loyalty, but Israel is the one who grounds its specific expectations in that reliability found in the whole creation.

The theme of the verdict about God and about the world in verses 18-22 is *steadfastness*. The theme looks back to verse 5, and that theme frames verses 18-22, occurring both at the beginning of the unit (v. 18) and at the end (v. 22). Israel's song moves from loyalty to loyalty. On that basis there is hope. Israel moves from hope to hope, well beyond the fear that marks the response of the world. Israel has eyes to see in the creation ground for hope in the creator.

The verses in the middle of the verdict, verses 19-21, give substance to the hope of Israel:

a) deliverance from real worldly danger (v. 19);

b) protection in every dangerous situation (v. 20); that Israel *waits* means it is not frantic but has every confidence of God's good order, without anxiety;

c) Israel is able to "trust" (בטח) because it knows the overriding name of God (v. 21), which gives reason for safety from every threat and confidence against every temptation.[25]

Now we can see why Psalm 33 begins by summoning the upright and the righteous (v. 1). It is because they are the ones who "read creation," who discern in its good order the loyalty of Yahweh and who therefore can live hope-filled lives. Not to be able to "read creation" is to live hopeless lives, not to know the real name of the Creator, not to be able to trust. To be able to *trust* (v. 21) is a response to the *steadfastness* of Yahweh. It is that perfect match about which the new song sings. The song is new because this evangelical certitude of God's reliability overrides every incongruity in which God seems not faithful and creatures do not trust.[26] Psalm 33 is a profound assertion about God, but also a bold announcement about true faith in Israel. This psalm discerns about creation that the truth of the world is not self-evident for anyone who takes a look; those who are not obedient may look and never see. Even creation is rightly read only through covenantal response, discerned through believing eyes.[27]

Psalm 8

Psalm 8 is yet another articulation of creation faith. The structure of the psalm is direct and obvious. It is framed in verse 1a and verse 9 by an envelope of praise to the regal Creator. Inside that envelope are two disproportionate elements. In verses 1b-2 there is a celebration of God's glory. The text is obscure and problematic. This doxology to God is matched in verses 3-8 by a comparable celebration of humankind, which is now the center and focus of God's creative work. This psalm is an advance beyond the others we have considered concerning creation, because here the human person is acknowledged to be God's regent in the governance of creation. Not only is creation well ordered, but the human agent occupies a crucial role in the governance of that order. In the creation psalms considered thus far, the human person has been primarily recipient, not agent.[28]

Verses 3-8 identify the role of humankind, first in relation to heavenly beings (v. 5), then in relation to all other creatures (vv. 6-8). In the first relation, humankind is marked by glory and honor. These attributes generally relate to God and are here assigned to humankind. In the second relation, humankind is authorized to have dominion over all other creatures, again an attribute characteristically assigned to God. Humankind has honor and glory in relation to the angels, not unlike God. Humankind has dominion over the other creatures not unlike God. Humankind is not unlike God.

This psalm, like the others we have considered, acknowledges that God's world is a well-oriented world, permitting confidence and security. And that assurance is here enhanced by acknowledging four larger contexts of this psalm which illuminate it:.

1. It is widely thought that this psalm is closely related to Gen. 1:1—2:4a, i.e., to the mainstream of creation faith. As the Bible starts with a line of defence against chaos, so our understanding of the Psalms begins with the celebration of good order. In both texts humanity stands at the crucial center of that good order.[29]

2. The humankind here celebrated is *royal* personhood. Probably Psalm 8 originated in the celebration of safe, luxuriant court circles. But now it is a mandate for all humankind to have authority and responsibility to order and care for God's world. In that connection, we may mention Psalm 72, which is a charter and mandate for a king, the true human person, who is to have dominion (v. 8) and whose authority is for the sake of justice and righteousness (cf. Pss. 33:5; 72:1-4, 12-14; 1 Kings 10:9; Isa. 9:7). See also Ps. 144:3, where the human agent is clearly royal.

3. Note that in Job 7:17-21 this psalm is used to express the intensity of God's care for humankind, which is too much for Job and is perceived as oppressive. The attentiveness of God to this ''power creature'' is carried to extremes, so that God's concern is an immobilizing burden. See also Ps. 139:7-12, concerning the inescapability of God.

4. While this psalm may be too much for Job, it is found appropriate by the New Testament church to understand Jesus as the one who will rule over all (Heb. 2:6-8).[30] Thus the new creation is one over which this true king presides. The New Testament takes the royal vision of humanity and uses it to identify and characterize Jesus, who is the true king. But in doing so, we must not fail to see that glory, honor, and dominion of the royal agent is profoundly transformed. Jesus is to be understood as the one who embodies all of this, who is indeed the one ''in whom all things hold together'' (Col. 1:17). But importantly, Jesus who has power and dominion has taken *the form of a servant* whose *governance* is in the form of *obedience* (Mark 10:43-45; Phil. 2:5-8). True kingship, which can order life in human ways, is now understood very differently, and permits a rereading of the psalm.

In light of that transformed reading, the structure of the psalm is worth observing closely. At its center is an affirmation of human power and authority. At its boundaries are affirmations of praise to God. The center (v. 5) and the boundaries (vv. 1,9) must be read together; either taken alone will miss the point. Human power is always bounded and surrounded by divine praise. *Dox-*

ology gives *dominion* its context and legitimacy. The two must be held together. Praise of God without human authority is abdication and "leaving it all to
God," which this psalm does not urge. But to use human power without the
context of praise of God is to profane human regency over creation and so
usurp more than has been granted. Human persons are to rule, but they are not
to receive the ultimate loyalty of creation. Such loyalty must be directed only to
God.

This psalm struggles with a delicacy not raised in the other statements on
creation we have considered. It recognizes that humankind is the crown and
pinnacle of creation, but even human power is shaped and qualified by doxology. Finally, it is glad and submitting doxology that receives and confirms the
well-oriented creation of God. These psalms of creation provide a sure and
bold beginning point for the full world of psalmic faith.

Songs of Torah

When the creation is celebrated, it is acknowledged to be a well-ordered
world. That order depends solely on God's power, faithfulness, and graciousness. That is why, in the face of the creation, Israel can only yield in praise. But
there is more to it. The good order of *creation* is concretely experienced in Israel as the *torah*. The torah is understood not simply as Israelite moral values, but
as God's will and purpose, ordained in the very structure of life. While the creation is sustained by God's faithfulness, it is also coherent and peaceable because of Israel's obedient attention to the way God has ordered life.[31] Thus
creation and torah are understood together, the torah articulating God's intention for Israel in the creation. That linking of creation and torah is particularly
evident in Psalm 19, which consists of two parts: verses 1-6 as a celebration of
the joy and wonder of creation, and verses 7-14 as an affirmation of the life-
giving power of the torah. To an outsider the themes may seem contradictory.
Creation is about God's sure *gift*; torah is about the urgency of Israel's *effort*, as
though the sure gift were conditional and not sure. But for Israel, torah is Israel's way to respond to and fully honor God's well-oriented world. That response in obedience is undertaken gladly in a posture of gratitude, without calculation or grudging.

Psalm 1

The most obvious and best-known torah psalm is Psalm 1. It surely is placed
at the beginning intentionally as a prolog to set the tone for the entire hymnic
collection.[32] It announces that the primary agenda for Israel's worship life is
obedience, to order and conduct all of life in accordance with God's purpose

and ordering of the creation. The fundamental contrast of this psalm and all of Israel's faith is a moral distinction between righteous and wicked, innocent and guilty, those who conform to God's purpose and those who ignore those purposes and disrupt the order. Human life is not mocked or trivialized. How it is lived is decisive.

In terms of our theme of orientation, this psalm, didactic in character, affirms that the well-oriented life fixed on torah expectations is one of happiness and well-being. The violation of that orientation is a sure way to diminishment and disintegration.

The structure of the psalm reflects the unambiguous structure of life as this tradition of obedience understands it. There is no middle ground, no neutral ground. Life—like the psalm—is organized in a sharp either/or. Either be a happy person who enjoys torah obedience and avoids alternative enterprises (vv. 1-2), or be like the wicked who refuse such delight (v. 4). Either end up like a luxuriant tree with plenty of nourishment (v. 3), or be like chaff which disappears (v. 4). Life consists of choices which are not obscure (vv. 5-6; cf. Deut. 30:15-20). There will be a judgment. One can stand or one can perish. But either way, it will be on the terms of the Creator. The connection between devotion and destiny is not negotiable.

Psalm 1 does not bargain or allow for ambiguity. It is the voice of a community that is familiar with risks, dangers, costs, and boundaries. It fully appreciates the givenness of God's world and has confidence that the torah is the only thinkable response to the givenness of creation. It probably is also a tract for socialization, by which the adult community firmly conditions the young into a "right" morality.[33] This community trusts its morality to be a way to fend off trouble.[34] It is life and death, and the young had better learn it while there is time (cf. Prov. 8:32-36).[35]

Psalm 119

Psalm 119 is not only the most extensive of the torah songs, but the longest of all the psalms. Unless its structural intent is recognized, it may strike one as monotonous and boringly redundant.[36] But its creation is in fact a massive intellectual achievement. It is an astonishingly crafted acrostic psalm. (We have already observed the device in Psalm 145, where each successive letter is used to begin a line, right through the alphabet. In that psalm the structure was intended to enable *full praise to be rendered*. Here the structure is intended to enable *full obedience to be offered*.) But the remarkable feature here is that each letter of the alphabet receives eight successive entries before the poem moves to the next letter. In terms of crafting, it is as though we have here eight acrostic poems all at once. That is what makes the psalm so long and so stylized. It is a pity that such an achievement is inevitably lost in translation.

In order to appreciate the psalm, we must ask why anyone would labor so intensely and rigorously on such a theme. Three possible reasons occur. First, the psalm is deliberately *didactic*. It reflects the work of a classroom teacher. Its intent is not casual. It wants to instruct the young in the "a-b-c's" of torah obedience. Second, the Psalm wants to make a *comprehensive statement* of the adequacy of a torah-oriented life. It affirms that torah will cover every facet of human existence, everything from A to Z. There is no human crisis or issue in which one need go outside the field of torah obedience to live fully. Third, the dramatic intent is to find *a form commensurate with the message*. The message is that life is reliable and utterly symmetrical when the torah is honored. And so the psalm provides a literary, pedagogical experience of reliability and utter symmetry. A torah-ordered life is as safe, predictable, and complete as is the movement of the psalm.

When one is aware of the form, not much more needs to be said about the substance. But we may make two observations. First, the torah is not a dead letter (cf. 2 Cor. 3:2-6), but an active agent which gives life. That is, torah is not just a set of rules, but it is a mode of God's life-giving presence.[37] Obedience to the torah is a source of light, life, joy, delight. Indeed, "delight" (שעע) is a repeated response to torah (Ps. 119:16, 24, 47, 70, 77, 92, 143, 174). The torah is no burden, but a mode of joyous existence. The active life-giving power of torah is also reflected in Ps. 19:7-9, in which it is the torah that restores life.[38]

The teachers of this psalm are not worried or seduced by legalism. They do not find the commandments restrictive or burdensome. Rather, they are persons who have decided some basic life-commitments. They know to whom they belong, and they will answer. Therefore, they know who they are, and they have settled in large part the moral posture they will assume toward life. There is a focus to life, an absence of frantic moral dilemma, a sense of priorities matched by an absence of anxiety. In a well-ordered world, such a decision can save one from an exhausting, endless reinventing of moral decision. Because the world holds together, the shape of obedience is reliable. And the result is not dullness or bitterness, but freedom. Twice the psalm uses the word רחב, "large place":

> I will run in the way of your commandments,
> surely you *enlarge* my heart (v. 32).
> I will walk in *liberty*,
> surely I have sought your precepts (v. 45).

Our modern bias that sees commands as restricting is countered. The commandments liberate and give people space in which to be human. This psalm instructs people in the need, possibility, and delight of giving settlement to the foundational issues of identity and vocation. Torah living does not require keeping options open about who we shall be.

Second, the teachers in this psalm are not simple-minded or reductionist. They do not imagine that life can be reduced to one-dimensional commandment-living. Rather, torah obedience is a starting point, a launching pad from which to mount an ongoing conversation with God through daily experience. Thus, the psalm is not narrowly naive about the torah, as first glance might indicate. It explores a range of issues related to faith. Torah keeping is not the whole of biblical faith, but it is the indispensable beginning point. Out of a solid orientation in obedience, the psalm then explores other issues. It includes a complaint against God that asks, "How long?" (vv. 82-86). It asks God to act out of steadfast love toward the covenant partner (vv. 76,124,149; cf. Ps. 33:5,18,22, already considered). It asks God to make his promise real and visible (vv. 58,76,123,133,154). It anticipates *shalom* (v. 165). To enter into the piety of this psalm we must break the stereotype of *retribution* regularly assigned here. It is not a psalm of bargaining, but a psalm of utter trust and submission. In some ways, it parallels the prose narrative of Job 1–2, which struggles against the same stereotype. In that narrative as well, it is not argued that "good people prosper and evil people suffer." Rather, it is simply a statement of trust and submission to a God who has been found to be good and generous.[39]

Psalm 119 thus is structured with delicate sophistication about the life of the spirit. On the one hand, the psalm understands that life with Yahweh is a two-way street. Torah keepers have a right to expect something from Yahweh. Obedience gives entry to seek God's attention and God's gift. Though close to it, this psalm does not bargain. This is the speech of one who has access not because of arrogance, but because of submission. The speech is not unduly deferential and certainly not strident. It is an articulation of legitimate expectation between partners who have learned to trust each other.

On the other hand, those legitimate expectations from God are given an evangelical cast. Finally having earned the right to speak, the speaker nevertheless throws himself on the mercy of God and waits for a move from God—a free, unfettered, uncoerced move from God. There is, to be sure, some comfort in recalling the torah (v. 52). But finally the psalm does not overrate torah. It is Yahweh who is the portion of the speaker (v. 57), not the torah nor one's keeping of the torah.[40] Thus the torah becomes a point of entry for exploring the whole range of interactions with Yahweh. Clearly this psalm probes beyond the simplistic formulation of Psalm 1. A life of full obedience is not a conclusion of faith. It is a beginning point and an access to a life filled with many-sided communion with God. It is by mercy and not by obedience that this one lives (v. 77).

Psalms 15 and 24

Under torah psalms, we may mention Psalms 15 and 24, though 24 is more complicated than that. Both psalms, in any case, regard torah obedience as a qualification for access to God in the sanctuary. In Psalm 15, verses 2-5a answer the question of verse 1. The substance of verses 2-5a is that a torah keeper, a genuinely righteous person is one who is permitted to enter the shrine and enjoy God's presence.[41] The same is true in Psalm 24:3-6, with torah provisions specifically in verse 4.

These two psalms taken alone may offend, because they suggest that only obedient persons may enter into God's presence. But it is important to recall that this spirituality reflects only the well-oriented community, one that has not yet addressed a theologically ambiguous or morally disruptive world. Life here is still to be comprehended in coherent categories. Since life is theologically secure, it is not inappropriate that access to God be measured in terms of conformity to what is known, trusted, and found reliable. In such a properly functioning world, such expectations have credibility and importance. There is as of yet, no crisis of *nomos*, no sense of approaching anomie. In that world, one does not sense that God is morally indifferent. How human persons obey or disobey matters decisively.

Wisdom Psalms

Another expression of a well-ordered, reliable world is in the wisdom psalms.[42] These tend to be didactic in tone and relatively amorphous in shape. They are best identified by their subject matter.

Psalm 37

This is the most obviously sapiential of all the psalms. Indeed it is a collection of sayings that might easily be found in the book of Proverbs. It appears to be a rather random collection of sayings without any order or development. However, there is an important qualification to that statement, for this psalm is acrostic and so is crafted with pedagogical purpose. That carefully ordered arrangement corresponds to the claim made for the substance of the psalm; that is, the world is exceedingly well ordered, and virtue is indeed rewarded.

1. The acrostic recital consists in a number of standard sapiential forms, each of which has an instructional intent. The most elemental wisdom form is evident in verses 1-2. It consists in two prohibitions, plus a motivation introduced by the proposition, "for" (כי).[43] The same form is apparent in verses 8-9, with three imperatives plus a motivation (cf. also vv. 27-28). There are also less didactic elements, including the dual observations of verses 10-11,

and verses 12-13 which state contrasts and present choices. See also verses 18-20, 21 for such constructs. In verse 16, we are offered a "better" saying, yet another wisdom form. But all the forms operate with the same assumption, namely, that the world is ordered, that conformity or nonconformity to this order has consequences, that the main issues of order concern social conduct. The theological point is that well-being (or lack of it) depends on knowing the order of creation, which is experienced in this community as social expectation.[44]

2. This poem, more explicitly than the torah psalms, articulates a close and predictable connection between *deed* and *consequence*. The purpose of such instruction (which indirectly attests the authority of the sovereign Creator) is to instill in the young socially acceptable modes of behavior. Such behavior contributes decisively to the well-being of the entire community. Thus the argument refers to God, but the case is made largely on utilitarian grounds—it works! And it reflects a community for whom most things work. Indeed, they understood themselves as the ones for whom "all things work together for good." And they understood themselves as "the ones who love God" (Rom. 8:28).

3. If we seek to find a more substantive concern in this psalm, we may find it in a series of reflections on *how to keep land and how to lose it*. Wisdom teaching generally reflects on the moral conditions whereby blessing is to be received and maintained, and land is the fundamental blessing.[45] This kind of reflection is linked to creation, for land is the specific experience of God's well-ordered creation over which humankind now has dominion.[46]

Psalm 37 offers five statements about land:

a) For the wicked shall be cut off;
　　　but those who wait for the Lord shall *possess the land* (v. 9).
b) ...the wicked will be no more...
　　　but the meek shall *possess the land*,
　　　and delight themselves in abundant prosperity (vv. 10-11).
c) For those blessed by the Lord shall *possess the land*,
　　　but those cursed by him shall be cut off (v. 22).
d) The righteous shall *possess the land*,
　　　and dwell upon it for ever (v. 29).
e) Wait for the Lord, and keep to his way,
　　　and he will exalt you to *possess the land* (v. 34).

It is evident that the statement about the "meek inheriting the earth" (Matt. 5:5) can and must be taken in a more general context of responsible conduct and land retention.[47] The connection is inescapable. The five statements that dominate the psalm are in fact synonymous. There is no development in the sayings, but each reiterates the main point. Land possession is closely linked to Yahweh, his governance and purpose. The psalm refutes every notion that the land can be had on our own terms. The land is not autonomous, nor are those who have it, but it relates to the Creator (Lev. 25:23) and true wisdom is to live in responsible awareness of the Creator and his intention. That basic affirmation is exposited through various other guidelines in the psalm, all of which seek to characterize acceptable *land-yielding behavior*.

Psalm 14

Psalm 14 is a reflective psalm. It embodies none of the conventional sapiential forms, but is judged to belong in this discussion on the basis of its subject matter. (The same psalm appears in 53:1-6.)

1. In its main theme the psalm is a statement about "practical atheism."[48] It reflects on one whose conduct is disordered and without focus, because it is not referred to God. A picture is drawn here of a creature whose life is not referred to the Creator. Notice in verse 1, the "fool" does not visibly announce atheism. It is only "in his heart"; i.e., he thinks and decides that way.

The result of such mistaken autonomy is the assumption that life is normless. Where God is not, everything is possible. The outcome is that the action of such a person is corrupt, without good (v. 1), without discernment, and therefore exploitative of other people (v. 4). The connection affirmed is clear. Where the Creator is not honored, creaturely life disintegrates and degenerates. The end result is a life filled with terror (v. 5a). There are no guards, limits, or boundaries, but everything is continually at risk. A person who follows that way has no supports for life beyond his own hopeless efforts, and those efforts are inevitably inadequate.

2. The psalm offers a countertheme. This is still God's world. A human life referred to God is still possible and worth living. God still governs from his heavenly throne (v. 2). God still sanctions a wise life, derived from proper worship (v. 2). God still attends to the kinds of folks who are righteous (v. 6). Thus the psalm is a reprimand and dismissal of those who deny the life given them in God's gracious sovereignty. But it does affirm that this reprimand and dismissal need not be.

3. Verse 6 makes an important and unexpected affirmation. One might conclude that life can ultimately be distorted by such disorderly living. But no. Yahweh still governs. This is the second use of God's name in the psalm. We have seen Yahweh mentioned in verse 2 as the ruling Lord. Now in verse 6, we are given the substance of that rule. Yahweh's business, even in a world distorted by fools, is to guard and keep the poor. They are not left to the capriciousness of the foolish (cf. Prov. 17:5). The ultimate mark of God's rule is not some ontological principle but the social certitude of Yahweh's solidarity with the poor. No amount of self-invention on the part of the rich and shrewd can

shake Yahweh out of a fundamental, nonnegotiable commitment to the marginal ones.

Thus, Psalm 14 is not simply a formal argument that Yahweh's governance survives the onslaught of fools who disregard it; it also asserts that God's governance is of a special kind.

4. Verse 7 is a rather odd verse, perhaps an addition. It is a wish and a hope for the rehabilitation of Judah and Israel. This is now the third use of Yahweh's name. Perhaps the verse is placed this way because at some point the poor who take refuge (v. 6) are recognized to be Israel and Judah. This verse interprets the preceding in terms of the community of faith.

The intent of Psalm 14 is to counter the temptation that humankind can manage the world in ways better than Yahweh's way (cf. Isa. 55:8-9). The alternative of the haughty ones is to reorder life's good for their own benefit at the expense of the vulnerable ones (cf. Ezek. 34:20-24). The psalm asserts and guarantees that life will not be so easily reorganized. God's will endures. God has made the world with some built-in protections for the weak against the strong, and that must not be mocked (cf. Isa. 10:12-14).

Songs of Retribution

Perhaps these should not be treated as a separate category, but rather grouped with the torah or wisdom psalms. But Psalms 111 and 112 are treated separately because they have a slightly different accent, an unqualified statement that the world is ruled by God with moral symmetry. That symmetry in the world is reflected in the disciplined acrostic structure of these two psalms. The world works so that persons receive the consequences of their actions (Gal. 6:7); this statement entertains no doubt about it.

Psalm 112

Psalm 112 is a clear example of such an argument.

1. The initial ejaculation of verse 1 credits the entire reliable system of retribution to the governance of Yahweh. Yahweh is praised because the world is reliable. Psalms 111 and 112 may belong together. Note that this opening formula is paralleled at the beginning of 111. If the two psalms belong together, then Psalm 111 provides the theological basis for the moral conviction of 112. The world is morally coherent because the Creator is mindful of his covenant (111:5), commands his covenant (111:9), and will be obeyed.

2. The main argument of the Psalm (112:1b-9) explores the proposition of 1b, that one who fears Yahweh, i.e., keeps torah, will be happy. Faithful obedience leads to well-being. The well-being of the happy persons runs the full range of human desire. It includes the most material yearning of wealth and

riches (v. 3). It also includes a steady heart that is not shattered by adversity, but has constancy in every circumstance (vv. 7-8; cf. Phil. 4:11-13).

The key phrase used to describe such a person is "righteous." All these psalms of orientation speak for a righteous person in a righteous society governed by a righteous God. Everything is all *right*. Thus, in verse 3, the righteous person's capacity to make things right endures. In verse 6 he is marked as righteous, which means he is himself integrated. He takes action to make right in his world. And in verse 9, his righteousness is again affirmed. This psalm reflects a clear and untroubled conscience.

The righteousness of the happy person is in the context of, and possible because of, the character of Yahweh, who is here known to be *gracious, merciful, and righteous*. That is the ground of human righteousness. This character of Yahweh is also stated in 111:3-4 (cf. Ps. 145:8-9) and likely appeals to the old creedal formulation of Exod. 34:6-7. Psalm 112 knows the best and most profound way in which Yahweh is characterized, and in this psalm we are dealing with a person in the image of this God, who corresponds to that image in the conduct of his life. Note that human life is characterized not by an *essence* but by faithful *actions*, as is Yahweh. This life is a happily oriented life because there is real harmony between creation and Creator. Israel's discernment of God and celebration of humanness come properly together.[49]

But the righteousness that makes this happy person is neither simply a quality of person nor an attribute. Rather, it is evident in the way he relates to others in his derivative governance of creation, i.e., in the way he exercises his dominion (Gen. 1:26-28). He gives generously (v. 5). He practices justice (v. 5). He cares for the poor (v. 9). We have seen in Psalm 14:6 that Yahweh is known fundamentally as a refuge for the poor. Now this person, faithful to this God, engages in the same practice. This psalm is a clear affirmation that virtue is relational. Goodness is not a condition or a property or a state of being, but a set of actions in social relations. Virtue concerns social relations precisely in relation to the distribution of economic justice. (Note this is also the mark of Job's claim upon God in Job 31:16-23.)[50] Generosity makes for joy in the life of faith.

3. Characteristically (as in Pss. 104:35; 145:20b), this psalm cannot resist a statement of contrast in verse 10. The stress is on the happy, righteous person. But to underscore the point, verse 10 asserts not only that the wicked do not act this way, but that they resist and are made miserable by their resistance. The wicked person is one who does not trust God's generosity and so cannot practice generosity. The wicked are not the morally bad, but those who grudgingly and grimly seek to monopolize and control rather than share. They are so grim, grudging, and greedy because they do not sense the enormous generosity of Yahweh.

In a way this psalm can be taken as a calculating guide on how to be happy. But its claim goes well beyond that. It asserts that giving life resources away to others in the community is the way to real joy. This psalm is echoed in Jesus' teaching, "Blessed are those who hunger and thirst for righteousness, for they shall be satisfied" (Matt. 5:6). Satisfaction and life fulfillment do not come from greed and self-filling and self-sufficiency. They come from trusting the generosity of God who always feeds us (Ps. 111:5), and we can in turn be generous. The happy person is the one who knows about the abundance of the Creator who withholds nothing needful from his precious creation. Believing that permits a very different social practice.

Occasions of Well-Being

All of the various psalms of orientation we have discussed thus far reflect a "peaceable kingdom." In all its parts, the "system" works, and the "system" refers to God's created order over which God presides in equity and faithfulness. The "system" also refers to a network of social relations, values, and expectations. On the basis of convincing firsthand experience the speaker in these psalms dares to postulate a correspondence between the way God orders the creation and the way in which society manages its choices. Everything is ordered and reliable. While the Psalms make that point theologically about God's governance *in heaven*, they also represent and reflect an *earthly* experience of the same order and reliability.

That orderliness and reliability is not a theoretical or abstract notion. It is known firsthand in the daily and seasonal experiences of life. Westermann has observed that confidence in creation is based on the pattern of blessings that are known especially in the family, household, and tribe.[51] The goodness of God is known here not by shattering intrusions but by quiet, unobtrusive sustenance. The regularity of creation is experienced in the predictable occurrences of birth, marriage, death, seedtime, and harvest. All these experiences testify to the Creator's regularity and reliability.

We may identify a number of psalms as occasional pieces that reflect and affirm God's goodness in the blessings of creation. In these God is nowhere visible, but is discerned as the guarantor of the critical points through which life is affirmed and enhanced.[52]

Psalm 133

Psalm 133 is an eloquent affirmation of family or tribal solidarity.[53] The structure of the poem consists in an opening affirmation (v. 1) and a conclusion (v. 3b) which enclose two metaphors. The opening line celebrates an experience. The conclusion identifies that experience as blessing. Only in the last statement does the name of Yahweh occur. Yahweh does nothing, but is acknowledged to be the hidden source of such well-being. But the reasoning is "from below," from experience.

The celebrated unity is articulated in two metaphors. First, unity is like "precious oil" (v. 2) which is a measure of extravagance and well-being (cf. Mark 14:3-9; Luke 7:46), of blessing beyond expectation. Second, the celebrated unity is like the dew (v. 3a) which is given miraculously and which gives life in an otherwise parched context (cf. Hos. 14:5).

All of the images point to what is "natural," the generous performance of creation, without condition, planning, or the concrete action of Yahweh. The main force of the language is that of "creation-blessing." The unity is as good as creation is said to be in Genesis 1. And the word *pleasant* (v. 1) moves in an aesthetic direction.[54]

Psalm 133 reflects Israel's capacity to appreciate the common joys of life and to attribute them to the well-ordered generosity of Yahweh. One can only hypothesize about the time such a poem was formed or used. It may be reflective of "family reunion," of the gathering of the tribe, of any social occasion of "brothers," clan leaders being together without conflict. The voice may be that of a relieved elder, anxious that the younger generation not destroy itself in conflict.[55] The poem anticipates the solidarity and harmony of all humanity as it lives without defensiveness in a creation benevolent enough to care for all.

Psalm 131

Psalm 131 is also a simple expression of submission to the reliable ordering of life. Verses 1-2 are likely the original form of the poem. At the outset Yahweh is identified, almost abruptly, as the one who will be credited with a well-ordered life. There is here a glad acceptance of life on the terms God gives. The body of the poem consists in two statements. The first is a negative denial or a statement of innocence (v. 1). It is marked by three negatives, with a fourth one understood: not lifted up, not raised too high, not walked in greatness, [not] in things beyond me. The speaker has not thought too highly of himself (cf. Rom. 12:3), which means he understands the proper relation to God. It is not a relationship between equals, but is one of subordination, submission, trust, which this speaker gladly accepts.

The positive counterpart in verse 2 is an affirmation of serenity and well-being from one who trusts in God's motherly care. It is a daring metaphor, approached in other ways in Num. 11:11-15 and Isa. 49:14-15. It is a characterization of relationship with God that grows out of observing the most trusting, elemental, and dependent relationship in all human interaction. The child does not try to be the equal of the mother or independent of the mother.

The need and claims of this psalm are contrasted most harshly in Isa.

2:6-22, where Israel is accused of being proud, haughty, lifted up, arrogant, and autonomous. That way, says the prophet, leads to destruction. The voice of this psalm announces the positive counterpart. This does not mean abdication or resignation, but the recognition of how life with God finally is.

The use of this remarkable domestic metaphor makes a stunning theological affirmation about the proper ordering of life. First, it affirms that creatureliness is contrasted with autonomy. The faithful human creature, like a small baby, like a tiny bird waiting for the mother to feed it, has no inclination for autonomy. Second, the poem understands that such glad, submissive reliance leaves one free of anxiety, for anxiety is wrought either in trying to be self-sufficient (which one cannot be) or in trying to be an equal of the mother-God, rather that a fed dependent.

The piety reflected in this psalm is directly opposed to modernity with its drive toward independence, self-sufficiency, and autonomy. It is worth noting that the Psalms deny the Oedipal inclination that there can be freedom only if the controlling, authoritarian father-god be slain or denied. The myth of modernity believes that real maturity is to be free of every relationship of dependence. But when the metaphor is changed from a harsh controlling father to a gently feeding mother, it is evident that the human goal need not be breaking away, but happy trust.

If Psalm 131 were taken as the whole of our relationship with God, one might judge it to be naive and romantic. Without taking it for the whole statement, it does provide for us a remarkable metaphor for some dimensions of faithful living that are lost in many of our other images for our relationship with God.

The third verse of the psalm appears to be added. As we have seen in Psalm 14:7, there seems to be a process by which intimate statements of faith are systematically reassigned to Judah and Israel. In this psalm, verse 3 has the effect of identifying Israel as the trusting child. The image of Israel is then of one who has ceased to insist on its own way and has submitted to the trustworthy will of Yahweh. That kind of submission is exactly what makes it possible for Israel (or any other) to hope. Unless there is submission, there will be no hope, for autonomy and self-sufficiency are finally postures of hopelessness in which free gifts are excluded and one is left to one's own resources. In this psalm (unlike Isa. 2:6-22) Israel is able to hope and to receive good gifts from this feeding God.

Thou didst hide thy face,
   I was dismayed.
To thee, O Lord, I cried;
   and to the Lord I made supplication:
"What profit is there in my death,
   if I go down to the Pit?
Will the dust praise thee?
   Will it tell of thy faithfulness?
Hear, O Lord, and be gracious to me!
   O Lord, be thou my helper!"

Psalm 30:7b-10

3

Psalms of Disorientation

The problem with a hymnody that focuses on equilibrium, coherence, and symmetry (as in Chapter 2) is that it may deceive and cover over. Life is not like that. Life is also savagely marked by disequilibrium, incoherence, and unrelieved assymetry. In our time—perhaps in any time—that needs no argument or documentation.

It is a curious fact that the church has, by and large, continued to sing songs of orientation in a world increasingly experienced as disoriented. That may be laudatory. It could be that such relentlessness is an act of bold defiance in which these psalms of order and reliability are flung in the face of the disorder. In that way, they insist that nothing shall separate us from the love of God. Such a "mismatch" between our *life experience of disorientation* and our *faith speech of orientation* could be a great evangelical "nevertheless" (as in Hab. 3:18). Such a counterstatement insists that God does in any case govern, rule, and order, regardless of how the data seem to appear. And therefore, songs of torah, wisdom, creation, and retribution speak truly, even if the world is experienced as otherwise. It is possible that the church uses the psalms of orientation in this way.

But at best, this is only partly true. It is my judgment that this action of the church is less an evangelical defiance guided by faith, and much more a frightened, numb denial and deception that does not want to acknowledge or experience the disorientation of life. The reason for such relentless affirmation of orientation seems to come, not from faith, but from the wishful optimism of our culture.[1] Such a denial and cover-up, which I take it to be, is an odd inclination for passionate Bible users, given the large number of psalms that are songs of lament, protest, and complaint about the incoherence that is experienced in the world. At least it is clear that a church that goes on singing "happy songs" in the face of raw reality is doing something very different from what the Bible itself does.

I think that serious religious use of the lament psalms has been minimal because we have believed that faith does not mean to acknowledge and embrace negativity. We have thought that acknowledgment of negativity was somehow an act of unfaith, as though the very speech about it conceded too much about God's "loss of control."

The point to be urged here is this: The use of these "psalms of darkness" may be judged by the world to be *acts of unfaith and failure*, but for the trusting community, their use is *an act of bold faith*, albeit a transformed faith. It is an act of bold faith on the one hand, because it insists that the world must be experienced as it really is and not in some pretended way. On the other hand, it is bold because it insists that all such experiences of disorder are a proper subject for discourse with God. There is nothing out of bounds, nothing precluded or inappropriate. Everything properly belongs in this conversation of the heart. To withhold parts of life from that conversation is in fact to withhold part of life from the sovereignty of God. Thus these psalms make the important connection: everything must be *brought to speech*, and everything brought to speech must be *addressed to God*, who is the final reference for all of life.

But such a faith is indeed a *transformed* faith, one that does not *conform* (cf. Rom. 12:2). The community that uses these psalms of disorientation is not easily linked with civil religion, which goes "from strength to strength." It is, rather, faith in a very different God, one who is present in, participating in, and attentive to the darkness, weakness, and displacement of life. The God assumed by and addressed in these psalms is a God "of sorrows, and acquainted with grief." It is more appropriate to speak of this God in the categories of *fidelity* than of *immutability*, and when fidelity displaces immutability, our notion of God's sovereignty is deeply changed. These psalms of disorientation are a profound contradiction to notions of an immutable God.[2]

But the transformation concerns not only God. Life also is transformed. Now life is understood to be a pilgrimage or process through the darkness that belongs properly to humanness. While none would choose to be there, such seasons of life are not always experiences of failure for which guilt is to be assigned, but may be a placement in life for which the human person or community is not responsible and therefore not blamed.[3] The presupposition and affirmation of these psalms is that precisely in such deathly places as presented in these psalms new life is given by God. We do not understand how that could be so or even why it is so. But we regularly learn and discern that there—more than anywhere else—newness that is not of our own making breaks upon us.

The linguistic function of these psalms is that the psalm may *evoke reality* for someone who has engaged in self-deception and still imagines and pretends life is well-ordered, when in fact it is not. The denial may be of a broken relationship, a lost job, a medical diagnosis, or whatever. The harsh and abrasive speech of a statement of disorientation may penetrate the deception and say, "No, this is how it really is." In such a case, *language leads experience*, so that the speaker speaks what is unknown and unexperienced until it is finally brought to speech. It is not this way until it is said to be this way.[4]

It is no wonder that the church has intuitively avoided these psalms. They lead us into dangerous acknowledgment of how life really is. They lead us into the presence of God where everything is not polite and civil. They cause us to think unthinkable thoughts and utter unutterable words. Perhaps worst, they lead us away from the comfortable religious claims of "modernity" in which everything is managed and controlled. In our modern experience, but probably also in every successful and affluent culture, it is believed that enough power and knowledge can tame the terror and eliminate the darkness.[5] Very much a "religion of orientation" operates on that basis. But our honest experience, both personal and public, attests to the resilience of the darkness, in spite of us. The remarkable thing about Israel is that it did not banish or deny the darkness from its religious enterprise. It embraces the darkness as the very stuff of new life. Indeed, Israel seems to know that new life comes nowhere else.

Whether this speech articulates, illuminates, or evokes experience, it does move the awareness and imagination of the speaker away from life well-ordered into an arena of terror, raggedness, and hurt. In some sense this speech is a visceral release of the realities and imagination that have been censored, denied, or held in check by the dominant claims of society. For that reason, it does not surprise us that these psalms tend to hyperbole, vivid imagery, and statements that offend "proper" and civil religious sensitivities. They are a means of *expressing* that tries to match *experience*, that also does not fit with religious sensitivity. That is, in "proper" religion *the expression should not be expressed*.[6] But it is also the case that *these experiences should not be experienced*. They are speech "at the limit," speaking about experience "at the limit."[7]

We may observe two factors that operate in the midst of this liberation of expression. First, the gamut of expressions employed here never escapes address to Yahweh. What is said to Yahweh may be scandalous and without redeeming social value, but these speakers are completely committed, and whatever must be said about the human situation must be said directly to Yahweh, who is Lord of the human experience and partner with us in it.[8] That does not mean things are toned down. Yahweh does not have protected sensitivities. Yahweh is expected and presumed to receive the fullness of Israel's speech.

Second, though this speech is liberated and expansive, it tends to come to expression in rather consistent and rigorous forms. That is not because the speakers are dull and unimaginative and cannot think of a fresh way to speak; it is rather that the speech itself imposes a kind of recurring order in the disorientation, so that it has an orderliness of its own that is known and recognized in the community. The speech thus serves in a remarkable way, both to speak about the collapse of all oriented forms, and yet to assure that even in the chaos of the moment there is a Yahweh-directed order.[9] The form itself testifies that "darkness and light are both alike to thee" (Ps. 139:12). As we shall see, this structured way is a means of leading the speaker into, but also through and out of, the darkness. Generation after generation has discovered that the form of speech holds, even in the darkness. As the speech has form, so it is discerned that the experience has form too. That form of experience is known in the form of speech.[10]

That form has been variously studied, first of all by Gunkel,[11] and then refined in a most discerning way by Westermann.[12] It will be understood that no single psalm follows exactly the ideal form, but the form provides a way of noticing how the psalm proceeds. That form has a dramatic movement that Westermann has usefully subsumed under two parts:[13]

1. *Plea.* A complaint that God should correct a skewed situation.

a) Address to God.   Albertz has shown that the address tends to be intimate and personal.[14] The complaint is not spoken by one who is a stranger to Yahweh, but one who has a long history of trustful interaction.

b) Complaint.   The purpose of the prayer is to characterize for God how desperate the situation is. While the situation may be variously one of sickness, isolation, imprisonment, or destruction, the imagery of the speech is most often about death. The rhetoric appears to overstate the case, hopefully to evoke from Yahweh an intrusive, transformative act. While it is not always the case, the complaint tends not only to describe a situation of urgent need, but to hold Yahweh accountable for it. The speaker intends to turn his problem into a problem for Yahweh, for it is Yahweh who is both able and responsible for doing something about it.

c) Petition.   On the basis of the complaint, the speaker makes a petition that asks God to act decisively.[15] This element is perhaps the most intense because it is spoken as a bold imperative. There is no suggestion here of either reticence or deference. The speaker assumes some "rights against the throne" (cf. Job 31:35-37), and so the urgency of the speech has a judicial quality. The speaker does, of course, ask for attentive compassion, but the speaker also insists on his rights. It is a plea for justice as much as mercy, with the suggestion that the unjust situation has arisen because of Yahweh's inattentiveness.

d) Motivations.   Less crucial, but most interesting, is the inclination of the psalms to provide motivations to give God reason to act. Some of this is less than noble, but it is the speech of a desperate voice that has no time for being noble. At times the motivation comes peculiarly close to bargaining, bribing, or intimidating.[16] But this also needs to be taken as a kind of parity assumed in the relationship. Among the motivations are these:

- The speaker is *innocent* and so is entitled to help.
- The speaker is *guilty*, but repents and seeks forgiveness and restoration.
- The speaker recalls *God's goodness to an earlier generation*, which serves as a precedent for God's goodness now. God should do once again what was done in the past.
- The speaker is *valued by God* as one who praises. If the speaker is permitted to die, the speaker will cease to praise, and the loss will be Yahweh's.
- The speaker finally goes beyond self and appeals to Yahweh to consider *God's own power, prestige, and reputation.* Finally, the loss in death will not be to the speaker, but to Yahweh who will be perceived as unable to care for his own. (This may be analogous to the inability of a national government to protect its own citizens in a hostile country. Although the citizen may suffer, the key loss is that the government loses respect and face among the nations.) The appeal is ''for thy name's sake,'' which means for the sake of God's reputation (cf. Ezek. 36:22-23).

Thus the motivation runs the gamut from conventional covenantal concerns to a less ''honorable'' appeal to Yahweh's self-interest. The speaker has no time for theological niceties, but must secure action for his own well-being.

e) Imprecation.   It is clear that such speech tends to be regressive, i.e., it moves into unguarded language that in most religious discourse is censored and precluded. Perhaps the most regressive element is the imprecation. This is the voice of resentment and vengeance that will not be satisfied until God works retaliation on those who have done the wrong. The most extreme statement of this, almost unrelieved, is in Psalm 109. But the same motif occurs elsewhere. While we may think this ignoble and unworthy, it demonstrates that in these psalms of disorientation, as life collapses, the old disciplines and safeguards also collapse. One speaks unguardedly about how it in fact is. The stunning fact is that Israel does not purge this unguardedness but regards it as genuinely faithful communication.

These five elements serve, on the one hand, to characterize how desperate is the need. On the other hand, these elements serve to lodge that need at the throne of Yahweh, so that it is made unambiguously Yahweh's problem, about which Yahweh must do something. Life may be disoriented, but even in the disorientation, Israel is clear about the place where the problem may be deposited. God is treated as the responsibly governing One, when all the conventions of governance have failed.

2. *Praise*.[17] When the psalm makes its next move, it is a surprising one. Things are different. Something has changed. We cannot ever know whether it is changed circumstance, or changed attitude, or something of both. But the speaker now speaks differently. Now the sense of urgency and desperation is replaced by joy, gratitude, and well-being. All of this Westermann summarizes as *praise*. This movement from *plea* to *praise* is one of the most startling in all of Old Testament literature. The *praise* element tends to include three factors:

a) Assurance of being heard. In the complaint discussed above, Yahweh is often accused of being absent, remote, unresponsive, not listening. Now that is changed. The speaker now is convinced that Yahweh has heard the petition. On the one hand, we may conclude that in stressful situations what we most yearn for is that we will be heard. That in itself is enough. Or alternatively, one must assume that if Yahweh has heard, he will act. It is not thinkable that God would hear and then not act. And therefore the crucial thing is Yahweh's hearing, from which everything else happily will follow.

b) Payment of vows. Apparently, the speaker in time of trouble had vowed that if delivered he would keep such and such a vow to give or pay something as an offering of thanksgiving and praise. Now in this moment of joy, the speaker has not forgotten. And so this is an act of faithfulness, of keeping one's word.

It is worth reflecting on the way in which coming through the depth of the plea to the praise permits one to be generous. When life is freely given to one in "the pit," it evokes gratitude that motivates the full giving of offerings. Conversely, we may surmise, when one does not enter the pit honestly, then there can only be grudge and not gratitude, and likely no generous keeping of vows.

c) Doxology and praise. The most important element of resolution is doxology and praise. The God who has been accused is now acknowledged as generous and faithful and saving. Now if one stands outside the poem, one may argue that this part of the psalm expresses the true character of God, worthy of praise. And the earlier accusation and protest are a misunderstanding and therefore unfair.

But if one enters into the poem and takes its movement as seriously reflecting the relationship between the two partners, then one must conclude that it is indeed the complaint which moves Yahweh to act. And each part of the psalm must be taken "realistically" as reflective of a real moment in this relationship. Thus the sequence of *complaint-praise* is a necessary and legitimate way with God, each part in its own, appropriate time. But one moment is not less faithful than the other. The doxology makes clear that things are changed.

The movement of the poem traces and evokes and makes possible the movement of the relationship. It is the honest address to God that moves the relationship to new possibilities of faithfulness that can only be reached through such risky honesty. In the full relationship, *the season of plea* must be taken as seriously as the *season of praise*.

d) We may consider what happened to make the movement *from plea to praise* possible. Clearly there was some kind of action or transaction in the unspoken space of the poem between the two elements. Thus, e.g., in Psalm 13, something happened between verse 4 and verse 5. In Psalm 22, something happened between verse 21 and verse 22. It is possible that this was an "inward, spiritual" experience. More likely it was an outward, visible act by some member of the community, mediating the fresh move of Yahweh to the speaker. If this prayer takes place in a liturgical or quasi-liturgical setting, then the "in-between act" may be a gesture or a word by someone formally authorized to do so, e.g., an elder, a priest, or some such functionary.[18] Whatever it was must have had a profound emotional, as well as theological, impact on the complainer, for a whole new world of trust and gratitude is entered into in that moment.[19]

The most used hypothesis about this move is that offered by Begrich.[20] He proposed that an authorized speaker answered the plea in a standard "salvation oracle." These speeches, now preserved in such texts as Jer. 30:10-11; Isa. 41:8-13; 43:1-7, originally stood at the in-between point in the psalm, but have now been separated into independent units in widely different parts of the Bible. The salvation oracle is a promise on God's part to be present with, to help, and to intervene on behalf of the complainer. The recurring feature of such a speech is the sovereign "fear not" of Yahweh. And that speech, so goes the hypothesis, resolves the desperate situation and permits the speaker to begin life anew in confidence and gratitude. It is argued that the "fear not" represents the primal communication that touches the deepest fears and angers and opens the most profound possibilities, when it is spoken by one who has consent from us to change our world. On purely literary grounds, Begrich's hypothesis has much to commend it, because it shows the detailed correlation of *complaint* (in the Psalms) and *assurance* (in Second Isaiah). But Begrich must argue that texts now widely separated have this intimate connection with each other.

The other factor that may illuminate Begrich's hypothesis is an experiential one. We are speech creatures. We do wait to be addressed. And when we are decisively addressed by one with power and credibility, it does indeed change our world. We must, of course, not forget that Begrich's proposal is only a hypothesis, but it is one that permits us to proceed with some awareness to the actual text.

What is clear in the text is that there is a covenantal-theological move from one part of the text to the next. Beyond that, we are engaged in speculation. We do not know concretely how this covenantal-theological move was made. What we do know, both from the *structure of the text* and *our own experience*, is that grievance addressed to an authorized partner does free us. That is the insight behind Freud's theory of talk-therapy, that we do not move beyond the repressed memory unless we speak it out loud to one with authority who hears. In our culture we have understood that in terms of one-on-one therapy. We still have to learn that this is true socially and liturgically. These psalms provide important materials for that learning.

There is a wide variety of songs of disorientation. Here I group together all the psalms that reflect (from one side or the other) the awareness that things between Yahweh and Israel are messed up. For that speech of disorientation, I take the personal lament psalm to be the clearest and most simple example. From that nearly pure type, we will consider a number of other such psalms, all reflecting disorientation, but some of them ranging far afield from the classic shape of the lament psalm. In the broadest sense, they have one partner or the other speak about the *disarray* into which the relationship has fallen. It is a disarray that concerns both partners in various ways.

Personal Lament

As will be clear in what follows, there is a great variety of psalms of disorientation. We begin our consideration of them with personal lament psalms for two reasons. First, lament psalms constitute a very considerable part of the collection.[21] We will advance our argument if we see that lament psalms are a quite standard and stylized way in which Israel articulated disorientation. Second, because the form is so clear in these, we will have easier access into the other psalms of disorientation when we see that the same issues are presented in a variety of different ways. The issue in all of these psalms is that something is amiss in the relationship, and it must be righted. This is not to suggest that the other psalms of disorientation are in any way derived from the personal lament, but that they participate in the same issues, which may be variously articulated.

Psalm 13

We begin with Psalm 13 because it most easily lets us see the form and the argument. Psalm 13 is indeed a speech of disorientation. Something is terribly wrong in the life of the speaker, and in the life of the speaker with God.

1. Verses 1-2. The psalm begins with four questions which in English are readily rendered as five. The questions addressed to Yahweh are rhetorical questions that do not seek an answer. Rather they are statements that describe a

situation of disorientation and intend to fix the blame firmly on Yahweh. They do not seek information but rather accuse Yahweh of being responsible for the trouble. The complaint is in two parts. First, in verse 1, the trouble is absence of God ("forget," "hide"), and where God is absent, there is disorientation. Second, in verse 2, the derivative trouble is pain, sorrow, and worst of all, the awareness that enemies prevail. Thus, the crisis in the *relationship with Yahweh* is at the bottom of the external problem of *troubles in the world*. The two cannot be separated for the seriously faithful. The speaker does not for a moment entertain the thought that the trouble comes from guilt or failure. It is because of Yahweh's irresponsible absence, which is regarded as not only unfortunate, but unfaithful to covenant.[22]

The speech begins abruptly and inexplicably. While the opening verse names the name of Yahweh, it is exceedingly terse. It is as though the pain is so acute that there is no time for convention or nicety. The speech is not reasoned. It is a barrage of someone in such sore condition that the accusation must be stated in its most vigorous form.

2. Verses 3-4 provide a *petition* and a *motivation*. The petition is in a triad of imperatives: "consider, answer, lighten." The psalmist is clear that the dread situation is beyond his own coping. There will be no way out of the trouble, unless Yahweh can act.

In verse 3, Yahweh is named a second time. Here, there is time for an address of intimacy, "my God." It is as though with the initial onslaught, the pent-up rage is released, and now there is opportunity to acknowledge and reaffirm the relationship necessary for the appeal. "My God" indicates a past relationship that is the proper ground and context for this urgent appeal.

The triad of imperatives is followed by the motivation. This also is given three times. In the RSV, "lest" is used for all three motivations, though the third is lacking in Hebrew: "lest I die...lest my enemy say..., [lest] my foes rejoice." The motivations communicate to Yahweh what is at stake. The psalm succeeds in making the problem into Yahweh's problem, because if Yahweh's partner be ridiculed, Yahweh is also diminished. We do not need to engage in any ontological speculation about whether God knows this before the speech is spoken. Inside the psalm the speech proceeds on the assumption that Yahweh is now being told what Yahweh needs to know. And that, of course, is the premise on which all serious prayer operates. In this serious exchange, the speaker provides data out of which Yahweh makes a new act.[23] The speaker does indeed impinge upon Yahweh in a new way.

Then the psalmist waits. It is a long wait after verse 4, a wait in the darkness of death, a wait in disorientation, a waiting "until hell freezes over." There must be such a wait, perhaps a long wait, because there is no other court of appeal. One must simply wait here until there is a response.

3. Then—we do not know how long the wait was—things are changed. When the psalmist speaks again, he is on the way to a new orientation. Verses 5-6, which resolve the situation of disorientation, are presented with three statements of trust plus a motivational clause: "I have trusted... my heart shall rejoice... I will sing... because... (כי)."

There are three self-announcements: "I... my heart... I." The language reflects a new liberated self-confidence. And this is matched three times by reference to Yahweh: "*thy* steadfast love... *thy* salvation... Yahweh." The psalmist is clear about the source of help. Equally interesting are the three verbs. The first one is completed action: "I have trusted." Presumably this means, the waiting in the dark space after verse 4 was not an act of distrust. There was a real wait—and now it is completed. The other two verbs are present-future and say what will now happen because of the satisfied trust: *rejoice* and *sing*. Life is broken loose in doxology. And the reason is because Yahweh has responded appropriately, giving the faithful what the faithful should and must have. The action of Yahweh about which we are told shows that life is not fundamentally disoriented, because faithful people are dealt with faithfully. And so, the speaker ends with a sense of disorientation overcome, released to a new, grateful, trustful communion.

The dramatic movement of the psalm from disorientation to (new) orientation is marked by three uses of the name "Yahweh." In verse 1, Yahweh is named, only to be assaulted. In verse 3, Yahweh is named with an appellation of intimacy as ground for appeal. And in verse 6, this accused Yahweh has now become the praised Yahweh, object of doxology.

Psalm 86

This Psalm is also a personal lament. It also speaks out of a situation of disorientation. As we shall see, its main moves are not unlike those of Psalm 13, but its rhetoric is much more complicated.

1. We may see the wording of this psalm weaving together three concerns:

a) There is the *petition*, which asks God to act on behalf of a needy covenant partner. These sayings are frequently accompanied by *a motivational clause* that gives God reason to act:

incline ... answer ... for (v. 1),
preserve ... for ... save ... (v. 2),
be gracious ... for ... (v. 3),
gladden ... for ... (v. 4),
turn ... take pity ... give strength ... save ... (v. 16),
show ... (v. 17).

At the beginning (vv. 1-4) and end (vv. 16-17) a strong, resilient urging is made upon Yahweh.

b) The actual *complaint*, which tells God how bad it is, is not very extensive. It is confined to verse 14. Unlike Psalm 13, there is no suggestion that Yahweh is responsible, or that the psalmist is angry with Yahweh. The situation of distress is also indicated in verse 13 ("depths of Sheol") and in verse 17 (concerning hate).

c) The third element concerns *resolve for a new life* after the deliverance, which is here utterly certain. Verse 11 concerns a new life of faithful obedience. In verse 13, remarkably, the completed verb is used, "Thou hast delivered." The same is true in the concluding line of verse 17: "Thou, Lord, hast helped me and comforted me." Thus the resolve of verses 11,13,17 form a double closure to the petitions of verses 1-4,6,16,17. The elements are not as nicely distinguished as in Psalm 13, but they are easy enough to identify.

2. This poem contains an abundance of address to God in direct speech, and that speech has the sense of *doxology*. It is not urging, or coercion, but it is the voice of those who freely praise God, even in the midst of trouble. We may distinguish four features of doxological address to God:

a) There are two statements of *God's uniqueness*:[24]

There is none like thee among the gods, O Lord (v. 8).
Thou alone art God (v. 10).

These two statements are quotes of rather standard formulae. It is not made explicit wherein Yahweh's uniqueness lies, but the body of the psalm suggests it is in Yahweh's attentiveness to poor, needy, desperate persons. Such a characterization may function as a motivation, by reminding God of who he is (cf. Psalm 82). But that point is not pressed.

b) There are also appeals to the rather stylized doxologies that form a group, seemingly derived from Exod. 34:6-7.[25] This provides a major catalog concerning Yahweh's character:

good and forgiving, abounding in steadfast love (v. 5),
great and doest wondrous things (v. 10),
a God merciful and gracious,
slow to anger and abounding in steadfast love and faithfulness (v. 15).

It is important that such conventional formulae are available to persons in distress. The psalm indicates that the creedal or catechetical formulae of Israel are not abandoned in such contexts of misery. Indeed, the faith of Israel functions precisely in such contexts, because Yahweh is known to be *a God peculiarly pertinent to seasons of disorientation*. In this connection, we may note the way in which Israel copes with seasons of darkness. In such times, Israel does not "free lance," or try *ad hoc* to make faith affirmations out of private "experience.'' It is in such times that Israel falls back on the tried and true formulations that seem to have special credibility in such times. That may be an important factor in using the Psalms, especially in a time of ''subjective consciousness'' as ours, which wants always to find ''meaning'' through personal feeling and inclination. Israel knew another way made available in this stylized speech.

c) This psalm has an unusual number of uses of the second person pronouns. These are of two types in Hebrew, though the difference is not evident in translation. The larger group are pronounal endings, attached either to verbs or nouns: ''thy ear'' (v. 1); ''thy servant,'' ''in thee'' (v. 2); ''to thee'' (v. 3); ''thy servant,'' ''to thee'' (v. 4); ''on thee,'' ''thou dost answer'' (v. 7); ''thou hast made,'' ''before thee,'' ''thy name'' (v. 9); ''thy way,'' ''thy truth,'' ''thy name'' (v. 11); ''to thee,'' ''thy name'' (v. 12); ''thy steadfast love,'' ''thou hast delivered'' (v. 13); ''thy strength,'' ''thy servant,'' ''thy handmaid'' (v. 16). This repeated use makes an appeal that presents the situation of trouble as squarely Yahweh's problem. The psalmist does not doubt Yahweh's capacity. The problem rather is making it Yahweh's concern, in order to mobilize God's mercy and God's power. Many of these psalms readily assume God's *capacity*. The psalm is concerned for God's *will* or *intentionality*, and so it engages in persuasion.

d) Finally we may note a rather remarkable usage, namely the direct use of אתה, the nominative pronoun used in direct address. In contrast to the dependent suffix, this is an independent element used to make a strong expression. The suffix is used inevitably and conventionally. The independent pronoun is used only intentionally for emphasis. There are six such uses, and they appear to be placed in a way that is worth noting:

> You (אתה) are my God (v. 2)
> > Surely you (אתה) O Lord (v. 5)
> > > Surely great are you (אתה)
> > > You (אתה) are God alone (v. 10)
> > You (אתה), O Lord (v. 15)
> Surely you (אתה), Yahweh (v. 17).

It is possible to suggest that these six uses of ''thou'' as an independent pronoun of direct address are arranged in an intentional, chiastic order. As the text now stands, the pronoun at the beginning and at the end of the psalm is a confessional statement:

> Thou art my God (v. 2).
> Because thou, Lord, hast helped me (v. 17).

The verbs accompanying these statements are very strong: *save* and *help*.

Strategically it is important that the first is expectant and the second is completed, reflecting the dramatic movement of the psalm.

Closer to the center of the psalm, the pronoun is used in verses 5 and 12, both times accompanied by אֲדֹנָי, "Lord," and each time containing a creedal formula:

> Good and forgiving, abounding in steadfast love (v. 5),
> A God merciful and gracious,
> slow to anger and abounding in steadfast love and faithfulness (v. 15).

And near the center of the psalm in verse 10, is a double use which in different ways articulates the uniqueness of Yahweh:

> You are great, doing impossibilities,[26]
> You alone are God.[27]

These six uses provide a structure for the psalm, and on them are hung all the doxological language that dominates this poem.

The movement of the psalm is parallel to that of Psalm 13, from trouble to confidence, but the moves are much more complex. What interests us here is the speaker's relentless reference to Yahweh. In the midst of the darkness, in the season of disorientation, Yahweh is affirmed, known to be the one who abides, who is not intimidated or alienated by the disorientation. The creedal claims of Yahweh are still credible in the darkness, perhaps especially credible here.[28]

Psalm 35

This is a third complaint psalm that articulates the common motifs, in yet another configuration. Obviously, it is much longer and more repetitious than Psalm 13, and the need is more desperate than in Psalm 86. That psalm still had some serenity, as if the speaker were able to discern himself above the trouble. Thus the mood is one of trust and doxology. Psalm 86 is the speech of disorientation that is not yet too severe, or which has not yet fully faced the darkness. But here in Psalm 35, the trouble is closer, the hatred is stronger, and the trust in Yahweh seems a bit more uncertain. While the Psalms cannot be firmly sequenced, this psalm evidences a situation badly deteriorated compared to that of 86.

1. The *petition* to Yahweh is very strong. Verses 1-3 begin abruptly with a barrage of military images. The petition is continued in verse 17. It is assumed that the trouble is Yahweh's business, if not his fault, and it is time that he act. Here the images have changed from *military* to those of the *jungle*. All such imaginative language is designed to get God to move on matters that are God's

proper business. Finally, in verses 22-24 there is an urgent request for God's presence, culminating in the word "righteousness." Note that the appeal is to the righteousness of God, to the capacity and will of God to act to make things right again. It is an appeal out beyond the speaker, who now cannot control the situation.

The language of war and jungle is regressive language, articulating the sense that things have gotten out of control. But the regressive language does not lead to hopelessness. Instead, it drives one from self-reliance to God. For Israel what is found at the bottom of the pit is not *despair* but *the rule of God*. Israel knows that the rule of God is the only alternative to despair. And the speaker dares to presume that some things are his due from Yahweh, even though beyond his own control. The word *righteousness* now introduces a different field of images, those of the *court*. (The language of v. 1b is that of the court, but it yields quickly to military metaphor and is not developed.) Here the request is for acquittal among all those hostile forces that treat one as guilty and deserving of threat. We have seen juridical language in verses 1 and 11, and here it comes to fruition in petition. But the language of the court serves a more basic presupposition, that of covenant. The speaker assumes a sound and abiding covenantal partnership, and here asks his partner to do what is owed him.

2. Psalm 35, reflecting its urgency, includes extended comment about *the enemy*, which we have not encountered in other psalms. So in verses 4-6 and verse 8, there is a wish that every thinkable trouble come upon the enemy. This is continued in verses 19, 25-26. Even as the speaker seeks righteousness for himself, this is matched by an urgent prayer for every possible trouble on his enemies.

This venom is supported in two ways. First, what "those people" have done is described so that God may know how awful they are and how deserving of retaliation from God (vv. 7, 15-16, 20-21). What they have not done is to speak שלום (v. 20). Clearly they are people who are not much interested in getting along or in enhancing the life of anyone else. They do not do righteousness. Second, the speaker describes the sorry situation in which he finds himself as a result of their enmity (vv. 13-14). This entire element in the psalm reveals the voice of one who is filled with rage, has a deep sense of unfair treatment, and finds it intolerable and unbearable for another instant. The speech is passionate, on the one hand, because it wishes to mobilize Yahweh (cf. v. 23). On the other hand, one may detect a note of *indignation*, or at least impatience about Yahweh (v. 17). It is as though the poet asks, "Where have you been, Yahweh? How much will it take before you do what is expected and what is, in fact, my due from you?" Relations with these folk have become exceedingly raw and unbearable, and only Yahweh has the capacity to change the present arrangement. The words suggest that some of that rawness has also contaminated the relationship with Yahweh, so that the rage is not all directed at the enemy.

   3. The third element is a *promise of praise*:

I will thank thee...
I will praise thee...(v. 18).
Great is the Lord (v. 27).

We may observe several things about these anticipations of praise. First, they are *sure* anticipations. The speaker does not doubt that it will happen. There is complete confidence that God is able and willing to act, presumably moved by the prayer. Characteristically these angry prayers uttered in deep disorientation are not acts of despair. They are acts of hope, for they are convinced that conditions need not and will not and cannot stay this way. There is no resignation, but an active insistence on change.[29]

   Second, these are *withheld* anticipations. The speaker does not yet engage in any praise. The poem only says what will happen as a result of transformation. It is made clear that there will be no praise until there has been an act on Yahweh's part. This withholding sounds like bargaining or threatening, like dangling a carrot in front of Yahweh. If Yahweh wants to be praised, then he must respond to this specific need with rescue and vindication.

   Third, we should note the actual *substance* of sure, but withheld praise. Verse 18 provides no content. It only addresses the possibility of praise formally, though the words "thank" (ידה) and "praise" (הלל) come together in a chiasmus that is worth noting. Much more important is the promised praise of verse 10, which asserts the distinctiveness of Yahweh. The claim is that when Yahweh delivers from this wretchedness, it will be known again that there is none other like Yahweh who delivers in such a way (cf. v. 9).

   The distinctiveness of Yahweh is further sketched out. As in Psalm 86, the distinctiveness of Yahweh is not in regal adjectives "from above," as in majesty and power and dominion. Instead, Yahweh is marked "from below," as the one who delivers the weak and the needy who cannot deliver themselves. Here we are close to the evangelical core of Israel's faith.[30] The speaker has presented himself as engaged in an uneven struggle with enemies, and is on the losing end. His prayer is that the uneven struggle not only be made even, but that it be made uneven in the opposite direction, i.e., in his favor. That change of leverage cannot be accomplished by the speaker himself, who has no resources for that. It can be accomplished only by Yahweh, who has the will, the resources, and the covenantal obligation so to intervene. So the issue is put "from below" to Yahweh: What kind of God will you be? What kind of praise do you want? Whom do you want to praise you? At least in this psalm, Yahweh's godness is drawn into the disorientation. If the *poor* are to praise, Yahweh must act for the poor. If the praise is about *incomparability*, then God must act in incomparable ways. Yahweh is here pressed to decide to be a God for those below.[31] God's incomparability is profoundly linked to the well-being of the helpless.

Thus, I propose a quite dynamic intentionality in this psalm, in which the God-questions are not all settled, even for God. They are here being worked out with God. But the decisive speaker in the resettlement of the God-question is this voice of the poor and the needy.

The final sure but withheld praise is in verses 27-28. Again a standard formula is used, "Great is Yahweh." But the content given that formula is noteworthy: first, because it gathers together the themes of the psalm, and second, it redefines *greatness* in terms of *rescue*. The verses refer back to the psalm in two important ways. First, in verse 24, the petition is "vindicate me" (שפט) according to your "righteousness" (צדק). In verses 27-28 the formula of praise is:

> Let those who desire my *vindication* (צדק) shout for joy...
> my tongue shall tell of thy *righteousness* (צדק).

The speaker will have experienced the desired "setting right." Second, in verse 27, God is great because he delights in the שלום (welfare) of his servant, the very שלום the enemies denied in verse 20. Thus God is to be celebrated for having resolved all the unsettled business. God is praised for doing for the speaking poor precisely what the enemies refused and denied. With the enemies, all of life is threat. With God who intervenes, all is changed, and life is wholeness, well-being, and joy.

In reflecting on the mood and movement of this prayer, two observations about psalmic piety are in order. First, the prayer life of the speaker is filled with anger and rawness. There is no attempt to be polite or docile. Psalmic prayer practices no cover-up. Real prayer is being open about the negativities and yielding them to God. The lament psalms we have considered portray the route by which they may be *yielded*. What is clear is that they are never *yielded* unless they be fully *expressed*.

Second, the relation to God in these psalms is not at all cozy, comfortable, or congenial. There is an edge of resentment and resistance here that involves some jeopardy of the relationship. The speaker has some of the "cards," which will be played only after Yahweh's lead. Yahweh will be freely praised, but only when there is specific reason for praise. This is daring theology, for it suggests that unless God *delivers*, God will not be *distinctive* (Ps. 35:10). Unless God gives שלום, God will not be *great* (Ps. 35:27). There is the hint that God is motivated by the possibility of praise, to act as he might not otherwise.

The psalmist appears to be skillful at "triangling," i.e., at lining up Yahweh with him two against one, against the enemy.[32] But this set for the triangle is not automatic. It takes some intentionality. This Psalm shows the speaker working passionately and knowingly at a relationship that will let him live. Such prayer is not at all disinterested, nor does it praise God with a sense of abandonment. Things are too dangerous for that. The speaker may come empty-handed, but not without a case to make, and a proper cause to plead.[33]

Communal Laments

It is probably easiest for us to resonate with these personal psalms of lament. Partly that is because they predominate in the psalter and we are more familiar with them, even if we do not use them easily. But the other reason is that the category of the personal, even psychological, has become our mode of experiencing reality.[34] We have, at the same time, experienced a loss of public awareness and public imagination.[35] So while the personal laments may parallel experiences of our own, the loss of public experience means we have little experiential counterpart to the communal laments. Given our privatistic inclination, we do not often think about public disasters as concerns for prayer life. If we do, we treat them as somehow a lesser item. We have nearly lost our capacity to think *theologically* about public issues and public problems. Even more, we have lost our capacity to practice prayer in relationship to public events.[36]

The psalms we now consider are statements about the religious dimension of public events of loss. They permit us to remember that we are indeed public citizens and creatures and have an immediate, direct, and personal stake in public events. The recovery of this mode of psalmic prayer may be important if we are to overcome our general religious abdication of public issues and the malaise of indifference and apathy that comes with the abdication. In a more general way, the public disasters of Israel were not unlike our own: war, drought, famine (cf. Job 5:19-22).[37] Quite specifically, public energy in Israel's prayer was focused in the destruction of the temple in Jerusalem by the Babylonians. That focus is not hard to understand. The temple had come to be the point of reference for all of life. Its destruction thus meant the loss of a center, and a profound public disorientation, in which public meanings and values are nullified or at least severely placed in jeopardy.[38]

The use of these psalms requires an imaginative identification of a "dynamic analogy," for the points of contact with our own experience are not so obvious and immediate as with the personal psalms.[39] In using them, we may in a preliminary way think about comparable experiences and possibilities. The overriding symbolic threat in our time is the nuclear threat, which may be analogous to the threat against the temple. I do not suggest that the destruction of the Jerusalem temple is "objectively" of the same magnitude, but as a *functioning symbol*, the loss of Jerusalem is comparable to the loss of the whole "known world" threatened in our time.[40] Reflection on our own threat will enable us to enter into the emotive power of these psalms that ponder the loss of the temple. On a lesser scale, every threat of war, every piece of bad war news, tends to mobilize public imagination. Or in more centered, localized places, it can be done by a storm, a mining accident, or an epidemic. Or in another sense, our most vivid memories of public desolation came in the deaths of the Kennedys and Martin Luther King Jr., in the 1960s. Whether one is conservative or liberal, those events articulated and made inescapable a darkness and disorientation that could be covered up; but their power could not be denied. These psalms give us some access to those sensitivities. Romantic liberalism had imagined that such evil could not move against public institutions that seemed so sure. These psalms are a visceral meditation on threats that now move against everything precious.

The communal laments are not so numerous in the Psalter, but they are important for the nurture of responsible faith.[41] The recovery of the personal lament psalms is a great gain, but unless the communal laments are set alongside, the record of personal religion can serve only privatistic concerns—and that is no doubt a betrayal of biblical faith. To gain access to these psalms, therefore, we need to think through the public sense of loss and hurt and rage that we all have in common. This may include the various massacres wrought in the name of authorized government, the endlessly exiled situation of Palestinians, the reality of worldwide oppression that is not "natural," but is caused by "the enemies" who trample on the public life and public future of large groups of people. It is stunning to think that prayer of this kind might indeed be the point of entry into the larger world of faith, where the Lord of the nations governs.[42]

Psalm 74

The temple has been violated. The key symbol of life has been lost.[43] Things in all parts of life fall apart—precisely because the center has not held.[44] This psalm of protest and grief does not concern simply a historical invasion and the loss of a building. It speaks about the violation of the sacral key to all reality, the glue that holds the world together.[45]

Our modern world has lost some sense of the power of such a centeredness. Indeed, it may be a mark of modernity to abandon such a notion of a center, but I suspect not. I suspect that the enormous power that nationalism and racism still evoke are signs of the center that is still desperately hoped for. Evidence may be found of the powerful attraction for many outside the church of the Pope as a sign of unity. The passion evoked by the issue of homosexuality in our culture may be evidence of a sense of an ordered whole that is kept from visibility but which has a powerful grip on our imagination. Acts of "impurity" are understood as a threat to that coherence.[46] The energy that can be mobilized by the gun lobby is at the same time a statement about disconnected individualism, and the finding of a common cause around a deeply held public value. This is not to suggest that any or all of these signs are healthy. They may indeed be unhealthy and destructive, as the temple in Jerusalem was also an ambivalent sign.[47] But whether healthy or unhealthy, whether true or idolatrous, the sense of a public center that holds our imagination is not as remote from us as we might imagine.

A psalm like this one permits us to reconsider a centeredness in life, a refusal to accept fragmentation, which leaves us abandoned, homeless, and open to brutalization, both as agent and object.[48] The loss of such a center invites totalitarianism, either political or religious, to satisfy that yearning when more responsible forms of coherence are gone. So, this psalm is for grieving Jerusalem destroyed, still a powerful symbol in its own way. But we can use the psalms in a derivative, translated sense for whatever it is that commands the center and holds the imagination as did Jerusalem, well beyond bricks and mortar.

Weiss[49] and Westermann[50] in different ways, have shown how Psalm 74 speaks to the three parties in the travesty: *the foes* who have done it, *the people* who have suffered it, and *the God* who must now deal with it.

1. Psalm 74 begins with an urging to Yahweh (vv. 1-3). It is telling that the first subject is not the ruined temple, but Yahweh. Israel makes its appeal out beyond the *hopeless temple* to *the ground of hope*. In the first instance, it is not Babylon who is responsible for the temple, but Yahweh. Jeremiah had made clear that the undoing of the temple was the action of Yahweh (cf. Jeremiah 7). In the initial assault on Yahweh, God is urged to do two things, to remember former times when things were right (v. 2), and to take a look at the present mess (v. 3). The contrast between *how it was* and *how it is* is calculated to get God to act, for he will find this present arrangement intolerable (cf. Job 29–31).[51] In the end, this is a poem of passionate hope. It does not believe the destruction of the temple is irreversible. God is not just a fixture in the temple. God is an agent who stands free from and has life apart from the temple. Yahweh is indeed Lord of the temple. And therefore, Yahweh can restore the temple (and anything else), perhaps in three days (John 2:19-21).

2. But Yahweh must be pressed and persuaded into action. Just in case Yahweh has not noted the depth of the problem, he is given a play-by-play account of the destruction: each shout in the holy place, each blow of the axe, each striking of the hammer, each crackling of the flames, is an assault on all

things precious (vv. 4-8). Note the wording. These are not our enemies. They are yours (v. 4). And you must act for your own honor and glory. Israel is baffled (vv. 9-11). There is plenty of motivation to act. Things seem not to be as urgent for Yahweh as they seem to Israel. Could it be that God is indifferent, that he has forgotten his own characteristic concerns?

3. If the memory of the older days (v. 2) and the sight of the tragedy (vv. 3-8) are not enough, then the urging must be escalated. If Yahweh cannot find motivation in the sad sight, then it must be found in Yahweh's own character and past commitments. So in verses 12-17 Psalm 74 reviews Yahweh's better days. This unit is dominated by *thou*, as though Yahweh needs to be reminded who he is and what he does and what is regularly expected of him.[52] So the classical memories of Yahweh's life with Israel are recited. Yahweh's great moments with Israel are those moments in the face of defeat when Yahweh performed against enormous odds to bring a new wholeness where it was not expected. Remarkably, after verses 12-15, a review of Israel's past with Yahweh, verses 16-17 move to the vast arena of creation, to make the most comprehensive claim possible. It is Yahweh's creative action which has overcome chaos. Now Israel faces a new chaos with the lack of a center. That is, the jeopardy of the faith as a way to explain what is happening does not lead to retrenchment, but to a new intellectual venture, to creation faith. Yahweh is known to be the answer to chaos, even as in the first combat against chaos.[53] Chaos with the loss of the temple is as acute as the first chaos.

4. On the basis of this appeal to Yahweh's own past, verses 18-23 are a series of *imperatives*. After God is reminded that he should act, now he is told what he must do: "Remember...and don't take this affront sitting down" (cf. v. 18). The images that follow are rich and varied. In verse 19 the helpless ones are mentioned, but the metaphor is intensified—a helpless dove against a wild beast—the dove has no other help. That need of the poor is echoed in verse 21. In verse 20, there is a different motivation, reminding Yahweh of his covenant commitments, with the unspoken suggestion that if Yahweh does not act, he is in fact reneging. The psalm concludes in verses 22-23 with a vigorous appeal for Yahweh's intervention, an imperative reminiscent of Israel's primal imperative to get God to act (cf. Num. 10:35-36).

5. Two observations may bring Psalm 74 closer to our own situation. First, there is a kind of double vision in the psalm. The speaker is utterly committed to the temple as the center and focus of all of life. That is why the poem is so passionate. And yet, at the same time, the speaker knows better. For even when the temple is destroyed, life remains focused on the invisible, but very concrete, presence of Yahweh. The psalm makes quite clear that the *loss of the temple* does not mean the *loss of Yahweh*. Yahweh can be present even where the temple, the sign of presence, is nullified. Yahweh's own presence

provides a center we had presumed. The psalm shows an inescapable tension between *a realizable focus* (the temple, which always tilts toward idolatry) and *an evangelical focus* (which finally leans on Yahweh and is free of religious structures). The temple is important, but it is not *ultimately* important, even for this temple speaker, who finally turns to "God my King" (v. 12). The juxtaposition is difficult. The psalm is clear that faith is in God, not in the temple. But such faith *in God* is always experienced in concrete, visible, even institutional ways. And therefore, the temple is not easily dispensable. The treasure is known only in such earthen vessels.

Second, we too face the conflict between the claim of the true, invisible, concrete, ultimate God and the claimants to visible ultimacy (race, class, nation, place, creed, or system). We live in a time when all our religious structures are jeopardized.[54] Perhaps the wonder is not that the psalm reacts so strongly to the loss of temple. The wonder is that in that loss there is still one to address, known by name. There is one to address who is still credible, who has a known past, who can receive imperatives, and who is therefore the ground of hope. The coming and going of the temple does not reduce Israel to despair. Instead, it drives to indignation, which properly is deposited at God's throne. So the psalm has a curious and surprising outcome, This psalm, ostensibly about the temple, is in the last measure not about the temple, but about the source of life and hope in the absence of the temple. This is a faith which is willing to "wait without idols."[55]

Psalm 79

This psalm repeats the themes of Psalm 74, but seemingly with more venom. The situation is the same: the temple is destroyed, Israel is bereft, and the conquering enemy gloats. Yahweh cannot afford to be a disinterested party. Appeal is made to the partisan holiness of God which works beyond visible religiosity. Israel here presses Yahweh to decide what counts with him.

The psalm has two major parts and a concluding resolution. What strikes one most is the guileless simplicity of strongly felt passion, which can be shared with Yahweh. There is no self-deceiving politeness, no attempt to protect Yahweh from how it really is.

1. First, in verses 1-4, there is a description of the trouble. The beginning of the psalm lays it out. The גוים, the ritually unacceptable outsiders, have come to Yahweh's special inheritance, the temple. The incongruity is unbearable. This incongruity is immediately intensified: "They have profaned (טמא) the holy place (קדש)" (v. 1). *Profanation of holiness* is the last galling act, an "abomination of desolation" (cf. Dan. 12:11). The psalmist only wants Yahweh to feel what we feel. It is like a patriot watching the flag burned, a lov-

er watching his beloved raped, scholar watching the library burn—a helpless revulsion that can scarcely find words.

2. And then there is an extraordinary appeal to Yahweh to act, for he is the only one who could possibly make a difference. Verses 5-11 are like an inventory of God's person, asking him to mobilize every possible part of his sovereign person. Reference is made to God's jealous wrath (קנא) (v. 5),

anger (המה) (v. 6),
compassion (רחם) (v. 8),
salvation (ישע) (v. 9),
glory (כבד) (v. 9),
vengeance (נקם) (v. 10),
great arm (גדול זרע) (v. 11).

All this is to be mobilized in a great inversion. The two-sidedness of Yahweh's person here is noteworthy. What is obviously needed is his *anger, destructive indignation*, exposed as wrath, anger, vengeance, power. But it is matched by his *compassion, salvation, deliverance, forgiveness*, attention to groans, even as he has heard groans from the beginning (Exod. 2:23). The mystery of this God is the juxtaposition of *vengeance* and *compassion*. Both matter here. Neither is available in the usual stoic gods of temple theology.

All of these appeals are for God's name's sake (v. 9), for the sake of his reputation, for the full announcement of who God really is. No doubt this prayer is a self-serving prayer on the part of an Israelite. Prayer in Israel is never disinterested, and we should not pretend that it is. But it is also a yearning that God should be fully God, to show God's self to friend and foe for who God really is, not to be blasphemed or trifled with, but to be taken with utter seriousness. The psalmist believes that there is a convergence of interest, Israel's self-interest, but also the transcendent interest of God. This troubled prayer is the activity of locating and articulating that convergence of interest.

The double-sidedness of Yahweh is necessary if our faith is to deal with us fully, our dark side as well as our piety. That double-mindedness is evident in verse 12. There is an urgent, militant petition to repay *sevenfold*, to crush some people and to punish sevenfold those who have done it to us. The prayer is an echo of the viciousness of Lamech (Gen. 4:24) who wants more than equity.[56] The poet uses the most radical memory that can be recalled for the settling of accounts by God.

Such a prayer may trouble us, and we would not think to pray that way very often, but it is thoroughly biblical. The speaker is *honest enough* to know that yearning, and the speaker is *faithful enough* to submit the yearning to God. Such a requirement of an "overkill" of retaliation is not to be used for casual affronts. It is only when "the temple" is undone that one does this. It is when the core, meaning, and structure of life are undone that one dares to go in this posture to the throne. But then one must go.

Yet this same speaker who authorizes such ruthlessness in verse 12 is the one who counts on forgiveness in verse 9. How could it be? Obviously one yearning is "for them," and the other is "for us." We do sort things out that way. But mostly the psalm reveals how divided and incongruous we all are. Perhaps the madness of that incongruity is because the temple is lost and the center is gone. When the center does not hold, we cannot will one thing. The temple destroyed permits moral chaos. So the prayer evidences a deep disarray and disorientation. It is the kind of prayer one would not have prayed while the temple stood and the center held. But when that is gone, all the deep forces are unleashed in our lives, and the darkness has its say.[57] The only hopeful thing in that raw contradiction that we know so well is that it is all submitted to Yahweh. Both reliance on forgiveness and hunger for vengeance are tied to Yahweh, who will deal with both needs in his utter sovereignty. Even in Israel's disorientation, the darkness is carried in prayer to the one who hears our yearning. And God handles both. On the one hand, the hunger for vengeance is processed by this God who gives distance between the venomous wish and the act of implementation, so that the judgment of God is not quite so direct and unmitigated. God processes also our need for forgiveness, so that it also is not so direct and sure, so cheap, so that the loss of temple is immediately resolved. As the vengeance is articulated, so the forgiveness costs and requires brooding. God is available to this desperate voice of prayer, but God is not available directly and immediately on the terms we presume. God is available in terms of God's own sovereignty, and even loss of temple does not change that.

3. The final verse articulates yearning for a new orientation (v. 13). It does not imagine that things must remain in such profound convulsion. It anticipates that Yahweh will right things, both with forgiveness and vengeance. So the new time to come is almost idyllic in its pastoral quality. The sheep–pasture metaphor of verse 13 calls to mind more familiar uses:

He makes me lie down in green pastures (Ps. 23:2).
We are the people of his pasture, and the sheep of his hand (Ps. 95:7; cf. 74:1).

The imagery offered here is like the bright day after the dark storm.[58] And so the psalm concludes with the chiasmus:

thanks. . .for ever,
generation to generation. . .*praise*.

It is to thank in specificity, to praise in grand abundance.[59]

But biblical faith never imagines that verse 13 exists by itself. New life is never a gift in a vacuum. It is wrought in profound and dangerous struggle as we bring to visibility the deep incongruity that marks our life. Our life is one in which all that is finally holy is violated, day by day. Yet, we dare hope for pastoral possibilities that move us beyond the wrenching, venomous indignation. Biblical faith is not romantic. It reckons with the evil, and it knows that the evil strikes at all that is crucial and most precious. Nonetheless, it dares affirm. It requires and permits us to move beyond the venom to the Lord of ruined temples.

Psalm 137

This psalm is better known, probably because it is one of the few psalms which contain a certain and explicit historical reference. It invites narrative specificity. It clearly comes out of the exiled community in Babylon after the destruction of 587 B.C.E., the community reflected in the pathos of Jeremiah and Ezekiel. It reflects the need of those who have been forcibly removed by the Babylonian imperial policies of relocation and yet who cling to their memory and hope for homecoming with an unshakable passion.

Psalm 137 may at first be an affront to us because of its vengefulness, but after we face that, I suggest it affronts because of the nonnegotiable, scandalous particularity of Jerusalem. No doubt the Babylonian managers of the exile regarded one place as good as another and were surely baffled by this insistent and uncompromising attitude. Indeed, the offer placed in the mouth of the Assyrian negotiator (2 Kings 18:32) fails to recognize that this rooted place is distinctive, and speaks as though places are for trading off, one as good as another (cf. also 1 Kings 21:2 for such a miscalculation). As much as any psalm, Psalm 137 requires us to face the Jewishness of the Psalms and asks us to think through how we as Christians embrace this Jewishness.[60] There are many forms of Zionism, even though Zionism is now popularly confused with Israeli militarism. But the Psalms require us to be some kind of Zionists, though not necessarily adherents to militarism. As we have it, the Psalter is a set of Jerusalem songs, concerned and convinced that our human future is somehow linked to that concrete place, for which there is no trade-off or equivalent. To some extent Christians have ''spiritualized Jerusalem.''[61] Already in Isa. 65:18-19, there is a renewed Jerusalem that stands in some tension with the old political capital of Solomon. That imagery is used for a new city coming down out of heaven (Rev. 21:2). But it is still Jerusalem, focus of peace and vision of one world. Psalm 137 invites us not to be talked out of the concreteness of our faith.

The mood in Psalm 137 is different from that of Psalms 74 and 79. These other psalms sound more like immediate, impulsive reactions from those who think the terror over the temple cannot be tolerated one more day. By contrast, Psalm 137 is the voice of those who have lived longer and have learned with anguish that things would not immediately be righted. One cannot storm the gates. Venom against imperial policy does not bring sudden change. So this is a psalm for the long haul, for those not able to see the change, but knowing that hope for change can be sustained for the long term. The psalm does not despair. Hope is resilient here. I suggest that the communal function of this psalm is to act out and transmit to the next generation the yearning and the hate that belongs to every dislocated Jew. It is important that generation after generation we remember with Jews that the present arrangements are not right, not acceptable, and not finally to be accepted. Psalm 137 draws its power and authority out of another vision, marked by homecoming, which seems remote, but is not for one instant in doubt. There will be a homecoming to peace, justice, and freedom. This psalm is the ongoing practice of that hope against enormous odds. It is always, "Lest we forget."

Most of the psalm (except for v. 7) is not even addressed to Yahweh. It is a musing, perhaps a statement of resolve for any who want to listen, not asking for response or even agreement. But it is a resolve not to be nullified. This is indeed hope against all the facts. Such hope must necessarily be visceral and unapologetic. Such a statement might be an embarrassment to bourgeois folk who have never lost that much, been abused that much, or hoped that much. But such a statement is not embarrassing to those who have been marginalized long enough. So the psalm could serve a Catholic in North Ireland, a black in South Africa, a Palestinian on the West Bank, and exploited women in our society. In such deep anguish, one dare never forget.

1. Verses 1-3 set the scene. This is the grief of those who have heard Psalm 79, who are utterly affronted at the גוים who have thoughtlessly and arrogantly gone into the holy place. This voice has a sense of Yahweh's abandonment. The grief is compounded by the torment of their overlords' requiring them to sing Zion songs in order to humiliate, to show how helpless and bereft they are. Such a scandalous scene was savagely repeated in the death camp of Treblinka, where Jews were forced to sing and dance of their Jewishness. It was a part of the humiliation intending to rob Jews of their identity, their dignity, and their hope. Such songs of Zion are not for public review. Indeed, the songs of Zion are pornographic when they are sung among those who do not hope in Zion.

2. But the resolve of verses 4-6 is that there will not be such a raid on our memory. We will not be talked out of that point of reference. On that the speaker is adamant. These exiles are clear. The vision of Jerusalem is more precious than body and self. "The body they may kill, God's truth abideth still." In this

tradition, God's truth is linked to this holy city of promise and hope. That is, our life is still centered, centered in Jerusalem, even if the temple is now an ashen crater. It is still centered where all "hopes and fears" are held in treasure. Not all of the evil of Babylon can take away that conviction. The temple may be in ruins, but it is nonetheless the temple. The memory may not touch very well the reality of destruction, but as substance for defiant hope, it is sufficient. Note then that this fix on Jerusalem is not neurotic religion. It is the maintenance of a counterculture posture, an act that asserts life is not controlled by Babylon. This psalm thus speaks of the kind of overriding meaning about which Viktor Frankl writes, to which the exploiters do not have access.[62]

3. The final unit of verses 7-9 shows the costliness of such resistant faith. The ruthlessness of such faith is extraordinary. It is not exactly a noble prayer, but such faith can have no mark of romanticism. To endure with sanity against despair requires an alternative vision and distance from the present forced feeding. If there be tolerance for or accommodation with the captor, the stubborn resolve of the victim will soon evaporate. And there would be no homecoming.

There is strong passion in this psalm; but we should understand its function. Passionate faith in Yahweh is here asserted with reference to actual life situation. There is no suggestion that the pathos-filled Jews in this psalm take any *action* against the "little ones" of Babylon. So far as the psalm is concerned, that is left confidently to Yahweh. But such vivid imagery must have energized fidelity for the long haul. Such a community of vitality and vigor in memory and hope could survive a long time, even against the pressures of imperial definitions of reality.

It is not for us to "justify" such a prayer in the Bible. Admittedly, it is not one of the noble moments of the Bible, but it is there. And it is there for good reason. It reminds us that the stark claims of the holy God override all our conventional humaneness. Of course, we are called to humaneness, but we must not be so reductionist as to imagine that commitment to the holy center can be translated into human kindness. Theological centering, faith in God, has its own say, and in times of stress it must needs be an affront.

We have evidence that the affront was not in vain. It was this very tenacity which led to the restoration of Nehemiah. A century later, it could still be said:

When I heard these words I sat down and wept, and mourned for days; and I continued fasting and praying before the God of heaven (Neh. 1:4).[63]

Nehemiah wept a century later as his forebears did in our psalm. It is remarkable that the memory and hope are kept so poignantly and immediately alive for so long, but that is the nature of our faith. Out of that history of weeping came resolve for new life. It is remarkable that the grief over Jerusalem did not lead to abdication or "heavenly religion." In Nehemiah it is clear that it leads to restoration, reconstruction, and reorganization of the city. It is hard for complacent bourgeois folk who have suffered little to understand the tenacity of affronted memory among the brutalized. Perhaps this psalm will be understood and valued among us only if we experience some concrete brutalization.

I am not sure how such a psalm fits with Christian faith. I suggest it asks about *faithful tenacity*. It asks about our capacity to endure, to maintain identity, to embrace a calling in situations of sell-out. Of course, we have present in our tradition—as do Jews—the call to forgive enemies. This psalm poses some questions: Can there be a claim that overrides *forgiveness* for the sake of *constancy?* Can forgiveness be a mode of coming to terms too easily? Could it be that genuine forgiveness is possible only when there has been a genuine articulation of hatred?

We may note this much in the psalm: the speaker does not take action. The speaker does not, in fact, crush the heads of babes against rocks. It is a prayer, a wish, a hope, a yearning. But even the venom is left in God's hands. Perhaps there is a division of labor here to be celebrated: Israel hopes; Yahweh avenges as he chooses. The capacity to leave vengeance to God may free Israel for its primary vocation, which is the tenacious hope that prevents sell-out. Indeed, one may speculate that if Israel could not boldly leave vengeance to God and had worried about vengeance on its own, Israel might have had no energy or freedom to hope. Perhaps it is precisely the capacity to turn that over to God which leaves Israel free to hope for the new Jerusalem.

At first glance, Psalm 137 strikes us as a childish outburst. On reflection it may be the voice of seasoned religion which knows profoundly what it costs to beat off despair. More than simply knowing the cost, this speaker is prepared to pay! What it costs is conceding even our wish for retaliation to the sovereignty of God who is beyond our ways of acting (Isa. 55:8-9). It could be that this psalm occurs in a context in which God's ways and thoughts for vengeance are "higher," but that does not keep Israel from speaking it honestly to the throne. It is an act of profound faith to entrust one's most precious hatreds to God, knowing they will be taken seriously.

Two Problem Psalms

The personal and communal complaints we have thus far studied are statements that still confidently addressed Yahweh with a sure hope. If we think of movement from orientation to disorientation as a move first *to the edge* of "the pit," then a more intense *entry into the pit* of disorientation, and then finally *a full descent*, the psalms we have studied are on their way. But they are not yet there.

Now we take up two psalms that are the voice of Israel in the very depth. They are psalms that pose difficult theological questions to any conventional faith. I will hope to show that they are also important theological and pastoral resources, precisely because they do not carry with them any articulated resolve of the issue. They leave us lingering in the unresolve, dangling in the depth of the pit without any explicit sign of rescue. That is an important statement to have in the repertoire, precisely because life is like that. Faith does not always resolve life. There is not for every personal crisis of disorientation a way out, if only we can press the right button. Too much pastoral action is inclined and tempted to resolve things, no matter how the situation really is. Faith is treated like the great answer book. Insofar as these psalms are witnesses to faith, they attest that faith means staying in the midst of the disorientation, not retreating to an old orientation that is over and done with, and not charging ahead to some imagined resolution that rushes ahead of the slow, tortuous pace of reality.

These two psalms also suggest that no "separate peace" is to be made with God, as though to compromise the reality of life for the sake of God's reputation. The psalms also hold God's feet to the fire in ways that seem an affront to more conventional faith.

Psalm 88

Psalm 88 is an embarrassment to conventional faith. It is the cry of a believer (who sounds like Job) whose life has gone awry, who desperately seeks contact with Yahweh, but who is unable to evoke a response from God. This is indeed "the dark night of the soul," when the troubled person must be and must stay in the darkness of abandonment, utterly alone.

1. The psalm opens with an urgent appeal to Yahweh (vv. 1-2). The initial address is one of intimacy, already suggesting what is needed and expected. The verses are dominated by this desperate speech: "I cry...my prayer...my cry." The appeal is reiterated in verse 9b, "I call upon thee...I spread out my hands." And again in verse 13: "I...cry to thee...my prayer comes before thee." This three fold cry (vv. 1-2,9b,13) forms the structure of the psalm. Characteristically when Israel cries, Yahweh hears and answers (cf. Exod. 2:23-35; Ps. 107:6,13,19,28). Indeed it is anticipated that a time will come when the answer will precede the cry (Isa. 65:24). But not yet, not here. Psalm 88 is adamant in its insistence, and it is harsh on Yahweh's unresponsiveness. The truth of this psalm is that Israel lives in a world where there is no answer.[64] We are not offered any speculative answer. Perhaps God is silent because the guilt of the speaker has driven Yahweh away, but we are not told that. Or one might take it to be a statement of God's transcendent freedom, so that God is not always on call (cf. Jer. 23:23).[65] But that is not suggested either.

The psalm is not interested in any theological reason Yahweh may have. The psalm is from Israel's side. It engages in no speculation. It asks no theological question. It simply reports on how it is to be a partner of Yahweh in Yahweh's inexplicable absence.[66] We may imagine that the situation is so desperate that even if a ''reason'' could be offered, the speaker would have no interest in it, nor would it help, because the needfulness of the moment supersedes any reasonable conversation.

2. The unanswered plea does not silence the speaker. Perhaps the speaker is in fact speaking to the empty sky, but that does not deter the speaker. The faith of Israel is like that. The failure of God to respond does not lead to atheism or doubt in God or rejection of God. It leads to more intense address. This psalm, like the faith of Israel, is utterly contained in the notion that Yahweh is there and must be addressed. Yahweh must be addressed, even if Yahweh never answers.[67]

In verses 3-9a, the speaker addresses a barrage at Yahweh. The speaker is not very cunning or calculating. The speech is not deliberately presented in order to evoke an answer. There is no playing up to God. There is only anger. If one wanted to tease or persuade Yahweh to answer, this is not the way to go about it, but this speaker has no leisure for such niceties. Yahweh should not need persuasion, for he is expected to answer.

Verses 3-4 are a standard complaint with reference to ''the Pit'' and to ''Sheol.'' This is the voice of a dying one crying out to the only source of life. ''The Pit'' is not final judgment or fiery place of punishment. It is only beyond the range of communion. For this speaker, communion with God is clearly everything. The notion of ''cutting off'' is expressed in verse 5 with three metaphors and a fourth climactic line: ''dead ... grave ... remember no more ... cut off.''

But then in verses 6-9a, the stakes are upped. This is an incredibly audacious speaker. Not only does death come, *but Yahweh causes it*:

Thou hast put me ...
Thy wrath lies heavy,
Thou dost overwhelm ...
Thou hast caused ...
Thou hast made me.

The speaker is utterly helpless. The fault is firmly fixed. In Job-like fashion, the speaker may hope that such an assault will evoke a response. But it does not—only more silence.

3. After the second cry in verse 9b, verses 10-12 offer a series of six rhetorical questions, or at least four questions, two of which have two parts. But the dramatic effect is six questions. All of them ask about Yahweh's capacity to

work his sovereign way in death. We have "dead/shades/grave/abandon/dark-ness/land of forgetfulness." That is the situation into which the speaker has fallen. The speaker will surely fall further if Yahweh does not act soon. And we are given six corresponding words that characterize Yahweh's usual action: "wonders . . . praise . . . steadfast love . . . faithfulness . . . wonders . . . saving help."

The pattern of two sets of words shows the incongruity between where the speaker is and what Yahweh does. The obvious response to the rhetorical questions is "no." Yahweh does not do his typical action in death, so, if it is to make any difference, what Yahweh does will have to be done prior to death (which is very near). The urgency of the speech is that at this moment Yahweh can still do his life-giving work, but not for long. If Yahweh does not act soon, the chance will be lost, preempted by the power of death. The speaker will be utterly lost, because the power of Yahweh has failed. But there is still no answer—only waiting. We may imagine a long dramatic, not very patient pause after verse 12. But there is no answer, and so the cry is resumed.

4. The final assault in verses 14-18 comes after the third appeal of verse 13. Now the poet moves to direct, unambiguous accusation. In verse 14, two questions place the blame frontally. Verse 15 describes the situation one more time, in case Yahweh did not hear it in verses 3-8,10-12. And then the poem culminates in its harshest statement: "thy wrath has swept . . . thy dread assaults . . . thou hast caused."

Finally, the speaker is shunned and in darkness. The last word in the psalm is darkness. The last word is darkness. The last theological word here is darkness. Nothing works. Nothing is changed. Nothing is resolved. All things deny life. And worst of all is the "shunning." It is twice articulated (vv. 8, 18), both times with הרחקת, so that the blame is fixed on Yahweh.

So what is one to do about that? Wait. That is what Israel has been doing for a very long time. I suspect that practically and dramatically, what one must do is say it over again, and again, until the speech and the speaker have genuinely reached the bottom. One has two options: either to wait in silence, or to speak it again. What one may not do is to rush to an easier psalm, or to give up on Yahweh.

What is a psalm like that doing in our Bible? Two things suggest themselves. First, life is like that, and these poems intend to speak of all of life, not just the good parts. Here, more than anywhere else, faith faces life as it is. Second, we observe that this psalm is not a psalm of mute depression. It is still speech. It is still addressed. In the bottom of the Pit, Israel still knows it has to do with Yahweh. It cannot be otherwise. Yahweh may not have to do with Israel. That is a problem for Yahweh, not for Israel or Israel's theologians. Israel has no option but to deal with Yahweh. That belongs to Israel's identity and character in the world. Israel must deal with Yahweh in his life-giving speech and answer. But Israel must also deal with Yahweh in the silence, in God's blank absence as in the saving presence. Israel has no choice but to speak to this one, or to cease to be Israel. In this painful, unresolved speech, Israel is simply engaged in being Israel. To be Israel means to address God, even in God's unresponsive absence.

This psalm accords well with Luther's theology of the cross. It certainly militates against every theology of glory, against every theology that imagines that things can be resolved, that there are answers, and that we go from "strength to strength." Psalm 88 shows us what the cross is about: *faithfulness* in scenes of complete *abandonment*.

Closer at hand, William Styron, in *Sophie's Choice*, has Stingo on his sad way by bus from Washington to New York to bury his two close friends who have committed suicide.[68] As Stingo gets on the bus, he is visibly bereft, without any resource. On the bus a black woman next to him sees his need and offers her best gift to him. She lines out Psalm 88. The words comfort. They may be the only words that could comfort. Easy words could not have comforted. But this psalm could, because the words assert, against all the facts, a tenuous link between the darkness and the Lord of life.

One might wish the assertion were from on high. Then it would be less tenuous. But when that voice from on high is silent, Israel must decide if a feeble line can be established from this side. We never know. This speaker does not know. But it is speech against the darkness. It is not cowed, but insistent, determined that if the Holy One chooses to answer, that answer must not be weak or trivial. When God next speaks, God must answer this charge. No doubt that is why God is not yet prepared to answer by the end of this psalm.

Psalm 88 stands as a mark of realism for biblical faith. It has its pastoral use, because there are situations in which easy, cheap talk of resolution must be avoided. Here are words not to be used frequently, but for the limit experiences when words must be honest and not claim too much.

Psalm 109

This psalm has no reason to be grouped with Psalm 88, except that they are both exceedingly problematic for our usual religious understandings. Whereas Psalm 88 is preoccupied with the *absence* and *silence* of God, Psalm 109 is concerned for *vindictiveness* toward other human beings who have seriously violated the speaker. I group them together because I believe the two psalms embody the main problems of Christian faith: the problem of *trusting a God* who seems not available, and the problem of *caring for a neighbor* who is experienced as enemy. The two psalms are negatively linked to the two great commandments (Mark 12:28-34). In Psalm 88 it is difficult to love a God who will not be present. In Psalm 109, it is difficult to love a neighbor who seems to be beyond love.

Psalm 109 is a problem precisely because it articulates a yearning for retaliation and vengeance of the sort that we do not expect to find in the "edifying" parts of the Bible. Before commenting on this general problematic, let us explore the movement and argument of this Psalm.

1. The poem is aggressively Yahwistic. It begins in a normal address to Yahweh that marks a complaint. The first verse not only asserts intimacy with Yahweh, but reminds Yahweh how much hinges on the action of Yahweh. The speaker hopes in Yahweh, no doubt because past covenant relations have invited such hope. The speaker hopes and believes that Yahweh will take his side and intervene to invert the present circumstance. That is what the faith tradition has made available.

That same sure covenantal appeal is elsewhere confined to verses 20-28, which are cast in much more covenantal language than is the remainder of the psalm. In this unit, there is one forcefully direct address: *But thou, Yahweh, my Lord* (v. 21). This is perhaps the crucial moment of the psalm when the speaker asserts to Yahweh that the sorry situation described is indeed Yahweh's problem and responsibility. This abrupt, direct address is surrounded by a series of imperatives: "deal with *me*, deliver *me* [v. 21]...help *me*, O Lord my God...save *me*" (v. 26).

The grounds for the appeal are of three kinds:

a) For thy name's sake (v. 21), i.e., to maintain your reputation, an appeal to God's *majesty*.

b) In verse 21 and again in verse 26, the appeal is to Yahweh's חסד, his covenant commitment, so there is appeal to God's faithfulness, to God's previous commitment.

c) In verses 22-25, a very different appeal is made in which the complainer portrays a sorry picture of himself. Here there is no reference to God. The speech is full of self: "*I* am poor and needy, and *my* heart...*I* am gone...*I* am shaken off...*my* knees...*my* body...*I* am an object of scorn."

Now the appeal is to God's *compassion*, believing that such a bereft picture will surely move Yahweh to action.

The combined appeal to *majesty, fidelity, and compassion* is as comprehensive a motivation as we could imagine. The second of these is central to a covenantal understanding of Yahweh, but the other two surely also address Yahweh's proper interests and inclinations. The speaker addresses every element of the relationship that has been learned out of the tradition. Israel's entire understanding of God is mobilized. At the same time the appeals and imperatives concern the needy speaker. The action urged here takes place between the two of them, and every element of it is consonant with covenantal commitments and expectations. Thus far there are no surprises and no great problem, given our understanding of the complaints that Israel regularly speaks.

2. But the great body of the psalm is of a very different kind. In the long section of verses 2-19 (and in a lesser way in vv. 27-29) we are in another world. There is here only one direct address of appeal to Yahweh, though Yahweh is named in verses 14,15,20,27. None of these strike me as being more than conventions. In this section, Yahweh is addressed only in verse 6 with the imperative "appoint."

Aside from that usage, this section is not a Yahwistic prayer or a covenantal speech. It is rather a raw undisciplined song of hate and wish for vengeance by someone who has suffered deep hurt and humiliation. The series of jussives suggests this is a recital of wishes that may be cast as prayer, but if need be, could be cast as free-floating wishes without reference to God.

In verses 2-4, the speaker makes a general complaint of having been wrongly treated, receiving evil for good, hatred for love.[69] In the key verse (v. 6), there is request for a *special prosecutor* who will look into every wrongdoing without fear or favor. It is like a special appeal to the judge, because the case is so sordid and shameful that normal investigative procedures will not work and conventional modes of punishment are inadequate. So the petition is for a רשׁע, an evil advocate, one who deals regularly in evil, to investigate and to punish. The parallel term usually rendered "accuser" is the term "satan," the one who tests things out.[70] The speaker is sure that in any serious court, the evidence will be overwhelming. He wants it all brought out. But the evidence is so horrendous that it will take one skilled in such matters, because a normal investigator might fail to notice its gravity.

But then in verses 7-20, the speaker wants to shortchange the investigation. The speaker has already determined the verdict. The evidence is so overwhelming that we do not need to engage in all the refined procedures of the court. This is a rush to judgment: "Guilty!" (v. 7).[71] So in his undisciplined indignation, he wants to rush to sentencing. Here his imagination runs wild, commensurate with his hurt and affront. He imagines that the sentence should include not only the person of the offender, but also the family and the property, so that there is no limit to the liability, just as there has apparently been no limit to the affront.[72] He hopes for the humiliation of creditors. He hopes that none will extend credit or kindness (חסד), the very kindness he himself wants in verses 21 and 26. He wishes not just for punishment, but for the social annihilation of this person, his memory, his name, his future. One who acts as this one has, has no right to social existence in this community.

And the reason for all this? We are lacking in specifics. We are given only the most general statements. The wicked one showed no חסד (v. 16). He exploited the poor and the helpless (v. 16). He cursed and did not bless (v.17).

He used opportunities to enhance himself at the expense of the easily
exploited.[73]

The speaker hopes that Yahweh will preside over and guarantee *strict retribution* so that the rewards and punishment should be precise matches for the
offense.[74] We may note three aspects of that correspondence:

a) The offender pursued the poor and needy (v. 16). The petition of verse
22 is that Yahweh should attend the poor and needy who are unjustly exploited.
It is clear that the speaker is not a disinterested observer, but is one of the victims and speaks for all the victims. There is a promise at the end that those restored needy (v. 31) are the ones who will praise. The motif of ''the poor''
moves from abuse (v. 16) to petition (v. 22) to praise (v. 31). The general claim
of the poem is that the accused is not attuned to the needy, as is Yahweh and the
entire ethical tradition of torah in Israel. The wish of verses 8-12 is that the offender become as poor and helpless as those he abused.

b) The accused did not practice חֶסֶד which any strong person must (v.
16). And so the counterhope is that there will be חֶסֶד (vv. 21,26). The speaker hopes to secure from Yahweh what could not be had from the wicked one,
even though there was every right to expect it. In verse 12, it is hoped that the
one who failed to show חֶסֶד will himself be denied חֶסֶד from every possible
source.

c) The accused clothed himself in cursing, wore cursing like a garment
(vv. 18-19). The hope is that he may be clothed with dishonor (v. 29). The image of clothes functions for a more general statement of blessing and curse. The
offender cursed and did not bless (v. 17). The prayer to Yahweh is that Yahweh
should bless in the face of such cursing (v. 28). The prayer further is that the
wicked should now be marked by the very curse he has worked.

The entire statement is a critique of a seemingly powerful person who had
a chance to act in ways that would give life, but chose to use his chance for self-
serving. Thereby he has brought misery, curse, and death. The characterization is a massive contrast to Job 31.[75] In that recital, Job is also a powerful man
who has a chance by his wealth and power to make a difference, and Job uses
his chance in life-giving ways. Perhaps the accused here has a Job-like future
of trouble without Job's ethical sensitivities and passions. Against such a one,
the speaker has recourse only to Yahweh, a recourse incidentally that did not
work very well for Job himself, until the final prose section (Job 42:7-17).

3. Finally, as one might expect, in verses 30-31, there is an anticipated
resolution—and, therefore, joy. Again the verbs *give thanks* and *praise* are
placed in a nice chiasmus. The speaker had hoped for sustenance from his
neighbor, but he has now come to see such a hope can be directed only to Yahweh (cf. Ps. 73:25). Yahweh is affirmed as the one who rescues the needy
where there is no other source of help.

This psalm moves in two quite different ranges of speech and concern. On the one hand, this is, as elsewhere, *faithful covenantal speech*, disciplined by the norms and expectations of covenant. It is this inclination that gives the psalm its overall shape. But alongside this, and not very well integrated into it, is a second kind of speech, not disciplined, not focused on Yahweh, not shaped by covenant—simply *a free, unrestrained speech of rage seeking vengeance*. The key to Psalm 109 is the delicate way in which these two factors are related to each other, the way in which the second is subordinated and surrendered to the first.

Clearly, in this juxtaposition, Psalm 109 is realistic about how it is in the human heart and in the human community. That is how it is with us who claim a covenantal bond to Yahweh. On the one hand, we do turn to Yahweh, our single source of help. But alongside that turning is free-floating indignation that is not easily supervised or disciplined, that wants direct and destructive access to "the wicked" without the discipline or chastening that comes with submission to Yahweh's sovereign, covenantal rule. This speech wants to circumvent "due process" by not submitting the rage to the rule of God, which is well beyond our rule. Thus the speech is an opportunity for realism that gives freedom of expression to those raw edges in our life that do not easily submit to the religious conviction we profess on good days. The raw areas do not easily submit to the reasonableness that we imagine on the days of our equilibrium.

It is not difficult to trace the movement of this psalm. Our main concern, however, is to ask how this psalm is to be appropriated in the life of faith. I suggest we had best begin with an acknowledgment of the reality of vengeance.[76] There may be some who are not keen on vengeance because life is lived in suppressed discipline. For others life has gone so well that this psalm may not be for them. But for the rest, this psalm deals in realism. It knows about the unfairness and exploitation that evoke rage. It knows that such rage is tenacious and will be expressed and not denied. It knows that the rage is rightly carried even to the presence of Yahweh, whose rule is marked by majesty, faithfulness, and compassion.

But such rage is not only brought into Yahweh's presence. It is *submitted* to Yahweh and *relinquished* to him. In the end this psalm shows the way in which free, unrestrained speech of rage is given over to the claims of the covenant partner. And that may be done just because Yahweh is known to be the God of vengeance, who will work his way with such destructive people (cf. Deut. 32:35-36, 41; Ps. 94:1). This is not a soft, romantic god who only tolerates and forgives, but one who takes seriously his own rule and the wellbeing of his partners. The raw speech of rage can be submitted to Yahweh because there is reason for confidence that Yahweh takes it seriously and will act.

Now in submitting one's rage as this speaker does, two things become clear. The submission to Yahweh is real and irreversible. It cannot be tentatively offered to Yahweh, and then withdrawn if Yahweh does not deal as we had hoped. Such a submission carries with it a relinquishment, a genuine turning loose of the issue. When God is able to say, ''Vengeance is mine''(Deut. 32:35; Rom. 12:19), it implies, ''not yours.'' The submitting partner is no longer free to take vengeance—may not and need not. So the submission is an unburdening and freeing from pettiness and paralysis for praise and thanksgiving. The second fact is that submitting to Yahweh is submitting to Yahweh's free action. Yahweh will avenge, but in God's own way and in God's own time—and perhaps not as we would wish and hope. Yahweh is not a robot. Yahweh does not implement our violent yearning, but passes it through his sovereign freedom, marked by majesty, faithfulness, and compassion. Thus what could have been a barbarian lashing out against a neighbor becomes a faithful activity in which the venomous realities are placed securely in God's hands. God is permitted to govern as he will. And the speaker is again free to start living unencumbered.

Psalm 109, then, is a marvelous act of liberation. On the one hand, it moves the speaker to freedom. On the other hand, it saves the social process from bloodletting, which can never be satiated.[77] But this psalm does not ask for cover-up or denial. Because it has such a vigorous notion of God, the vitality of vengefulness can also be fully articulated. If God were less robust, the speech of rage would need to be toned down; but there is no need. The covenantal conviction about God is a worthy match for the unrestrained yearning for retaliation.

This speech is precious because it shows that Israel understood that what is *healthily human* intersects with what is *vitally faithful*. One can think of only two alternatives to this articulation, submission, and relinquishment. One alternative is repression, when the rage and hunger for retaliation are never brought to speech and perhaps not even recognized as a power. When they are not brought to submitting speech, they may smolder and wait for a more opportune time. The second alternative is that they may be brought to speech and acted out, but not submitted to Yahweh. Then it may serve to justify yet another act of Cain against Abel. Either alternative is destructive, unhealthy, and unfaithful, The way of *repression* is likely to destroy the one who suppresses; but *expression without submission* is likely to lead to overt acts of anger.

This psalm places Yahweh clearly in the line of our cry for vengeance, but Yahweh's presence does more than block or censor. It releases us and promises that soon or late, in God's wisdom, the retaliation will be more sure and more profound than we could imagine. The psalm is not simply a siphoning off of hate. It is a channeling of it in effective ways, in covenantal shapes. In either repression or overt acts, when one keeps possession of one's need for vengeance, one does in fact withhold that part of life from the covenantal sovereignty of Yahweh. When we reserve for ourselves the drive for vengeance, it means that we do not trust Yahweh sufficiently to submit that to his governance.

One may conclude "This psalm does not concern me, because I have never been that angry." Such a response may be spoken as though it were a virtue, but I suggest it reflects someone who is only half living. It is a good idea, when encountering a psalm like this, to ask, "Whose psalm is this?" If I am not able to pray that way today, then I can ask, who needs to pray that way today? Who is justified in praying that way today? It could be the voice of a woman who is victimized by rape, who surely knows that kind of rage and indignation and does not need "due process" to know the proper outcome. It could be the voice of a black in South Africa (or here?) who has yet again been brutalized or humiliated by the system. Or it could be a Palestinian peasant weary of war, resentful of displacement.

Through this psalm the believer may join in the prayers of those who take God seriously and whose destiny is so heavy that they need others to join in these prayers with them. For such as these, the rage must be carried to heaven, because there is no other court of appeal. "Love of neighbor" surely means to go to court with the neighbor who is grieved. Our prayer life is selfish if it attends only to our own needs. We are invited to join in such prayers for others, to help with the *articulation*, with the *submission*, with the *relinquishment*, even if the psalm seems remote from our own life. It could happen that this "going to court" (which is what prayers of intercession are about) may lead to other interventions, also on behalf of those abused and needing a vocal friend in court.

Finally, Psalm 109 is an affirmation of God's governance. The psalm moves from the sure and strong conviction that this is a moral universe, that Yahweh governs with equity and is not indifferent, that the exploitative ones finally do not go unbridled, but must be called to answer. Such a conviction may not be urgent in our comfortable lives, but this psalm is for all those who surround our little oases of satiation with hurt, indignation, and hatred. Here it is affirmed that hatred is one mode of access to the God who cares for his *majesty*, honors in *fidelity* and is moved to *compassion*. At the moment, we may not be poor and needy enough to pray with such venom, but there are poor and needy who need such prayers and who need others to join in their articulation. This is the voice of disordered life yearning for a new order from the throne. The very address to the throne is an act of hope that disorder is not the last word. Such prayers must be prayed until the full order of God's kingdom comes among us.

"A Second Opinion" on the Disorientation

If one is alone in the world, disorientation may be handled by an uninterrupted monolog. Since there is only "us," we do all the talking. Our speech does not then evoke a response. Or if one believes that orientation and disorientation come in natural sequence, then the unsettlement may be viewed simply as a "passage" through which we must move. But in Israel, disorientation is not seen in either of these ways. It is not seen as a normal "passage," because real disorientation is a threat, and it evokes other responses than embrace. It is also not seen as monologic, because in Israel life is always understood covenantally and dialogically.[78] Changed situations always concern both parties, God as much as Israel. Israel is expected to listen as much as speak. In the psalms we now consider, we have a "second opinion" about the disorientation, that is, how it looks to Yahweh. From these psalms we see that Yahweh views the matter in a very different way from the view in Israel that we have presented in our last several sections.

Disorientation is not viewed as a faceless situation nor as a passage, but as a *trouble in the relationship*. When God properly guarantees and when Israel properly responds in "trust and obedience," life will be well-oriented. Or at least that is the buoyant affirmation of the fully oriented. When orientation collapses, it is taken to mean that one of the two parties in the relationship has failed the other party. Trouble is lodged with one party or the other. Characteristically, each party assumes that the fault lies with the other.

In the psalms we have thus far considered under the rubric of disorientation, the speech is that of Israel addressed to Yahweh. On the whole, it is assumed that the trouble has happened because Yahweh has not adequately guaranteed a stable life. That is a conclusion that can easily be drawn if one trusts the affirmations of the songs of creation and torah. And so the speech urges Yahweh to act in a fresh way. We say, "on the whole," because that generalization is modified by one important factor. A third party in the skewed situation, in addition to Israel and Yahweh, is "the enemy."[79] Sometimes disorientation comes, as in Psalm 137, through no fault of either Yahweh or Israel, but through the action of other human agents. But that does not alter the main dynamic of these prayers. Even when disorientation is caused by an enemy, the appeal is still to Yahweh. The appeal is not to the enemy that the enemy should desist, for that is a hopeless plea. The appeal is that Yahweh should intervene to right the situation and to punish the destabilizer. Sometimes Yahweh is blamed, and sometimes not. But when Yahweh is not blamed, he is nonetheless regarded as the only one who can intervene in a decisive and helpful way.

Not all the songs of disorientation are Israel's speech to Yahweh, and not all present Israel's view of reality. Not all songs of disorientation assume that the disorientation is Yahweh's fault, or Yahweh's to correct. There are a few psalms that put the shoe on the other foot, that assume that Yahweh speaks against Israel and calls Israel to repent in order that there may be restored covenant. Only in the most general way can these psalms be said to share any features of the genre of lament. Westermann has indicated that there are some laments of Yahweh against Israel, but these are most likely to be in the prophetic literature.[80] Indeed, the prophetic lawsuit form does function as Yahweh's "complaint" against Israel. Thus the psalms we consider here may seem to have more in common with prophetic than with psalmic literature. We take them up here not because they are laments of a common genre, but because they show another way of addressing the experience of disorientation (cf. also Psalm 95).

Psalm 50

This psalm is the speech of God, who addresses his covenant partner concerning matters of violated covenant. After the narrative introduction of verses 1-6, it is all one extended speech in the form of a decree with no room for negotiation.

1. Verses 1-6 appear to be a stylized description of a theophany, a majestic overpowering coming of Yahweh in his royal splendor. Israel has a tradition of such a powerful coming *from Sinai* (Judg. 5:4-5; Hab. 3:3; Ps. 68:8). But here the tradition has now been reassigned to the temple of *Zion* as the place from where God now comes to hold court (Amos 1:2). Originally the theophany may have been a reference to a storm (cf. Ps. 29:3-9), so that this language is standard fare.[81] But now the images are used to articulate a concern about covenant and disobedience to the royal will. In verse 4 there is a summons of the heavenly court, so that the drama of the meeting is not unlike that Isaiah experienced in his call (Isa. 6:1-8). The myth of the heavenly court is put in the service of the covenant.

But in verses 5-6 there is a somewhat different note. We are no longer concerned with the broad formulae of the temple tradition, but with the concrete language of the Mosaic covenant. Four words suggest this, "my faithful ones" (חסידי), "covenant," "righteousness," "judge" (though it is possible that this latter shoud be read "justice," thus giving a parallel to "righteousness"). Either way, the meeting concerns the serious and disappointed expectation Yahweh has for his covenant partner.

2. Verses 7-15 are a remarkable statement in which God testifies against

Israel (v. 7) by asserting his sovereignty, his independence, his otherness. This is one of the most exalted statements we have of God's ''Godness.'' This God has no need to be fed by Israel's action in worship, in this or in any other way. Verse 8 suggests that sacrifice is a proper and acceptable form of worship to which Yahweh has no objection, but Israel ought to be under no illusion about such worship. God does not need or want such sacifices and does not rely on them for nourishment as if this great God were to be nourished by such a pitiful human effort. God is here disentangled from any necessary bond to Israel. Israel knows and relies on God's abiding engagement with Israel. On Yahweh's part, however, that engagement is one of free passion, not of necessity.

What follows is a complete inventory of food that might be offered to God: bull, he-goat, beast, cattle, birds. Yahweh commandeers the whole creation on God's own terms (cf. Exod. 19:5), and does not depend on Israel.

In verses 14-15 Israel is told what then is proper. First, it is acceptable and accepted that there will be offerings and sacrifices. Second, perhaps more crucial, a real relation to God is to call upon Yahweh, to rely upon him. In this statement, which is a rebuke, there is also a terse promise, ''I will deliver.'' In a right relation with God we do not treat God as an equal or as a needy, hungry partner, but rather call upon God and know that God is ready to save. So it is *call* and *save* that shapes this faith. The alternative that is rejected is *need* and *feed*. ''Call...save'' keeps priorities clear. It affirms that the relationship is grounded in God's rule and his will to save. A religion of ''need...feed'' distorts this truth and draws God into a pattern of need and satisfaction in which this God will not participate. Psalm 50 resists the notion that Yahweh is a consumer or a client of Israel.

We do not know what issue this statement addresses, for we are not told. But the words suggest that the psalm is a protest against perversion of the God-Israel relationship so that it has become increasingly friendly, cozy, and bilateral. The peculiar and decisive initiative of God is lost or compromised in a tendency to reduce this relation to an equality in which each party does some gracious service to the other.[82] In the ancient world, perhaps this slippage had to do with devising a *legalistic* sacrificial system. Our contemporary version might be a friendly collapse of God's *holiness* into a blind *graciousness*. Against every such temptation, this psalm asserts the distance and the qualitative difference between God and Israel, so that the saving gifts move only in one direction. The surprising and decisive word is the assertion of readiness to *save*, a graciousness that yields nothing of God's freedom from Israel.

3. The final section of the poem, verses 16-23, is a special harsh word to the *wicked*, those who do not honor covenant, likely those who presume excessively upon God and do not recognize the qualitative difference in God which has just been asserted. This is now an implementation of the justice signaled in

verse 6. It is as though verses 7-15 are a kind of parenthetical comment to underscore the seriousness of the violation. Clearly, God is not interested in *equity* with Israel, but with *obedience* that is full and unquestioning. The charge now brought against the wicked makes clear who causes the disorientation that lies behind this psalm. It is not God who causes the disorientation, but Israel. It is done by a trivialization of torah when covenantal statutes are recited and then completely disregarded (vv. 16-18).[83] The wicked are those who ignore covenantal requirements (v. 19) and do what they please. What they please may be theft, adultery, slander (vv. 18-20), allusions to the second half of the Decalog.[84]

Finally, in verse 21 we are given the clue to the entire argument. We are told now why the warning of verses 7-15 is so sharp and why the loose conduct of verses 18-20 could happen, ''You thought that I was one like yourself.'' Israel had judged God by the same criteria with which Israel judged itself. This is not so much an elevation of humankind as it is a minimization of God.[85] The word *God*, i.e., Yahweh, has ceased to carry for the wicked the weighted (כבד) claim of holiness. And when God is not honored but is reduced to an average household idol, i.e., when the first tablet of the commandments is not taken seriously, it is certain that the second tablet of neighbor relations will lose its power and its compelling authority. Then there is judgment (v. 21b). The reality of God as ''Other'' guarantees the humaneness of human life. If there is disorder in the human community, its root is found in the loss of God's sovereign sway. The result (v. 22) is that the God who promised to save (v. 15) will not do so. The God who saves is also the one who tears (Job 5:18; Hos. 6:1). Those who violate covenant cannot count on the guarantees of the covenant Lord. They choose for themselves disorder, and they get what they choose. Where the holiness of God is trivialized, human life will be cheapened. Where human life is cheapened, the saving power of the holy God will not be known.

4. The last verse assures Israel that there is an alternative to this abandonment. There is a right sacrifice. It is thanksgiving, acknowledgment that God transforms life.[86] Those who live their life out of such a posture are those who go ''in the way,'' in the way of obedience, trust, and proper acknowledgment. These, God saves. But saving can only be given to those who let God be God.

The true honor of God here is not theological or liturgical recital. It hinges on commandments and the right, obedient ordering of human relationships. This God is relentless about that linkage. In contrast to the lament psalms we have considered, Israel never speaks here. Israel is only to listen (v. 7). And when Israel listens, it must face the sovereignty of God. That is the key issue in a fully oriented life.[87]

Psalm 81

Psalm 81 is a close companion to Psalm 50. If anything, the lines of the argument are even clearer here.

1. Verses 1-5 are a summons to a confrontation, like Ps. 50:1-6, but the mood is different. Here there is not as much of the mythic awesomeness, because now the invading speech of God is lodged in a liturgical festival. The scholars of a generation ago located this in a regular ceremony of covenant renewal.[88] While we are not now so enamored of that hypothesis, that may still be the case. We have what sounds like a liturgical procession, the coming of God midst festal music.

The specific meaning of verses 4-5 is uncertain, but they do seem to assert that from the very beginning, from the time of the exodus, Israel has been under a special decree. That decree becomes the basis for what follows. It is impossible to speculate on what is meant by such a decree, but the verses allude to the exodus deliverance which sets Israel over against Egypt. If that be so, we may suggest that the primal liberation decree was that Israel now belongs to Yahweh, as Egypt does not. Therefore Israel must take care to respond to this liberation Lord and not succumb to any other form of bondage. That distinction is perhaps asserted in Exod. 11:7, and is given substance in Lev. 25:42, "For they are my servants, whom I brought forth out of the land of Egypt; they shall not be sold as slaves." That decree of difference is echoed in Gal. 5:1, which asserts that the people of God are ordained to freedom in the gospel and must not compromise by serving any other lord. This decree of distinctiveness and liberation is under review in this psalm.

2. Verses 5b-10 provide a review of Israel's faith memory. Von Rad has shown how this is a recasting of the primal version of Israel's salvation recital.[89] It begins with the exodus by alluding to subservience. Then it uses the crucial words "called...delivered...answered," on which everything hinges (cf. Exod. 2:23-25; 3:7-10). Then it moves in verse 7b to the initial events of the wilderness sojourn.

Verse 8 is a pivotal verse. It moves the recital from the saving deeds to the commandments.[90] Thus it is an echo of Deut. 6:4, asserting that Israel's foundational requirement is "to listen" (שְׁמַע). In this version of that imperative, one may already detect a reprimand. The history of covenant begins with an invitation to hear, but the course of that history is a refusal to hear. Here in the Psalm it is a subdued note that surfaces later.

Verses 9-10 contain the main claims of Israel's faith. Verse 9 is the primal commandment and may be taken as an allusion to the entire Decalog. In a shorthand way, it summarizes the entire torah. We are given a clue to the main problem: Israel listens to other voices. Already at the exodus the decree warned

against that, because the tradition knows that other voices lead to other obedi-
ences and the end result is slavery.

But the recital does not end in command. It ends in a saving deed. Verse
10 reverts to the initial point of verses 6-7a and reasserts the exodus deliverance
as foundational. Moreover, verse 10b is anticipatory. The offer still holds.
Yahweh promises to feed Israel, to make Israel full and safe (precisely the
things Israel cannot do for Yahweh in Psalm 50). Israel need only come fully
under Yahweh's protective sovereignty.[91]

3. Until this point everything is in the foundational past. Only now does
the speech arrive at its point: the people invited to *listen* have *not listened* (v.
11). In refusing to listen, they refuse sovereignty and therefore God's saving.
Let there be no lingering doubt about why there is trouble or judgment or disorientation. It is very simple: "not listening leads to *death*." Yahweh let Israel
have what it wanted. Israel wanted other lords and other gods, and now Israel
has them—in the form of oppression. The argument here closely parallels that
of Deut. 32:37. The people who are faithless are abandoned to the gods they
have served and trusted.

With scorn and perhaps pain, Yahweh sees that the other gods are not
gods and cannot save. As Beyerlin has seen, the same theology governs the
book of Judges.[92] When Israel goes after other gods, Israel gets the oppression
that accompanies it. Israel has indeed been liberated (vv. 6-7, 10), but disregard of torah can undo the exodus and set Israel back into misery.[93] That is a
sure road to disorientation.[94]

4. The remarkable thing about this psalm is that Yahweh moves on (vv.
13-16). It is obvious that Israel can never go back to the good old days of exodus and miraculous feeding. But it is equally clear, by the mercy of God, that
Israel need not forever linger in the mess of verses 11-12, which Israel has
made for itself. The wonder of Yahweh and the news of this psalm is that Israel
is again invited to *hear* (v. 13). It is a wistful urging, a yearning with pathos on
the part of Yahweh. Yahweh does not want Israel left to its fate. Yahweh is
ready to move on to a new life together. There is no need for lingering punishment. There is only need for a signal from Israel to enter now the covenant of
faith, obedient listening.

Verses 14-16 are a recital of new blessings now available. They have always been available. But the wonder is that they are *now* available in a new beginning, notwithstanding the indictment just articulated. These verses are a
characterization of what the new orientation could look like:

   *a)*Political liberation for a people oppressed. Oppression is ended as the
     community practices justice (vv. 14-15).
   *b)*Economic abundance (v. 16) in which the "filling" of verse 10 is now

implemented. Crops will grow. Famine and shortage will end. The rock will be more miraculous than in the wilderness. There will be genuine satiation.

And the price is simply the listening that concedes there is no other source of satisfaction.

In a rather precise way Psalm 81 articulates the entire pattern of orientation-disorientation-new orientation. The old saving deeds (vv. 6-10) indicate a memory of well-being. In verses 11-12, we have the disorientation, and in verses 13-16, an anticipation of what is yet to be given. Each of the three is marked by the verb שׁמע (hear):

a) *Hear*, O my people (v. 8).
b) But my people did not *listen* (v. 11).
c) O that my people would *listen* (v. 13).

The speech of God here comprehends the whole way of Israel with Yahweh.

In considering the lament psalms, we have suggested the notion that the disorientation is laid at the door of Yahweh. In considering 50 and 81, a counterargument is made that the disorientation is due to Israel. Both judgments are biblical, and both need to be heard. But I do not suggest by placing them in the sequence I have, that the second argument (in Psalms 50 and 81) is the better argument and supersedes the argument of the laments. That would be to return to the argument of the psalms of orientation, that trouble is only because of disobedience. We could as well have presented these psalms in the opposite sequence. The pivotal observation is that both arguments are made. Biblical faith must not be forced in one direction only. A sensitive pastoral use of the Psalms requires deciding which articulation is personally and theologically faithful in any given circumstance. The "second opinion" is not always correct. Sometimes the first opinion needs to be held to tenaciously.

"The Seven Psalms"

Many psalms concern experiences of disorientation in which life between partners is skewed. The psalms of disorientation we have considered thus far tend to focus on disorientation experienced as an external matter. That is, because of *Yahweh's abandonment*, or because of *Israel's infidelity*, or because of *third-party hostility*, the speaker has experienced circumstances that are unhappy, unbearable, and, at least in part, unmerited. They are the kinds of situations not anticipated by the covenant community when the covenant is properly functioning: sickness, isolation, prison, abuse, death. Such psalms of disorientation are "external" in that they point to visible situations of negativity. They are also external in the sense that they seek redress through formal legal transactions. They are still discussions that take place according to the categories of a stable orientation, and in some sense yearn for its return.

Now we focus on psalms that experience the disorientation as an internal-spiritual-introspective issue of intimacy. The distinction between *external* and *internal* must be made cautiously and tentatively, because Israel never posits any kind of dualism and bifurcation. Certainly these psalms are not ''internal'' in the sense that they are privatistic or without reference to the bodily life of the community. That would be a serious misunderstanding. Perhaps a better word than *internal* would be *intimate*. Whatever term may be used, I refer to the awareness in these psalms that formal categories of explanation and insistence are inadequate for the intensity of the issue. The two parties, Israel and Yahweh, are thrust directly onto each other. Neither has recourse to conventional modes of distance. Between them something new must be wrought, and it can be wrought only by an acute struggle. In making this distinction, I do not want to harden it into a distinct category, but mean to refer only to inclination and nuance.

In these psalms we find different sensitivities and different modes of speech and different questions being faced. These psalms show the speaker readily inclined to concede guilt. Here there is no fault attributed to Yahweh or even to a third party. It is as though the public bombast is spent, and the two parties must get down to the case. Clearly the guilt conceded results in disorientation. But the speaker, and God as well, are not as much preoccupied with disorientation as with the possibility of the relationship. What we have is a probe of new possibility that moves out of the old categories, the old orientation that tends to destroy.

The grouping of these seven psalms is a long-established tradition in the liturgical life of the church.[95] They have been treated as a kind of special corpus in the service of penitence, and Luther found in them special resources for his articulation of a new righteousness.[96] They are indeed statements of an intense moment in the relation of God and Israel when something new is required. And that required newness makes a demand on both Israel and Yahweh. (Our discussion will be limited to four of these psalms, which present the themes common to the entire group.)

Psalm 32

This psalm is easily divided into three parts, with the middle portion holding the most substance for us.

1. Verses 1-2 are a general thesis statement cast as a sapiential teaching. The formula is like that used in the Beatitudes in the Sermon on the Mount. The statement describes ''the lucky ones.'' The lucky ones are not those free of transgression, but those able to move beyond it. In a didactic way, the psalmist

announces the conclusion at the beginning of the teaching. Such beatitudes are regularly a conclusion drawn from reflection on a long deposit of experience. The conclusion is that for the living of a full life, there is nothing like being forgiven. The psalm does not trouble over the speculative question of a life free of transgression. It assumes transgression. It has observed the killing burden of sin unforgiven, and it knows that forgiveness is the power for new life. Genuine forgiveness permits freedom to get on with living.[97] The word "imputes" (חשב) in v. 2 is important because it is a usage parallel to Gen. 15:6, where Yahweh "reckoned" righteousness to Abraham. Here Yahweh may "reckon" iniquity.[98] But in a genuinely forgiven life, Yahweh *need* not do so, and Yahweh *does* not do so. No continuing guilt is assigned by Yahweh to those who are in fact forgiven. It is possible to live in a *resolved* relation with Yahweh. This is not the same as a life never touched by such abuse. But what a gift this is, given our situation with Yahweh!

2. In verses 3-7, the psalmist shares his own experience, which has given rise to the conclusion of verses 1-2. This part of the psalm retells a particular occurrence in the long history of transgression and forgiveness. The most powerful testimony is first-person narrative that stays free of speculation but only tells what in fact has happened. That experience is in two parts, negative and positive. First, in verses 3-4, the psalmist describes what happened when the burden of guilt was heavy but unclaimed—unacknowledged to God and unrecognized by self. Notice that the sin is real. It is an objective theological datum, a substantive force between self and God. This is no psychological reductionism, no reference to "guilt feelings," but the honest recognition that sin blocks life with God. That blockage can go on unnoticed, for we have a deep capacity for self-deception.

That blockage works on its bearer. There is here a profound and uncomplicated understanding of psychosomatic realities. The body pays for covenantal disturbances. There is weight loss and discomfort, restlessness and weakness.

The positive statement is in verse 5. It describes the incredible release that comes with articulating the guilt to Yahweh. That is all that is needed. The verse uses the three basic words for sin in a chiastic structure:

> sin
>   iniquity
>   transgression
>   iniquity
> sin

This is matched by covenantal activity of a quite simple kind:

I confessed/you forgave (נִשְׁאת/אֽוֹדִיעֲךָ).

There is nothing between the two moves. The act of *forgiveness* follows the act of *confession* directly, without condition or mediator. The whole difference between the diminishment of verses 3-4 and the forgiveness of verse 5 is acknowledgment to Yahweh.

Obviously, everything is changed in verses 6-7. These verses make a sharp contrast to the immobilization of verses 3-4. It is available to everyone (v. 6). But the main point is the personal experience of verse 7: God hides me, God preserves me, God surrounds me with shouts of rescue. That is the way to fend off the "great waters" (v. 6) of death.

The middle part of the psalm states the movement concisely: paralysis (vv. 3-4), acknowledgment (v. 5), rescue and well-being (vv. 6-7). No wonder the conclusion of verses 1-2 is announced. But the simple statement should not cause us to miss the insight offered. Everything in the disorientation, everything for future life, everything in relation to God—*everything* depends on making known, not concealing, confessing to Yahweh. The key verb "acknowledge" (יָדַע) is contrasted to "be silent" (חָרַשׁ). Long before Freud, this psalmist understood the power of speech, the need for spoken release and admission, the liberation that comes with actual articulation to the one who listens and can respond.

At a theological level, this psalm makes an assumption so obvious we may miss it in our convoluted modernity. There is no doubt here about the reality of God, the reality of accountability, the clarity of expectation, and the need to come to terms with that clear, unavoidable relationship. God is not an elective or a hypothesis, but a definitional and determinative partner who establishes norms and with whom we must deal. Guilt can be destructive. It is in this psalm for a reason. But guilt fully embraced and acknowledged permits movement, a new reception of life, and a new communion with God. Only then can the guilt be resolved and genuinely relinquished. There are, the psalm asserts, no alternatives, no substitutes. The body will not be deceived, even as God will not be mocked. Freedom from guilt requires embracing it and having it dealt with by the mercy of God.

3. In verses 8-11, after sharing the unarguable experience of what has happened, the psalmist returns to the didactic stance of verses 1-2. The one who has found this way to freedom wants to share it. Indeed, verse 8 suggests that the sharing may be more than anybody else wants to hear. In verse 9 the listener is chided not to be stubborn (cf. Isa. 1:2; Jer. 8:6). We could be stubborn and miss the whole point. Perhaps better to be like a mule, who never knows guilt and never has to deal with it (v. 9). Jeremiah knows about such mulish resistance (Jer. 18:12). But that need not be our destiny. Psalm 32 concludes with

a choice (v. 10). One can resist and live in pain unrelieved. Or one can experience Yahweh's restored חֶסֶד. One can have it either way. But only the second way leads to freedom and power and joy. The "narrow gate" to new life is the way of coming to terms with God, facing God's holy will and the contrasting failure of our life.

Psalm 32 can be handled in many different ways. I fear this exposition may be taken as a "tool" for self-righteousness that knows the parameters of forgiveness and tenaciously reduces everyone's experience to moralism. That, I think, is not the point of the psalm. It is not an invitation to a fearful moralism. Or the psalm can also be taken as an invitation to the deep and basic escapism of our culture. But the guilt to be acknowledged is not, I submit, a set of religious sins. It concerns rather the idol-making ideologies of our day, which reduce all of life to management and reduce the terror of God's holiness to a set of religious niceties. The restoration to communion here offered involves a programmatic critique of our culture which binds us into restlessness and weakness. The psalm could lead us to think through the ways in which our culture denies and suppresses and covers up all in the name of competence, prosperity, and success. For what the psalm finally commends is *yielding*. Against that, our social values are oriented to *unyielding control*.

There is a temptation for the religious to prate about the *instruction* of verses 1-2, 8-11, but to neglect *the transformational act* of verses 3-7, which costs. Otherwise, we might long since have done it.

Psalm 51

Psalm 32 testified to the need of confession, and in 32:5 we are offered a brief statement of it. But Psalm 32 is mainly *a proposal* that sin should be confessed. Psalm 51 moves closer to the center of the crisis of alienation and offers *a model* for actual confession. Here we see the psalmist actually doing it.

1. Verses 1-2 provide for us the basic themes and vocabulary of confession. The remainder of the psalm may be taken as an exploration of the implications of this initial statement. On the one hand, the basic words of forgiveness and graciousness are given. Everything Yahweh needs to show is listed: *mercy, steadfast love, mercy*,[99] together with three cultic words, *blot out, wash, cleanse*. The petition addressed to Yahweh involves two systems of words, covenantal and cultic. Yahweh needs to take a fresh initiative with this one whose actions have distorted everything. The covenantal words urged and the cultic actions requested are not mutually exclusive, nor are they the same. The psalm does see that the cultic acts of forgiveness are a mode through which the actual pardon of Yahweh is made available. Cultic action is real, transformative action.

On the other hand, the psalm has the speaker again use the primary vocabulary for sin as we have seen it in Psalm 32: *transgression, iniquity,* and *sin.* At the outset the speaker holds nothing back. He exhibits the attitude of the later hymnwriter, "Nothing in my hand I bring." This is the prayer of an empty-handed person. So the words provide a proper evangelical match. Complete *forfeiture of self,* on the one hand; *desperate trust in God,* on the other.

2. The actual confession is presented in verses 3-5. The governing word is "I know" (I make known, I acknowledge, I admit), the same word used in Ps. 32:5. There is no argument. The speaker concedes that all that is wrong in the relationship is on his side. There is here no abrasion toward Yahweh, but a genuine admission that Yahweh is utterly in the right. That basic *knowing* is supported by three statements.

a) Real sin is a violation of relationship with God. Tradition (and the superscription) has this as David's prayer of confession occasioned by his meeting with Nathan (2 Sam. 12:13). On the face of it, most sin is played out in the social arena. It is sin against the neighbor, as was this. But here the psalmist sees that sin is a *theological* problem—not moral, ethical, social, or psychological. The problem is that sin violates God. This does not mean that others are not also hurt. But the righting of the wrong concerns the "godness" of God, and none other. In the flat world of modernity, this psalm affirms to us a forgotten reality. Our skewed lives finally must deal with God.[100]

b) God is utterly in the right (צדק, v. 4). That is not a common affirmation in all of the lament psalms. We should not generalize from this psalm, because in other psalms it is argued that God is not always in the right. When we take into account all the texts, biblical faith always leaves open the charge that God is not in the right, a charge vigorously urged by Job. But here the point is not argued. It is, as Barth repeatedly argues, the righteousness of God that makes the reality of guilt so dismal.[101] Here, as much as anywhere in Scripture, the radical difference between God and a human creature is made clear. That difference is relational. The problematic aspect concerns God's righteous holiness and God's partner, who is neither righteous nor holy.

c) The statement of verse 5 can be readily misunderstood. It does not mean that sex is sinful, nor that this speaker has a perverted beginning, or that the mother is morally implicated. Rather the speaker asserts that he is utterly guilty, in principle, from the beginning. There never was a time when this speaker was not so burdened. I take this to be not a clinical statement, but an expression of theological candor as the speaker exposes himself to God's righteousness. One may say that it is a piece of liturgical hyperbole, as is much of the Psalms. We do not need to take the statement ontologically as a "doctrine of man." What is important is that in this moment of drastic confrontation, the speaker has no claim. There is indeed "no health in him."

3. The long middle section of verses 6-14 is a set of imperatives that ask

God to do for the speaker what he cannot do for himself. Verse 6 is a strange and noteworthy statement. It speaks of God's *fidelity*, God's wish that the speaker should be reliable, trustworthy, true. This wish of God is contrasted with the actual life of phoniness that is here brought to the throne. So the prayer is for *wisdom*, the kind of *discernment* that will make a new, responsible life possible. The prayer is a departure from the old life, which surely is marked by a foundational foolishness.

Then come the imperatives addressed to God: purge, wash, fill,[102] hide, blot out, create, put, cast not, take not, restore, uphold, deliver. The speaker covers the full range of the actions God can take that will bring life. In several modes, the speaker asks God to make a new life possible.

In verses 7-9, we are dealing mainly with cultic language, with words already used in verses 1-2. The speaker is apparently ready to undergo ritual washing physically to remove the stain and shame of sin (cf. John 13:8-10).[103] This is indeed going public with the acknowledged burden. In verse 8, as in Ps. 32:3-4, it is as though some physical problem has arisen out of the guilt, so that ritual healing restores the whole person. Note that in verse 6, there is a request for wisdom, and here a petition for restoration of bones. The two motifs are brought together in Prov. 3:8: "[Wisdom] will be healing to your flesh and refreshment [medicine] to your bones." Psalm 51 suggests a great deal of work to be done in our understanding of the material fact of sin in our lives and what that does to our bodies. If the reality is material, then we have work to do about the ritual (visible, bodily) ways of overcoming the problem. The psalm suggests that more than "talk therapy" is needed for the really foundational disorder among us.

Verses 10-12 ask for restored personhood, again with reference to the body. A "clean heart" means a new beginning, a capacity for new living.[104] In these verses, three times there is reference to "spirit/wind" (רוח). The first is a request for a new spirit (cf. Ezek. 36:26), a chance to begin again. The latter two are a recognition that the "wind" to live is a gift from God. One should not make anything doctrinal of "holy Spirit" in verse 11, for the phrase simply acknowledges that a genuine life-giving wind is wholly God's gift. The petition is for bodily restoration. But at the same time it knows that the body depends on the fresh wind of God. Notice this is not conventional dualism, but a way of speaking about the need for God's gift to be given in each moment; without it the bodily person is unable to function (cf. Ps. 104:29-30).

If this text can on any ground be linked to David, we may note that in the beginning of the David narrative (1 Sam. 16:13), David received the wind/spirit, which enabled him to rule. Indeed he could not rule without it. The tradition recognizes that in his unthinkable act against Uriah and Bathsheba, David has lost the power of Yahweh authorizing him to rule. The wind to gov-

ern is gladly given by Yahweh (cf. Isa. 11:2), but it is never possessed. It is always held in trust. Sin can destroy God's royal mandate for David, and for us.
Such utterly alien sin can leave us powerless and without authority for living
our lives. That much this psalmist knows. He places himself utterly at the disposal of Yahweh and asks for a reissue of gifts that make a regal life possible.

We have much to ponder in this insight. We have operated as though the
wind to rule is our property, to be used as we choose. And now we may wonder, given the demise of humane governance in our world, whether such cynical abuse of the trust of power has caused the wind to depart, and we are left
with only our own imagination and our technology. A survey of the modern
world might cause us to wonder if any among us any longer have the gift of
God's power which authorizes real life-giving rule. This act of deep repentance
assumes a posture in which the gift of power for governance might be given
again.

This section concludes in verse 14 with a decisive plea, but also with a
hope. This speaker who has utterly relinquished self to God dares now to look
ahead, beyond the emptiness of the moment. Already here something of the
new wind has been given, as it is to those who yield themselves fully. And with
that gift, the psalm is on the way to new orientation.

4. Though this psalm is of a very different kind with a very different intent
than the lament, it still holds to the basic structure of the lament. After verse 14
comes the decisive turn. In verses 15-17, the mood has changed. It is as though
some assurance has already been given. Now the חנן, חסד, רחם (grace,
steadfast love, compassion) requested in verse 1 have perhaps been granted.

The very lips which diminished the self are now able to exalt God (v. 15).
This verse is frequently used as a liturgical prayer. As in so many such uses, it
may be intuitively correct. But when taken out of context, its force is greatly
weakened. The full psalm shows that one cannot ask for lips to praise until one
has engaged in a profound yielding and emptying. That is because the God of
this psalm wants no religious conventions (the kind often given after the liturgical prayer) but only a dismantled self. The dismantled self, characterized in
verse 17, requires a shattering of one's spirit, a brokenness of one's heart (cf.
Isa. 57:15). True worship and new living require a yielding of self to begin
again on God's terms. But the brokenness may not be a psychological
dismantling. It may as well be an economic unburdening, a political risking, a
stepping away from whatever form of power we have used by which to secure
ourselves. Our handling of this psalm has often been narrowly reductionistic,
when in fact the emptying that most needs to be done may take very different
forms, depending on who prays the psalm.

5. The concluding verses, 18-19, are a rather odd addition. They are
clearly added by a Jerusalem enthusiast who must have come along later, and

who seems to contradict the statement of verse 16. But perhaps we may find a more subtle explanation concerning the intent of these verses. In verses 16-17 it is clear that God wants no sacrifice, but a yielding (cf. 1 Sam. 15:22; Hos. 6:6). Could it be that when one has really yielded, then everything, even conventional worship and animal sacrifice, can be a proper gesture? But only after yielding. That is, what is *prohibited* in verse 16 *before* verse 17 becomes *acceptable* to Yahweh in verse 18, *after* verse 17. The Bible is not interested in making lists of what is acceptable, as much as it is interested in *transformed intentionality*. Given such transformation, what had been precluded now may be a form of legitimate worship.

In any case, this psalm traces the anguished way by which a deeply disoriented life can begin again. We might consider briefly the traditional placement of this psalm in the life of David (as in the superscription).[105] Such a placement is not impossible, though in general scholarship has not inclined to credit such claims. What we have is a quite concrete confession not attached to any specific situation. It could be that a connection to the David-Uriah-Bathsheba incident has a heuristic value, whether it is historically correct or not. For the sin of that episode is not finally sexual violation (against Bathsheba) or murder (against Uriah), but it is the sin of pride against Yahweh, of imagining that one is autonomous and can live one's life without reference to Yahweh and Yahweh's commandments. The sin is thinking the commandments can somehow be superseded. As the psalm now stands, it underscores both moments in the life of faith, *the seriousness of the disorder*, for which responsibility must be taken, and *the possibility for new life*, which cannot be coerced from God, but only freely given. These two affirmations together constitute the heart of evangelical faith, in which this psalm is so firmly rooted.

The psalm comes dangerously close to our own situation. For we imagine we are, like David, "come of age." We order our common life, make public policy, build our institutions on such a premise. We may find, like David, our life grinding to an anguished halt, because the "wind" may be at the moment of departure. We may be more like Saul than David (1 Sam. 16:14). The issues in this psalm do not concern guilt of a moralistic, privatistic kind, nor of a tortured conscience.[106] They concern rather the realities about how to live and die in a world where the only wind that counts is God's holy wind. And we are left in a delicate relation to it, yet having to exercise, or pretend to exercise, power as rulers of the creation.

Psalm 143

We have been considering in turn the psalms that concern the external dimensions of disorientation and then the internal aspects of the same reality.

Psalm 143 is of particular interest because it holds those two dimensions together, as finally they must be.

1. The main body of the text (vv. 3-10) is unexceptional in portraying the normal elements of a complaint psalm.

a) Verses 3-4 describe the situation of need. The problem is caused by the deadly work of the enemy. The result is loss of self; the speaker is reduced to hopelessness and helplessness.

b) Verses 5-6 are a statement of deep trust in Yahweh, perhaps as a motivation to Yahweh. First it is recalled that Yahweh has been powerfully attentive in the past. And then verse 6 is an act of yielding the self, with the telling metaphor of "parched land." This one beset by other enemies turns to the only source of help. There is here no word of vengeance, but only a desperate, hope-filled surrender.

c) The petition of verses 7-10 is vigorous, with an extended series of imperatives. It asks for answer, to be saved from the Pit, on the basis of God's חסד and the trust of the speaker. There is resolve in verse 8b, and verse 10 leads to a new life of obedience when rescued from the trouble. So the sequence of complaint–motivation–petition is what we might expect. Thus far the psalm addresses the external circumstance caused by the enemy, and expresses full confidence that Yahweh can correct that situation.

2. But what interests us in this text, as indeed it interested Luther, is the theological sensitivity in the opening of verses 1-2 and the conclusion of verses 11-12. Here attention is largely turned away from the external problem of the enemy, though the note is present in verse 12. Instead, the speaker focuses on how this needy person dare intercede with this awesome God. Indeed, all our prayer must be aware of and take into account the utter mismatch and the boldness of such petition. How dare one like this pray to a God like this? What is the basis for any hope that Yahweh will hear and heed such prayer? The bold answer is given in verses 1-2. The basis for prayer is found in "*thy* faithfulness, *thy* righteousness."

Psalm 143 articulates utter confidence in Yahweh's חסד and אמנה. There is no need for confirmation, qualification, or any other augmentation. Such confidence is enough, and it is the only basis for such a prayer from the Pit. Note well: the basis is not in the one who prays, but in the one addressed.

The following verse states the countertheme. The speaker is quite aware that what is needed and sought is an act of Yahweh's graciousness, the ground for which is found in Yahweh's inexplicable inclination. Verse 2 is clear that one must depend upon the righteousness of Yahweh, because the righteousness of the petitioner will never suffice. There is no adequate motivation to be brought from the human side. There is no persuasive reason found in human righteousness. The speaker seeks graciousness, not justice, for justice will not suffice.

The psalm sharply contrasts the *righteousness of Yahweh*, God's uncondi-
tioned inclination toward Israel, and *Israel's righteousness* which will carry no
freight in time of trouble. The psalm understands the vast and unbridgeable distinction between the two parties. The contrast is the very one found in Rom.
10:1-5, where Paul contrasts the righteousness of God, which is *the righteousness of faith*, and the *righteousness of the law*, which is found wanting. No
wonder the tradition of the Reformation has found this to be a crucial psalmic
affirmation, for it portrays guileless faith throwing itself without reservation on
the good intention of God.

The conclusion of the psalm in verses 11-12 returns to that theme. The triad of appeal is "thy name's sake, thy righteousness, thy steadfast love." The
vocabulary has shifted slightly from verses 1-2, but the reality is the same. And
this is reenforced by the last statement, "I am thy servant." That is, "I am at
your disposal, utterly dependent on your move toward me."

The middle body of the psalm is rather conventional. But the framing of
verses 1-2, 11-12 is distinctive. This psalm moves some distance from the usual speech of complaint, which appeals to rights rather than to need. That move
is difficult in a culture that prides itself on competence and the capacity to work
one's way in the world. Perhaps for that reason it is an important one to carry
out.

Psalm 130

In the group of psalms we are considering, this psalm is the clearest and
most terse. Compared to 32, 51, and 143, it is uncomplicated.

1. The basic address of verses 1-2 is standard for a complaint, an address
to Yahweh in trouble. Yet the placement of the voice *in the depths* adds to the
power of the prayer. In fact, the prayer is an act of inordinate boldness. In one
sweeping rhetorical move it proposes to make a link between the ruler of reality
enthroned and the most extreme, remote circumstance of human need (cf. Isa.
57:15; Deut. 10:14). The psalm thereby strikes one of the most poignant evangelical notes in all the Psalter. From where should the ruler of reality be addressed? One might think it should be from a posture of obedience, or at least
from a situation of prosperity and success, indicating conformity to the blessed
order of creation. One ought to address the king suitably dressed, properly po-
sitioned, with a disciplined, well-modulated voice.

But this psalm is the miserable cry of a nobody from nowhere. The cry
penetrates the veil of heaven! It is heard and received. This prayer makes available to us again and again the cry of Exod. 2:23-25 with which our history of
faith began. The gospel affirms that the cries from the depth are the voices to

which Yahweh is peculiarly attuned. This God is palpable, available—a staggering comment both about God and about the speaker. Moreover, the Lord is attentive to and moved by the beggar. A new solidarity is forged in the moment of speaking between the Lord and "the least," a new binding between the throne and the depths.

2. The next move in verses 3-4 indicates that this straightforward statement has a shrewdness of its own. The speaker acknowledges he is unqualified to approach the throne. That is not contested, but that disqualification is countered and overridden by the statement of verse 4: there is forgiveness with Yahweh. That is not a derivative act, not a result of some other act. It is the first act, the base line, the promise for all else, genuinely *ex nihilo*. There is forgiveness, and from it everything else flows. It is not "grounded" or reasoned or explained. It is the first fact of new life, of the new age. This is the center of the entire prayer. It is the ground for such bold prayer. There is in this One the readiness and capacity to cancel the iniquity and to begin again. At every crucial turn in Israel's life, that has been the court of appeal.

The surprise of that conviction is what follows. One might imagine that forgiveness serves to open things up to joy and to freedom, that forgiveness is the key intent of the transaction, the pivot on which everything in the future depends. But it is not. Forgiveness is instrumental to the real purpose: "That thou mayest be feared." One might have expected things in reverse sequence. One might have thought fearing Yahweh would be a ground for forgiveness. But this psalm scandalizes all our calculating notions of religion. The move comes the other way; the gift goes before the obedience. The result is that the heard beggar fears the king. The psalm surely suggests that as the relationship is transformed, so the depths are transformed as well.

But what does it mean to *fear* Yahweh? The answer may range from *reverential awe* to *utter terror*. Probably it comprehends all of these. Our first answer to the question may come from Exod. 20:20, where there is a remarkable play on the word *fear*:

Do not fear; for God has come to prove you, and that the fear of him may be before your eyes, that you may not sin.

"Do not fear...that you may fear." Do not live under *threat of Yahweh* in order that you may *embrace God* for the sake of utter obedience. The fear intended here is to begin anew, a life freshly oriented, finding in obedience new vitality.

3. But the second answer comes from within Psalm 130 itself, in verses 5-6. *Fear* leads to *hope*:

I wait (קוה) for Yahweh, my life waits (קוה)

for his promise my life hopes (יחל).
more than watchmen.

The terms *wait* and *hope* are rough synonyms. The waiting–hoping is like a watchman at night, waiting early and expectantly for the relief that comes with daybreak. Fear of Yahweh means to have confidence that things as they are (in the depth), are not as they will be. Life will be transformed. Forgiveness leads to liberation from life as it is presently organized.

4. The last two verses of the psalm (vv. 7-8) are perhaps tacked on at a later time, around the catchword *hope* (יחל). The function of these verses is to generalize the new situation from a speaker in the depth to the whole community of Israel. The rescue and forgiveness of one "feared" permit the whole community to have new life. Now, because of that bold cry from the Pit, all Israel waits for חסד, for redemption, for liberation from sin and all that blocks new life. The single speaker enacts how it is for all Israel. That single speaker might be any one in the depth who risks enough to cry. The news is that the cry is answered by forgiveness, which sets a new life in motion.

After the Deluge—Thou!

We have considered psalms that are unrestrained expressions of *rage and passion*, lashing out at anyone available. We have also considered psalms that assume God is in the right and take a posture of *submission*. Now we consider yet another response in the season of disorientation. These psalms are conventionally regarded as wisdom teaching, and that may be a useful preliminary identification.[107] However, we are mainly concerned about the *function* in a time of disorientation. They appear to be more reflective statements, somewhat removed from the intensity of the first shock of disorientation. They reflect some distancing after the first visceral articulation has spent itself. These psalms no longer have an urge to lash out, though the issue is still very real. They evidence a working through and coming to terms with the realities of the situation. But for such working through and adaptation, there is nonetheless a confident restlessness that affirms that God is a reality who will finally override all the negative realities that may now seem decisive. There is here no escape from realism, but it is a realism now reread and made provisional by God's sovereignty.

Psalm 49

This psalm, reckoned as a wisdom psalm, seems to have a didactic intent. Its general structure reflects a teaching of "the two ways," the way of life and the way of death (cf. Deut. 30:15-20; Prov. 8:32-36). The purpose of the teaching is to set the record straight, because some have their head turned and are deceived and regard the way of death as the way of life (cf. Isa. 5:20-21). That is, there is a profound confusion about what in fact makes for life. However, as we shall see, a straightforward pedagogical reflection develops in a way that shows there is more at stake for the speaker than a general theoretical question.

1. Verses 1-4 are a general summons to teaching, the kind that is standard among wisdom teachers. The vocabulary of verses 3-4 concerns ''wisdom, understanding, proverb, riddle.'' This suggests a wisdom instruction similar to Prov. 1:1-7. And these words also suggest that what is about to be taught is not obvious common sense. It is something hidden and inscrutable, and therefore likely to be confusing. Indeed, the teaching offered here is against the ''obvious'' truth of common sense. It is something that can be known only to the wise, i.e., those who are not misled by the ideologies and habits of the day.

In this summons the teacher already hints at the substance of instruction. The summons of rich and poor ''as one'' invites all to listen. But that is also the main point of the teaching. They are to be *taught together* because they are *equal*. It is false teaching to teach them separately, because they are not in fact different or unlike. And if they study separately, they will wrongly imagine they are unlike and unequal.[108] This is a proposal for egalitarian education as the only way one can learn egalitarian lessons, which is the point of the instruction. The instruction seems to understand that the experience of learning together is essential praxis for what is taught.

The *act of pedagogy* seeks to overcome imagined economic differences. The *substance of instruction* means to deny the difference. The issue facing both the substance and the pedagogy concerns a false reading of reality, namely, that wealth and poverty are somehow measures of worth and really matter. This teaching makes the point, already in its summons, that such criteria and distinctions are not only irrelevant but misleading and false.

A fine linguistic point on this lack of differentiation is lost in translation. RSV renders verse 2 ''both low and high.'' But the Hebrew contrasts אדם (royal person) and איש (weak person).[109] As we shall see, the psalm is concerned with אדם, with royal-rich persons who imagine they are superior in worth and merit.

If we are to deal with this psalm under the heading of disorientation, we suggest the psalm is the voice of resentment and doubt. It wonders why the torah keepers end up so poor while the schemers come out on top. This question of *theodicy* is the question posed by Jeremiah (12:1) and by Job (21:7-15). The question is not speculative or theoretical. It is an experiential question of one who is resentful at being cheated by virtue unrewarded. It is the voice of one who has asked whether indeed life is a moral jungle in which there is no relationship between deed and destiny, but only a moral indifference. It is Job's issue: do the faithful serve God without benefit (Job 1:9)?

The language here is not so passionate as that of Job. We are now on the other side of the question from Job. The question has now been resolved. The resolution is not subtle or complicated. Imagined human difference is resolved by the relentless, indifferent reality of death, the great equalizer. The well-being and power that the rich imagine they have is in fact of no consequence.

2. The remainder of the psalm (vv. 5-20) is a reflective teaching made to those assembled in verses 1-4. While there is no regular form or pattern, there are interesting rhetorical features that may inform our reading.

a) The issue is stated in verses 5-6: why should I fear? It is not immediately clear why the question is posed as one of *fear*. Perhaps the wealthy are a threat because their rapacious ways are always too aggressive. Perhaps the fear is to draw a theological conclusion that God is indifferent, so one's moral confidence is jeopardized. In any case, it is an honest question. Rhetorically it is answered in verse 16 with an admonition not to fear. Thus: "Why should I fear..." "Do not fear." Coping with the disorienting reality of prosperous evil people means not taking these facts with too much seriousness and not reading these facts as the last word.

b) The parallel statements on *fear/fear* (vv. 5,16) are answered in verses 8-9 and 17-19 with *verdicts*. The former is introduced by "surely"[110] and the latter by "surely." Verses 8-9 assert that no one can save his own life. Enough money is not available to pay the ontological ransom, to buy one's way out of death. Apparent wealth is as nothing in the face of death. So the poet stays with an economic agenda. Death trivializes human capability and human resources. The same answer is given in the second verdict of verses 17-19. Verse 18 quite literally says, "He can't take it with him." So the advantage is a quite temporary one that touches no real issue in one's life. It only seems to.

c) A more general teaching is given in verses 10-14, which argue that death is the great leveler (cf. Job 3:13-19). There are ultimately no differences. In the long run, the differences in verse 2 in the summons are nonexistent. Thus far the teaching seems to be evenhanded. But in verses 13-14 the speaker discloses his resentment against the "conspicuous consumers." The death to come is not here offered as the fate of the poor, only as the fate of the rich. Verse 14 does not rejoice that the poor will go to Sheol or have death as a shepherd. It may be true of them as well, but it is not said here and is of no interest to the speaker. Indeed, it does not need to be said, for everyone knows that the poor are vulnerable. What everyone apparently does not know and now needs to learn is that the same is true of the wealthy. In the real issues they are as vulnerable and undefended as all the others. And that is the inscrutable riddle that the teacher promised to elucidate (v. 4). It is against obvious common sense that imagines that somehow the wealthy are protected, immune, and safe. Societal standards do not function effectively at the raw, holy, dangerous places of life, because the power of reality does not respect artificial lines of distinction.

d) The other structural factor is the refrain of verses 12 and 20, which draws a conclusion.[111] One cannot "dwell" on the things one treasures.[112] The rending of the RSV, "pomp" (יקר), is curious. The reference is to what is treasured, precious, dear, presumably because it is scarce and not generally available. But the possession of scarcity does not differentiate, because at death, even the wealthy are like any other animal that dies (cf. Jer. 22:19), abandoned, helpless, worthy of no great respect, and not grieved. It is worth noting that the "man" mentioned in these verses is אדם (as in v. 2), the big man, the real man, the man born to power. Rhetorically the poem means to strip the pretense so carefully constructed.

3. But the most interesting verse we have saved until now. One might imagine this a simple, reasonable, instructive discourse. But verse 15 is a confessional statement that surprises us. The teacher shows that he is not a disinterested, objective observer. This is a boldly confessional statement in a context of didactic rhetoric. This single line is a wondrous faith affirmation. It begins with an asseverative: "surely, indeed" (אך).[113] This speaker is very sure. There is no "riddle" about this. This one verse is quite atypical of wisdom instruction, for the speaker here is not disinterested.

The agent now is God. This is the only positive reference to God. (The one other use, and that negative, is in verse 7, where God is the object.) Here God is an active agent who is set to save. Elsewhere in the poem, God is not even an active judge, much less a savior. The power of death works its inexorable way without divine direction.[114] But in this single verse it is different, for this is a statement of evangelical faith.

Here God "redeems" (פדה; the poet stays with economic metaphor). The rich cannot redeem themselves (v. 7), but God can and does redeem those who trust in him. We see again the theme of God's righteousness contrasted with the ineffectiveness of human power as in Ps. 143:1-2. The speaker is sure, for he asserts, "God will receive (לקח) me." The rendering *receive* is weak, for the verb is stronger, the same verb used in Gen. 5:24; 2 Kings 2:3, 5, 9. The same verb is used in verse 17, perhaps in intentional contrast: "God will *take* me...[the rich] will *take* nothing away." God "takes" to save. The rich cannot "take," for they have no power for life.

This psalm is of course not symmetrical. Whereas the negative reality of the rich is subjected to analysis and explanation, the positive affirmation of verse 15 is left unadorned. No more needs to be said. God, the agent of freedom and surprise, gives the lie to all usual conventions. That can only be announced, not argued or proved. This assertion about God changes everything. If God be removed from the issue, then things are open and unresolved. But God is the key factor, lodged at the center of the psalm. It is this that constitutes wisdom, that resolves the riddle, that keeps the apparent moral chaos bearable.

4. Our entry into this psalm may hinge on these recognitions:

a) What purports to be an objective reading of reality is in fact a partisan polemic. That is how the Bible works out the truth—by a conflictual engagement. This speaker asserts the truth against the dominant class.[115]

b) It is asserted that God joins this partisan argument. For all its urbaneness, the wisdom tradition understood the peculiar alliance of God and the poor (Prov. 17:5). Creation is peculiarly biased in this direction. It is sheer ideology to deny God this special commitment.

c) Psalm 49 may grow out of a particular conflict, but it now serves a more systemic analysis. As in the prophets, the case made against the rich has to do not only with greedy persons, but with institutional and ideological means of self-service. To read the psalm simply as a statement against individual acts of individual persons is to miss the force of the argument.

d) In the consumer capitalism of our society, this poem is important. We have enormous sorting out to do. In our affluence, it is difficult not to value the things the rich one valued. The psalm invites a long view that provides a criterion for criticism. But this is not simply an analysis of a "natural" process. It is an evangelical statement of the power of God, who seeks out for new life precisely those marginalized in the present system. That is the claim of verse 15. Wisdom has to do with the way economic power works. It discerns in the midst of economic process a factor that uncritical observers may not notice. The word *trust* (בטח) is used only once, negatively (v. 6). The psalm inquires about the source of fundamental trust. Trust has to do both with economic reality and religious commitment (cf. Matt. 6:21).[116] Choices must be made that hold the two together. One cannot avoid the issue by spiritualizing the gospel (cf. Mark 10:24; Luke 18:9; 1 Tim. 6:17). The parable of Luke 18:9-14 is addressed to those with false trust, whom God will not "take" at death. Such as those wind up "praying to themselves" (Luke 18:11).[117]

Psalm 90

Psalm 90 is one of the most magisterial of the psalms. Its attribution to Moses is no clue to authorship, but it may invite us to conjure a situation. There is no basis in the tradition, but I suggest that the psalm be heard as though Moses were now at Pisgah (Deuteronomy 34). He has come to the end. He stands looking at the promised land to which he has been headed all his life (cf. Heb.

11:23-28). Now it dawns on him that he will not go there. He embraces that painful reality that his life-pursuit of fidelity will stop short of fruition. He submits to that reality from God—but that does not stop the yearning.

1. The pivotal point of the text, I suggest, is the goal of a "heart of wisdom" (v. 12). That is the point of the prayer. The first 12 verses are a probe into the true situation of the speaker with God. The psalm affirms that the goal of true prayer, piety, and spirituality is finally to have "a wise heart."

Obviously a wise heart does not refer to knowledge, skill, technique, or the capacity to control. Instead, it seems to mean the capacity to submit, relinquish, and acknowledge the decisive impingement of Yahweh on one's life. Wisdom means to appropriate what the best sapiential tradition in Israel might teach: on the one hand, that things are connected in inscrutable ways and will not be mocked; and on the other hand, in the frame of that connectedness, human persons have great *power, freedom,* and *responsibility.* On this phrase we may bring to bear the expectations of the wisdom teachers (cf. Prov. 10:13; 14:33; Eccles. 1:17; 2:3). In relation to Moses, note the Priestly phrase in Exod. 31:6; 35:35; 36:2. The phrase is "wise heart" which in these Priestly texts the RSV renders as "ability." But the text clearly refers to more than the technical ability of a craftsman. It refers to a disposition that is responsive to and congruent with the purposes of Yahweh. Thus "wise heart" means discernment of the purposes of Yahweh.

2. The first part of Psalm 90 (vv. 1-2) is a meditative reflection on the realities that may result in such a disposition of trust, obedience, and submission.

a) Verses 1-2 lay down the parameters of faith. The psalm makes an abrupt and strong beginning with a rather bold address, "Lord." No finesse or intimacy, but simply a frontal acknowledgment. It is instructive that this term is the generic word for sovereign, אֲדֹנָי. It is not until verse 13 that the historical name of *Yahweh* is used, and then it is used only once in the entire psalm. It is used only at the turn of the psalm into the lament. Here it is enough to establish sovereignty as the context for all that follows. Perhaps that submissive ejaculation is the first mark of a truly wise heart. The psalm announces at the beginning and clings to the confession of *thou* as the focus of all that follows.

b) The first acknowledgment made is that Yahweh is the speaker's home, den, shelter, refuge, belonging place (cf. Ps. 91:9; Deut. 33:27). This is an extraordinary affirmation, of extraordinary importance. It qualifies all that follows. First, it affirms that the speaker is not homeless.[118] There is a center to prevent fragmentation. There is a belonging to preclude isolation. Second, it affirms that the speaker need not and cannot fashion his own belonging place. It is a gift. God is indeed the undoubted "home-maker," letting us be at home without anxiety (cf. Matt. 6:25-34). Real home is always gift, never achievement. Third, notice that it is not a reference to place, but to person. It is not said that Yahweh provides or makes a home, in the sense of temple, city, or land. But *Yahweh is home*. The thirst for *place* is resolved in the gift of *communion*. Moses, short of the land, can celebrate such a *place* in a *relation*.

The confidence of this first affirmation is overriding. Therefore I do not share the somber, tragic reading of the psalm offered by von Rad.[119] There may be wistfulness, even chagrin, but Psalm 90 is not a meditation on *futility and death*, as much as on the *power of God* even in the face of human reality.

c) Verses 3-11 are a reflection on the limitedness and transitoriness of human life. The speaker is aware that the human creature is a "dust creature," destined for dust (v. 3). The human creature is like grass that wilts and dries (vv. 5-6).[120] The two metaphors of *dust* and *grass* serve to characterize the true relationship between God and speaker.

The reality of disorientation is intensified with reference to "anger, wrath" (v. 7), "iniquities, sins" (v. 8), "wrath" (v. 9), "anger, wrath" (v. 11). The speaker of this psalm has a sense of deep fault, and the guilt is related to the shortness and fragility of life. In that sense, the speaker can concede that trouble in life stems not from the inscrutable hand of Yahweh, but as just punishment for sin. The statement stays close to the simple retribution presuppositions of some wisdom teachers. There is no suggestion that such judgment is other than just and fair. But seen that way, even the transitoriness of life is not tragic. It makes sense in terms of sin. The psalm stands a considerable distance from Ecclesiastes and such resignation.

d) The middle section of verses 3-11 contains two themes of transitoriness and guilt in an odd tension. It is Israel working at its peculiar sense of *guilt* in relation to a more general recognition of *finitude*, and in the psalm the tension is not resolved. It is not said that finitude results from sin. The two motifs are simply left there. That is an odd and interesting juxtaposition.

But the more telling tension is the juxtaposition of verses 1-2, 12, and 3-11. Verses 3-11 suggest negativity and resignation, but this is countered by verses 1-2. The speaker does not suggest that the assurance, "in all generations," "from everlasting to everlasting" (vv. 1-2), has been nullified by verses 3-11. The speaker holds to the initial claim. The abiding constancy of Yahweh as home is the overriding religious reality of the psalm, and the middle portion does not diminish that reality.

I suggest that the "heart of wisdom" in verse 12 is not simply one that is realistic about human transitoriness and guilt, but one that knows there is "at-homeness" in God's governance. That is the overriding character and definitional mark of the human situation. Such a reading of reality is against the evidence, even against the evidence offered in the psalm itself. A "heart of wisdom" is one that is not captured by the evidence, is not overly impressed by the

data at hand, but one that attends to the persistent reality of Yahweh's Lord-
ship.

3. If verse 12 is the pivot, as I take it to be, then it is remarkable that in the
remainder of the psalm (vv. 13-17) we are treated to very different rhetoric.
The sense of "at-homeness" which is the mark of a wise heart might lead to serenity, calmness, stability. This could lead to a kind of fatigued resignation.

But it is characteristic of the faith of the Psalms that it does not lead to this.
For these final verses are a vigorous complaint. It is like being glad to be at
home, but then immediately announcing that the home is not adequate, and
there is need for a serious transformation of things. One could most easily take
these verses of complaint as subsequently attached, as not integral to the
Psalm; then we have no problem with the incongruity.

But the incongruity may provide us a main clue to the psalm. It is this: being confident of God does not lead to passive acceptance. It leads to a vigorous
pressing of the issues, an insistence on transformation that can only be wrought
by God. Still in the midst of the disorientation, this persistent faith does battle
toward newness. Trust in Yahweh leads to a zealous insistence on change, and
the change is wrought through a lament.

a) The opening words of verse 13 are lament or complaint. The most interesting rhetorical feature is the intense imperative, "return" (שׁוּב). It is the
same word used by Yahweh in verse 3. Yahweh turns humankind to dust. Now
Yahweh is summoned to make a turn. It is Yahweh's work to turn misery to
joy. The following word, "Have pity" (נחם), is the one used in Isa. 40:1 for
the ending of exile. This speech seeks a transformative act from Yahweh and
does not doubt that it can be given.

b) The standard features of a lament are present in these verses which seek
to urge God into a decisive intervention. Yahweh is named by name. And then
the verses are dominated by a series of three pairs of imperatives or jussives:

> satisfy/make us glad
> let us see/let [your] favor
> establish/establish.

What is remarkable is that these six imperatives challenge the perspective of
verses 1-12, which assumed that God is eternal and humankind is transitory,
and nothing can change that arrangement. The prayer is an act of courage that
refuses to settle for that scheme of things and insists that something drastic be
done about it.

The most revealing nouns attached to these verbs are "steadfast love"
(חסד), and "favor" (נעם). The first of these is a request for an intense
covenantal engagement. The speaker refuses to settle for the distance of verses

1-12, and insists that Yahweh be involved with Israel and in question. By the use of "steadfast love," Yahweh is drawn out of the rather safe detachment of the preceding verses and back into Israel's (or Moses') dangerous history. The second word, *favor*, is a rather peculiar word to be used here. It is not, as the translation, "favor," might suggest, a close parallel to חסד. Rather it has an aesthetic dimension to it, suggesting serene loveliness, as might be found in the temple (Ps. 27:4). The word is used especially in wisdom contexts (Prov. 3:17; 15:26; 16:24) in the sense of pleasantness. Thus, the two terms together, חסד and נעם, have a range from passionate covenantal speech to sapiential concern for the pleasing. It is a prayer asking that the dimness of verses 3-11 be overcome, in full confidence that Yahweh can do that, and only Yahweh is able.

In the climax of verse 17, we have again the powerful word "Lord" (אדון) matching the abrupt beginning point of the psalm. The name of God then at beginning and end is אדון, Lord, and in the middle with the lament, "Yahweh." The repetition of Lord at the beginning and at the end is qualified by the covenantal term, "our God," so that the Sovereign One now belongs with us and for us, and is not free to enjoy his own eternity indifferent to our well-being. The psalm moves from a God who is outside human circumstance to a God now deeply drawn into our paths.

The temporal language used here matches the shift to covenantal language. In verses 1-2 the time reference for God, in contrast to that of humankind, is "from generation to generation [RSV, "in all generations"], from everlasting to everlasting." But in verses 15-16 the time references are more modest, specific, concrete, and limited, probably a deliberate contrast with verses 1-2. In verse 15 the time request is not for generations or everlasting; it ʾs only *days* and *years*, asking for as many times of blessing as there have been of curse. In verse 16, there is a hope for the generations, but the exact demand is much less than "generation to generation," asking only one generation ahead. The speaker does not request the grand doxological promise and finds that irrelevant unless the promise is true specifically to this people in this circumstance. The *eternity of God* is pressed toward a *daily concreteness*. The shift in time is correlated with the introduction of חסד as the immediate concern of the speaker.

Finally, the speaker twice uses the phrase, "work of our hands." We would not have expected the psalm to end with this. Indeed the psalm would seem to be a dismissal of such a concern. Certainly Yahweh has works of his hands on a cosmic scale (cf. Pss. 8:3; 19:1). But in the face of Yahweh's power, this psalm ends with a passionate, perhaps pitiful, plea for the "stuff" from our side. The phrase surely refers to human goods and human achievements. Israel knows that God can bless the work of our hands (Deut. 16:15; 24:19). But Israel also knows that God can be vexed by such equipment (Deut. 31:29) because the work of our hands may be idolatrous (Pss. 115:4; 135:15). Nonetheless, the crowning petition here is not one of yielding to God's majestic power (as one might expect with a "heart of wisdom") but one of wanting this "withering grass" to be given durability. This last petition, along with the entire lament, seems to fly against the claims of the first half of the psalm.

Now one can argue this is an act of pitiful, stubborn defiance in the face of theological reality. But one can also argue that it is the *majesty* of God (vv. 1-2) translated into *faithfulness* (v. 14) that gives rise to *hope* (vv. 14-17). This sequence of *majesty...faithfulness...hope* means that the last petition is not an act of defiance but is precisely an act of fidelity. The petition is the natural outflow of God's majesty when that majesty is articulated as covenant faithfulness. If it were not so articulated, then hope would be an act of willful autonomy. But when God's majesty is transferred to covenant faithfulness, it invites this kind of hopeful petition. The prayer "hopes" that God is mobilized for the long-term valuing of human reality.

It could be that such a prayer in a time of disorientation is deception and denial. But I think not. The speaker has looked it all squarely in the face (vv. 3-11). The speaker has concluded that our situation is not finally defined by dust and grass, but by the one who makes us at home safely. That assurance evokes and permits an insistent prayer that is relentless against "the Pit," insisting on new life, and that not empty-handed. It is the covenantal rendering of God's sovereignty that permits human assertion that in other contexts might appear as Promethean presumption. But here it is a believing response to God. In the midst of the reality, the *thou* of God invites prayerful Israel to move on in hope.

Psalm 73

We come now to what may be the most remarkable and satisfying of all the psalms. We treat it last among the psalms of disorientation, because in the career of faith it seems to be the last word on disorientation, even as it utters the first word of new orientation. The very process of the psalm itself shows the moves made in faith, into, through, and out of disorientation, into new orientation, which is marked by joyous trust. One can trace the moves formally as we will do. But we should not fail to notice that this psalm is an act of faith. It is a mighty *engagement with God, a struggle against God* and a wondrous *communion with God.* The formal factors must not distract from the theological power of the experience made available here.

1. Verse 1 lays down the premise of the psalm. It is this verse that causes us to regard the psalm as a wisdom psalm. However, such a judgment is not without problem. Wisdom characteristically deals with moral coherence, free-

dom, responsibility, and mystery. And while these motifs are present, they are
not prominent. Rather this is an intensely *religious* statement, disclosing a rich
interiority of faith that wisdom teachers characteristically do not probe. There
is a kind of profundity and sensitivity not usually associated with wisdom.
While the presenting problem may be "theodicy," the course of the argument
and the resolution are on terms other than sapiential. By the end of the psalm,
the issue of theodicy is dealt with by a move from *questions of equity* to the
power of communion.

Much hinges on how the first phrase is rendered. It is conventionally rendered, "God is good to the upright." But that is a reading which must change
the text. The Hebrew has טוב לישראל, "good to Israel." The changed reading has טוב לישר אל. The division of the word dissolves the reference to Israel and treats it as two words, "upright/God." The textual change is com-
mended by the forming of an attractive parallel with the second phrase, "good
to those who are pure in heart." If this change be made, then the formula
sounds very much like sapiential teaching, because it makes a general affirmation, without reference to the historical community of Israel. Such a reading is
a long-established one which can be appropriately pursued.

What argues against such a reading is that the text has "good to Israel."[121] Obviously there is more at stake than grammar. The change from "Israel" to "upright" changes the religious world in which we do our interpretation.[122] In this exposition I will want to insist that the one who prays here is an
Israelite, who prays as only a child of the commandments can pray.[123] In a
general way, this psalm deals with the question of theodicy. But it is an Israelite way of putting the problem, and certainly the resolution is an Israelite resolution. The question and the answer of theodicy are set in the context of the *tradition*, in the authority of *torah*, in the *promise* made to this people.

Verse 1 sets the premise for the psalm, which is also its conclusion. But it
is a different statement when it is conclusion than when it is premise. When it is
premise, it may be taken as pre-hurt, pre-doubt, pre-anguish. It is then a buoyant statement of naivete. But as a conclusion, the affirmation is on the other
side of hurt, doubt, and anguish. While the words may be the same, they now
bear different freight. Now the unuttered words of resentment have been uttered. Now the unthinkable thoughts of hostility have been thought. This
speaker has been surprised to find the truth of the tradition emerge in fresh
form. It is as though the speaker is saying, "Come, I will show you how I
learned to make this faith affirmation in an adult world of hurt, envy, and inequity." Psalm 73 is an assault on any naive faith. It arrives tortuously at a second, knowing naivete.[124]

The opening ejaculation, "surely" (אך) is the same as in Psalm 49:15. In
both cases it is an utterance that is against the presumed knowledge. The psalm

proposes a counteropinion to what must have been a *new* consensus organized against the tradition. It is as though others (along with the speaker) were close to giving up on the Israelite claims of faith, because the evidence showed it wasn't worth it.[125] This speaker makes the case with passion that the old claims of Yahweh's faithfulness are claims of vitality that will hold in the fatigued world of cynicism. This speaker is not content to reassert the old claims, but provides experience to substantiate the claims afresh. Of course, the Israel to whom God is God is not a careless, indifferent Israel. It is the "pure in heart" in the covenant community, who take ritual practices seriously (cf. Ps. 24:4). This promise of verse 1 is for those who genuinely participate. The pure in heart shall see God (Matt. 5:8). No one else shall see God. This psalm concerns the truth of seeing God, how it happens and what is wrought by it in Israel.

2. Verses 2-16 are a statement of the problem posed for this psalmist. The "But as for me" at the beginning of the unit seems to suggest that the established assumptions of Israel (stated in v. 1) are problematic for this speaker. The personal *experience* of the speaker does not mesh with the claims of the *tradition*, so the speaker wants to make a quite personal statement. In retrospect, these verses are like a confession of sin. The confession is stated in verses 2-3: "*I was envious.*" Then we are told the basis of the jealousy, which is essentially an act against God's sovereignty.

Verses 4-11 are dominated by "they," the affluent, cynical, well-off who seem to thrive. Their daily existence seems to affirm either that God is good to the גוים who do not keep covenant or honor torah. Or their existence affirms that God is irrelevant. Either way, the special claim of Israel is in deep question. "They" are described in great detail, indicating not only that the speaker is a careful observer, but that he has been intensely, almost obsessively, fascinated with the subject. They are people who take easy, happy trips to the beach and come home suntanned (v. 4). They are untroubled and seem to have no hang-ups with "middle-class morality" or attentiveness to the "less fortunate." They are exceedingly well-fed, and their bodies are well cared for. They engage in self-care and self-love to the point of self-indulgence. They live for themselves, and they evoke resentment from those schooled passionately in the care of the neighbor, who are exhausted and perhaps "burned out."

The speaker makes a shrewd economic critique. People who live like that are not disinterested. They are not well-off because they are lucky. Such wealth and comfort, the psalmist argues, is based on violence (v. 6) and oppression (v. 8). They are skillful and adept at self-interest and have no shame about it. They are genuinely atonomous people who look after themselves (v. 11). The psalmist is troubled with the obvious conclusion: it works!

Then in verses 12-16, the psalm carries the fascination into tension with the tradition. Verses 3-11 are without reference to the tradition, pure description. But now we must take another look. In verse 12 the speaker issues a verdict: "Behold, these are the wicked." This is not, I suggest, to be taken as a condemnation, for that would be dismissing them. The speaker is not ready to dismiss them. Rather the label "wicked" is simply a social identification. These are the ones my tradition has told me would suffer. According to the tradition, they live so that trouble must come upon them. And it does not come. Thus the "wicked" begin to look like a viable alternative way to live which makes the Israelite tradition seem terribly provincial and not "with it."

Then the speaker tells about a sudden doubting awareness in the pit of his stomach. The particle beginning at verse 13 is lost in translation. It is "surely" (אַךְ), the same as in verse 1. The speaker using this disruptive language wonders whether Israel's tradition of moral responsibility is nonsense: it is useless to keep a clean heart. With a different adjective, the psalm returns to the initial proposition of verse 1. God "is good to those who are pure in heart." But now the psalmist suspects that a pure heart is useless. The speaker is seduced to a "superior" way in the world, a way not judged by *fidelity*, but by *pragmatism*. Clearly, the alternative way works. Indeed, it works better than the way of Israel. How can it be bad if it produces such happy results?

In verses 15-16, the dawning begins, when the speaker "comes to himself" (Luke 15:17). The point that sticks in the craw is this: "What will the children think?" "Is this how I want to be regarded by them?" "I would have violated the trust the coming generation has placed in me." Note well that the sobering moment does not come to an isolated person, even to an upright person, but it comes to a member of the community who must act responsibly toward that community. Reference to the community of hope makes clear that "they" are not who I am. Attractive as "they" are, I cannot live that way. Perhaps it is said with some regret and wistfulness. The point is not yet fully established. The speaker still has decisions to make, but his unease grows. There is a readiness for movement.

3. That movement occurs in verse 17, the center of the poem. The verse is brief. We would like to know more, but we are given only a hint. The speaker was attracted "until." The "until" is a decisive time, a turn in perspective. A new orientation was wrought; a refocusing of reality happened in "the sanctuary of God." The holy place offered another look and freed the speaker from the mesmerizing evidence so close at hand. In some ways—perhaps liturgical—the reality of God's holiness caused the speaker to reperceive the tempting alternative. Now he takes a long view and sees "their" destiny. This moment is a moment of utter inversion. Now the psalm moves on, but in a quite different direction. Thus far, the entire narrative has been confined to the horizontal interaction between "I" and "they."

4. In verses 18-28 we see a refocused faith that stands in complete contrast with verses 2-16. First we have a dismissal of the alluring alternative (vv. 18-20) and then an exploration of what real faith means.

a) The dismissal of the tempting alternative (vv. 18-20) is begun with yet another "truly" (אַךְ), the third such use in the psalm (cf. vv. 1, 13). It is now clear. These self-indulgent, autonomous people have an end coming which is harsh and unavoidable. They had thought they could pick their own destiny. But as in Psalm 49, such social standing does not give one special voice in one's future. The speaker then reiterates the best claims of Israel's moral tradition: such a life won't work. (Notice that the argument is still pragmatic.) The disorientation of the speaker is not so deep or massive that there is no longer a moral coherence. Life still holds, and the result for those who deny the holding shape of life is slippery places, ruin, destruction, terror, an unreal dream. This is now how life in fact is. So we will not live in opposition to the claims of God, because such life cannot endure. The reality of God shows the futility of such an autonomous effort.

b) Verses 21-22 are a painful reflective moment, corresponding to verse 15. The speaker in retrospect sees how silly the fascination was. He recognizes that in this fascination he violated the only relationship he really values. The verses are a statement of regret, for this stupid infatuation with another' way threatened the only real relationship he knows. How utterly insensitive, as if he could finally ignore this relationship with God which defines all (cf. Isa. 1:2).[126]

c) But the psalm does not linger with remorse. In verses 23-28, we arrive at the kind of intense faith that leads to the trusting conclusion of verse 1. The self-announcement, "but I," is precisely parallel to that of verse 2. There it is removed from the community of tradition. That is, the "I" of verse 2 wants to separate from the way of the community. Now in contrast, the "I" is restored to fellowship and to the claims of the community. The symmetry of "But I" in verse 2 and "But I" in verse 23 traces the dynamic of this life with God. And this is preceded by a parallel "surely" (אַךְ) in verses 1, 18 which provide the intellectual, religious, and moral point of discontinuity with what had been assumed until this point. Thus the psalm narrates two break points. The first is "surely" (v. 1) and "but I" (v. 2), which breaks with the premise of verse 1. The second is the "surely" (v. 18) and the "but I" (v. 23), which breaks with the destructive fascination.

The "but I" in verse 23 is a moment of remarkable disclosing power. In that instant, the speaker discerns what is most foundationally true: "I am continually with thee." But this is not a statement of resolve or fidelity. The substance of that claim is given in verses 23b-24a. The ground for "I am with thee," is in *thee*. After the temptation of this psalm, the redemptive utterance is

thou: "Thou dost hold my right hand. Thou dost guide me." The speaker is recipient, not agent. Life with God is gift, not achievement. The confession contrasts with the cynical dismissal of God in verse 11. The assurance celebrated
here is like an enthronement formula (Isa. 41:10, 13; 42:6; 45:1). Royal power is related to God's grasping, upholding hand, a point used Christologically
in the Apostles' Creed, "He sits on the right hand of God."

The final statement of verse 24 is most enigmatic. The "afterward"
(אַחַר) of the faithful is contrasted with the "afterward" (אַחֲרִית; RSV,
"end") of the גוים in verse 17. Their end is ruin, destruction, terror. The contrasting end of the speaker is glory and honor. The verb "receive" again is
לקח, "take," the same strong verb we have seen in Ps. 49:15. The language
must be left metaphorical. Some commentators take this as an allusion to life
after death, but that is a highly speculative reading that seems to fall outside the
purview of this psalm. It is enough to see that the destiny of the faithful is well-
being from God and with God. This verse is consistent with the tradition of the
Westminister Catechism that one's "chief end" is to "glorify God and enjoy
him forever." That is exactly what is happening here.

d) Verses 25-26 are a reflective spin-off from the decisive affirmation of
verses 23-24. The speaker now has a clarified commitment. After the way-
wardness and inventiveness of verses 2-16, the speaker has "come to his
senses." He now understands and confesses that there is no other source of life
(cf. John 6:68). There is none in heaven (no other god), none on earth (no attractive alternative) that has power. This, only this, is his genuine delight. Notice there is nothing here of moral weightiness. He now regards Yahweh as his
best friend,[127] the one who does "friendship" (v. 1).[128] And as there is no
other help outside self, so verse 26 denies self-resources as a way to life. He
has lusted after the "portion" of the self-indulgent. But Yahweh as portion
(חלק) is contrasted with the "slippery place" (חלק) of the wicked, which
leads to ruin (v. 18; cf. 1 Sam. 2:11-16; Mic. 2:1-2). The portion that is Yahweh is safe and reliable (cf. Ps. 16:5; 142:5), unlike those portions among the
wicked, which end in disaster.[129]

e) In verses 27-28, a final didactic conclusion is drawn. The "behold" at
the beginning of verse 27 matches the "behold" in verse 12. There it was a
startling discovery which is now seen to be false. Now a second crucial
discernment is made. Those distant from God die. Autonomy is a harlotry that
does not work.[130] Then in verse 28, we have a third "but I" (cf. vv. 2, 23),
with an unembarrassed self-announcement of nearness. The psalmist is now
unabashedly a companion of Yahweh and without apology. The nearness
(קרב) of the speaker is contrasted with the distance (רחק) of the others. As
distance leads to death, so nearness leads to "good." Psalm 73 ends with a
sense of well-being. One who ventured out has discovered how pleasing is the

haven of God's fellowship. It is striking that only here in verse 28 is the name of Yahweh finally uttered. It is as though it has been withheld and must not be sounded until the right moment, the moment of happy resolution and serious fidelity. To speak the name before then would be a mockery.

5. Clearly this is an intricately crafted speech. As Buber has noted, this psalm is a meditation on the *heart*.[131] The term occurs six times:

a) the pure in heart (v. 1)
b) the heart overflowing with follies (v. 7)
c) a well kept heart as futile (v. 13)
d) a sour heart (v. 21)
e) a failed heart (v. 26)
f) a strengthened heart (v. 26)

The psalm impresses one in its remarkable insight and candor. It is the tale of a heart seduced and then healed, a heart isolated and then restored to fellowship. It provides clues to the moves into disorientation and out. One goes there with unqualified honesty, but what faith finds in the disarray is the memory and hope of God. I am not inclined to read the crucial encounter (v. 17) as a mystical experience.[132] Rather the turn is triggered by a thought of the coming generation (v. 16) and their verdict. But it is in the holy place (v. 17) where one gets free of the ideology of self-sufficiency, affluence, and autonomy long enough to recognize that the decisive reality is a move on the part of the faithful God. The denial of God (v. 11) does not change the reality of God (v. 23). This psalmist has arrived at new orientation, a decision to maintain an alternative reading of reality.

Thou hast turned for me my mourning into dancing;
  Thou hast loosed my sackcloth
  and girded me with gladness,
that my soul may praise thee and not be silent.
  O Lord my God, I will give thanks to thee for ever.

Psalm 30:11-12

4

Psalms of New Orientation

I have tried to show that a major move of the Psalms is the move from an ordered, reliable life to an existence that somehow has run amok. The Psalms give expression to that new reality of disorientation, when everything in heaven and on earth seems skewed. We may believe that such psalms not only express what is already experienced. They also articulate and evoke the new situation of disorder, so that it may be experienced. That is, it may not be fully experienced, embraced, acknowledged, unless and until it is brought to speech. We have seen that the experience of disorientation is experienced and expressed in many different ways. These different ways embody very different theological readings of reality, which cannot be explained by, understood through, or reduced to any single formulation. We have spent a major portion of our time and space on that reality in the Psalms because that is the part of the Psalter that has been most neglected in church use. In the present religious situation, it may be the part of the Psalter that is most helpful, because we live in a society of denial and cover-up, and these psalms provide a way for healing candor.[1] It may also be so because we live in a society in which the disorientation is not only personal but also public. The "sacred canopy" is clearly in jeopardy, and that jeopardy must be dealt with as a religious issue.[2]

But obviously the move into disorientation is not the only move made in the faith of Israel or in the literature of the Psalms. While the speaker may on occasion be left "in the Pit," (as in Ps. 88), that is not the characteristic case. Most frequently the Psalms stay with the experience to bring the speech to a second decisive move, from disorientation to new orientation. That is, the Psalms regularly bear witness to the surprising gift of new life just when none

had been expected. That new orientation is not a return to the old stable orientation, for there is no such going back. The psalmists know that we can never go
home again. Once there has been an exchange of real candor, as there is here
between Yahweh and Israel, there is no return to the precandor situation.

Rather, the speaker and the community of faith are often surprised by
grace, when there emerges in present life a new possibility that is inexplicable,
neither derived nor extrapolated, but wrought by the inscrutable power and
goodness of God. That newness cannot be explained, predicted, or pro-
grammed. We do not know how such a newness happens any more than we
know how a dead person is raised to new life, how a leper is cleansed, or how a
blind person can see (cf. Luke 7:22). We do not know; nor do the speakers of
these psalms. Since Israel cannot explain and refuses to speculate, it can do
what it does best. It can tell, narrate, recite, testify, in amazement and gratitude, "lost in wonder, love, and praise."

Westermann has argued that the full form of the lament psalm is the most
basic rhetorical pattern in Israel's faith.[3] That is because the full form constitutes a dramatic whole that moves from wretchedness to joy.[4] It is important
that the form, as currently understood, includes not only a statement of the
problem. It also includes a statement of *resolution*, culminating in praise and
thanksgiving. In the first instance, an act of praise and thanksgiving is a statement about *trouble resolved*. Thus the praise and thanksgiving forms in this
case are not independent forms, but are partial forms. Initially every such statement has as its backdrop a situation of need and trouble. It is evident that these
celebrative statements of resolution then break off and become independent
speech forms, standing alone without their proper rhetorical forerunners. That
is, we can have free-standing statements of new orientation for which God is
gladly credited, but we will be helped to see that such statements of new orientation always have in their background statements of trouble. Israelite praise
characteristically comes out of the depths, out of the Pit from which we are surprised to come, because the situation seemed unresolvable. This is easy
enough to see in the psalm of thanksgiving, for that song is often a lament recited now from the side of resolution, but with the remembered trouble still
quite visible. It is not so easy to discern with the hymns, for they have a much
more independent posture. And yet even the hymn in its primal assertion is a
statement of *victory* that has happened in a situation that could have ended in
defeat but did not. Thus the *celebrated victory* in the hymn is correlated with
the *resolved troubled* of the song of thanksgiving.[5]

The break point of the lament form which turns *from plea to praise* is of
course a literary phenomenon, but it does not illuminate how we receive the
new experience of orientation. It simply gives expression to it. The question of
how the move is made is not a literary, but a theological matter. Israel sings

songs of new orientation because the God of Israel is the one who hears and answers expressions of disorientation and resolves experiences of disorientation. This evangelical reality must be fully appreciated for what follows. No amount of literary form or structure or habit will account for the new experience. Along with *the literary habit* which dominates these psalms comes *the theological experience* of the will and power to transform reality. All these prayers and songs bespeak the intervening action of God to give life in a world where death seems to have the best and strongest way. The songs are not about the "natural" outcome of trouble, but about the decisive *transformation* made possible by this God who causes new life where none seems possible.[6]

I have grouped the Psalms this way to try to make a point that is decisive for pastoral experience: the lives of people and of communities are never static. They are always on the move, and I have structured it, either into orientation or out of orientation. Both moves are helped by pastoral sensitivity, theological honesty, and liturgical, rhetorical drama of the texts themselves. That is why I have organized this study in this way. Human experience strangely corresponds to the flow and form of these texts.

But having done that, I must acknowledge two methodological factors. First, one must make an exegetical decision, not always objectively, whether a psalm speaks of old orientation or new orientation. Some psalms are rather clear on this point, with little ambiguity. But in some other instances, it is a matter of interpretation as to whether a psalm articulates the surprise of *new grace* or whether it speaks of the *enduring graciousness* of God, which always sustains and so is rather taken for granted.[7] Indeed, as Goldingay has suggested, that depends on *how the psalm is used.*[8] That implies that one's hermeneutical stance toward the psalm might determine how it is to be classified in terms of function. This classification of function is much less stable and much more dynamic than the usual classification of form, which tends to be stable and even static.

Second, it is evident that the psalms of new orientation offer a variety of solutions on a continuum of continuity and discontinuity. The new orientation is seldom utterly removed from the old orientation.[9] Yet there may be such significant new factors that the major point is indeed the newness of life just now given. We shall see that the experiences and expressions of new orientation are rich and varied, for the newness of the treasure outdistances all the conventional modes of speech.[10]

Thanksgiving Songs

The most obvious song of new orientation is the thanksgiving song. The speaker is now on the other side of a lament or complaint.[11] The occasion for the song is that the speaker has complained to God and God has acted in response to the lament. The result of God's intervention is that the old issue has been overcome. The speech concerns a rescue, intervention, or inversion of a quite concrete situation of distress which is still fresh in the mind of the speaker.

Psalm 30

This psalm is a quite clear example of the thanksgiving song, which Westermann labels as a declarative narrative.[12] That is, the psalm tells the story of *going into the trouble* and *coming out of the trouble*. We may note, as we proceed through the psalm, how closely correlated to the lament psalm is this way of speaking. Indeed, one might be helped in reading it to try to articulate the lament psalm that must have been expressed by the same speaker on the other side of the trouble, before the resolution.

1. The psalm begins in praise (vv. 1-3) for a quite specific reason. The speaker has just been given a new lease on life. It is our experience that we need to recite over and over the details of the death of a loved one. In parallel fashion, this psalmist needs to recite in detail the rescue that has just been accomplished. The statement is dominated by four action verbs credited to Yahweh:

> You have *drawn* me up (v. 1);
> You have *healed* me (v. 2b);
> You have *lifted up* my life (v. 3a);
> [You have] *restored me to life* (v. 3b).

The statement lacks concreteness about the problem. Whatever the problem might be, it is covered by the imagery of death. The speaker knows the specificity; it does not need to be spelled out. This is a genuine experience of resurrection, whatever the specifics might have been.[13] Life has indeed been inverted. The psalm is useful to us because we may bring our own specificity to the text.

The countertheme linking it to lament is evident. There is reference to the Pit and Sheol, usual terms in laments. There is reference to crying and foes rejoicing. The same intimacy of address is evident, three times naming Yahweh. Indeed, the psalm throughout delights to utter the name of the rescuer, for to speak it is to give praise and thanks.

2. Verses 4-5 are a general invitation to the community to join in the praise, because the thanks are more than one individual person can adequately render. These two verses are a standard hymnic form, matching the two imperatives to praise with a reason given, so that the reason for praise, when spoken, becomes itself the act of praise. The simple praise formula is:

Imperative: Sing praises...(זמר)
Imperative: Give thanks...(הודו)
Motivation: For...(כי)

Two items are worth noting. First, the key verb is הדה, "give thanks," (ידה) which means a confessional acknowledgment of who it is that has given the new life.[14] Thanks is more than just being grateful. It is a confessional statement, in some sense relying upon and committing one's self to the other. To thank is to make commitment. Second, the *reason* is a brief review of the disorientation (anger, weeping) that had just happened, and a hint of new orientation (favor, joy; cf. Isa. 54:7-8). The psalmist does not deny that there has been trouble, but it has been powerfully overcome. We are given no concreteness about the trouble, and we are given no clue about how it has been overcome, because Israel never knows that. The move from weeping to joy (cf. John 16:20) is as reliable as the move from night to daybreak. The power of daybreak is a new enactment of God's sovereignty, which is the ground of praise.

3. The middle portion of Psalm 30 (vv. 6-10) provides confirmation for our general scheme. We have seen that verses 4-5 trace the move from disorientation to new orientation. Now these verses articulate the prior move from old orientation to disorientation:

Old orientation: I said in my prosperity, "I shall never be moved" (It can't happen here) (v. 6).
Disorientation: Thou didst hide thy face, I was dismayed (v. 7).

The absence of God destabilizes the scene of prosperity. Then in verses 8-9, we are given a quote from a previously used lament, a lament not unlike those we have considered: I cried; I offered motivations for God to act (v. 9); I uttered a petition (v. 10). Thus the psalm narrates a whole career of the relation to Yahweh from *well-being* (prosperity) to *Pit*, to *new life*.

4. The conclusion (vv. 11-12) is parallel to verses 1-3 in acknowledging and celebrating the decisive transforming actions of Yahweh:

You have turned,
You have loosed,
[You] have girded (v. 11).

Because of new life given only by God, silence is impossible. New life requires doxology, the end of sullenness, depression, numbness, despair. The last word in the psalm is הדה, confession. The mark of new life, inexplicable and unexpected, is confession expressed as thanks. Such thanks, which articulates a new life commitment, is possible only among those who vividly remember their prerescue situation. The purpose of the psalm appears to be to keep that memory alive, so that the occasion of transformation is kept alive. In that movement of transformation are found both the power to life and the passion for praise of God.

Psalm 40

This psalm is of special interest because verses 1-10 constitute a song of thanksgiving, whereas verses 11-17 are a lament psalm. We shall consider the two parts and then reflect on their relationship.

1. The beginning of the psalm is a familiar phrase, "I waited patiently." This is a weak rendering. The text has an infinitive absolute which might better be translated, "I hope intensely for Yahweh." Indeed all other hopes were exhausted. Verses 1-10 tell that this passionate hope was fulfilled and not disappointed. The hope was against all the evidence in the conviction that Yahweh could work a genuine newness. The hope was not disappointed.

2. Verses 1b-3 tell about the rescue that was hoped for and granted: he inclined, he heard, he drew me up, he set my feet, he put a new song in my mouth. In verse 3, as elsewhere, the psalmist is eager to assert that this is not a private matter. The personal rescue is a matter of public interest and benefit, for Yahweh's trustworthiness in this instance leads others to trust (בטח). The phrase, "new song," is a sign of new orientation. The new situation of well-being requires a break with old liturgical claims and practices. Perhaps the phrase originally referred to the public commissioning of a new song for a fresh public occasion such as new year. Here it is used to say that life has begun anew for this person, and it requires new lyrical speech to match the gift. Elsewhere the phrase refers to historical liberation (Isa. 42:10), liturgical renewal (Pss. 96:1; 98:1), and finally to a great new opening of public life for those who "hope intensely" in the gospel, like this psalmist (cf. Rev. 5:9).

The verbs of thanksgiving are of interest. No doubt they refer to a personal experience, but the words have imaginative power because they also touch and allude to the primal memories of Egypt and the exodus. That God inclines and hears, brings up, and sets feet in new places is the experience of all of Israel (cf. Exod. 2:23-25; 3:7-15). The new song is enacted there in the Songs of Moses (Exod. 15:1-18) and of Miriam (Exod. 15:21), though the phrase is not used. When one uses this psalm, one stands in solidarity with, participates in, and relives the whole saving memory of Israel.

3. The remainder of the thanksgiving (vv. 4-10) consists in three spin-offs from the deliverance that leads to new life.

a) In verses 4-5 are combined two very different themes. Verse 4 is a wisdom saying that sounds like a beatitude. Perhaps it is placed here because of the use of the word "trust," echoing verse 3. Trust in Yahweh is here contrasted sharply with trust in idols, who are no proper source of hope. And in verse 5, that contrast leads to a celebration of the distinctiveness of Yahweh: "Who is like thee?" Answer: "None." The psalmist, as the Bible generally, draws broad and universal conclusions from the particulars of verses 1-3. But then, that is what Israel has been doing since the exodus, (cf. Exod. 15:11). What Yahweh has done for this speaker is taken as characteristic of what Yahweh does all the time for everyone. It is a claim made both by Job's friends (Job 5:8-9) and by Job (9:10). Yahweh as deliverer is the one who causes surprises and newnesses and miracles in the historical process and in creation. No other god does so. This God is the proper source of hope and trust.

b) Further reflection of this speaker in the new situation leads to a clarification of what God wants from newly rescued people. Yahweh does not want more conventional religion; that belongs to the old world of fatigue. Those habitual practices are not condemned, but they are recognized as irrelevant. So what does the one with the "new song" do? He engages in new obedience, an embrace of the torah which is not burden but delight. In our subjective culture with its preoccupation with repression and the need to "be me," we imagine that the new life is one of utter freedom without expectation. But not here. The new life is one in which obedience to torah is an utter delight. Even in the great promise of Jer. 31:31-34, the new covenant is intensely oriented to *torah in community*. In his summons to new life, Jesus obviously has obedience in mind for the new age (Mark 10:21). This speaker has the torah in his "guts" (מעי, v. 8). That is exactly where Jeremiah promised the torah would be.

c) Along with the distinctiveness of Yahweh and the embrace of new obedience, the third spin-off is readiness to go public (vv. 9-10). The statement of thanksgiving here is quite close to the resolve of the lament in Psalm 22: 22-31. The speaker is at great pains to indicate he has not squandered the news of his new life:

> I have told the glad news (בשר),
> I have not restrained my lips,
> I have not hid your saving help (צדקה),
> I have spoken of your faithfulness (אמונה) and salvation (תשוע),
> I have not concealed your steadfastness (חסד) and faithfulness (אמת).

The great congregation is mentioned at the beginning and end of these verses. The vocabulary expresses the main agenda of biblical faith: good news, righteousness, faithfulness, deliverance, steadfast love, reliability. The whole gospel of Yahweh's new life is presented. All of it is gladly on the mouth of this thanks-giver. All of it, in the most sweeping way, is grounded in the concreteness of this personal inversion.

It is not too much to suggest that verses 4-10 provide a comprehensive proposal for what the new life should look like:

   a) singular reliance on Yahweh (vv. 4-5);
   b) glad obedience to the torah of Yahweh (vv. 6-8);
   c) ready testimony to Yahweh's actions (vv. 9-10).

4. After that affirmative statement, we are scarcely prepared for the abrupt move in verse 11 to a song of lament. The fundamental motif, as we might expect, is the actual petition for rescue which is pervasive (vv. 11, 13, 17) with the telling conclusion, "do not tarry" (v. 17). This sense of urgency is matched by several motivations: in verse 12, the threat of evil is offered, and in verse 17, the complaint is repeated. Likely the anticipated doxology is also a motivation. In verses 14-15 there is an imprecation that hopes for the punishment of the enemies. Because we have already considered lament psalms, we need not further explicate this part of the psalm.

5. What interests us is the juxtaposition of lament and thanksgiving. We have seen that in the standard form, the lament culminates in anticipated thanksgiving, but here the elements are in reverse sequence. The easiest way to handle such a surprising configuration is to say that they have been casually or accidentally joined without intentionality, as though the matter is mechanical and not integral.

But one can observe very close linguistic ties between the two parts, suggesting that there is a quite deliberate and meticulous use of the song of thanksgiving to add power and credibility to the complaint. We may observe the similarities, some of which are peculiarly close, some of which are less so:

Thanksgiving	*Lament*
I have not restrained (כלא, v. 9);	Do not thou, O Lord, withhold (כלא, v. 11);
I have not concealed your חסד and your אמת (v. 10);	Let your חסד and אמת ever preserve me (v. 11);
Your torah is within my heart (מעי, v. 8);	my heart fails me (לבי, v. 12);
I have spoken of your faithfulness and salvation (תשוע, v. 10);	May those who love your salvation (תשוע, v. 16);
I delight (חפץ) to do your will (v. 8);	Who desire (חפץ) my hurt (v. 14);
[wonders, deeds] more than can be numbered (מספר, v. 5);	Evils have encompassed me without number (מספר, v. 12);
all who seek thee (בקש, v. 16).	seek (בקש) to snatch my life (v. 14).[15]

In addition, we may suggest two pairs of phrases that are linguistically parallel. First, the thanksgiving has a doxology, and the lament anticipates one: "None can compare with you (v. 5)....Great is Yahweh" (v. 16). Second, the beginning and end of the psalm balance and complement each other. The thanks begins, "I have hoped intensely" (v. 1). The lament concludes, "Do not tarry" (אחר, v. 17). The intense hope is the ground for the concluding prayer.

It is possible that the parallels we have noted occur routinely because of the stylized and limited stock of phrases used, but it appears to be more than that. It appears that the lament is composed with precise reference to the thanksgiving song so that the thanksgiving song adds weight to the complaint.

Understood logically, the sequence is wrong. A complaint should not come after the joy of the new song, but experientially the sequence is significant. It reminds us that the move from disorientation to new orientation is not a single, straight line, irreversible and unambiguous. Life moves in and out. In our daily life the joy of deliverance is immediately beset and assaulted by the despair and fear of the Pit. So the one who hopes has to urge God against delay. The one who has not "withheld" praise has to ask that Yahweh not "withhold" mercy. There is a realism to the psalm, but it is a realism set in a profound trust. It is to Yahweh that Israel turns in deep need, to Yahweh and to none other, in trouble as well as in joy.

Psalm 138

As in other songs of thanksgiving, this prayer remembers a time of need that has now been resolved in deliverance. What is special here is that the circle of praise is expanded, both in heaven and in earth.

1. Verses 1-3 summarize the main action of thanksgiving. This unit begins with a fourfold self-announcement of praise:

I thank,
I sing,
I bow down,
[I] thank.

The location of the doxological enterprise here seems to be the divine court of the gods in heaven (v. 1). It is as though it is testimony time. Each god has witnesses to what he or she has done lately (cf. Isa. 41:23; 44:8). Psalm 82 asserts that the only god who does not die is the one who cares for the poor. Psalm 138 offers supportive evidence for Yahweh's credibility in that company. Indeed, in verse 2b, the exaltation of Yahweh may be in relation to other gods.

The reason for the thanksgiving is first stated in general covenant terms, Yahweh's חסד and אמת. But then in verse 3, that חסד and אמת are made quite concrete with reference to the speaker. What all of that general matter of faithfulness means is that God is faithful *to me* in this particular situation. This prayer is bold to imagine that the main issues facing God are to be resolved with particular reference to me.

2. Verses 4-6 are a reiteration of the same themes. Only now the community of praise is on earth. In verses 1-3 the gods in council are forced to see that the rescue of the lowly constitutes real godness. Now the kings of the earth are also pressed to confess (ידה) to Yahweh. The reason is the same as for the gods. It is acknowledged that Yahweh is great in his glory, i.e., in his regal power and splendor (v. 5). Kings do take notice of that. That is, on their own turf, by their own norms, they are able to see this one as extraordinary. But in the new world here articulated verse 6 contains the evangelical surprise. In what does Yahweh's great glory consist? The clue and pivot point is in verse 6. He is high, but attends to the lowly (cf. Isa. 57:15). That is, unlike the other gods in verse 1 and unlike the conventional kings in verse 4. Characteristically kings and gods are high, but do not notice the lowly. The whole history of Israel is evidence to the contrary, and that is why Israel is a scandal among the nations, and why Yahweh is an embarrassment among the gods. This verse, the ground of the entire thanksgiving, is revolutionary in its disclosure. Mention of the high, the lowly, the haughty introduces political reality and political awareness into the prayer. The seeds of social transformation and historical inversion are present when this agenda is articulated.

3. Such a radical claim for Yahweh and such a radical hope for Israel is not grounded in grand theory, but in the specific experience of the speaker (vv. 7-8). The conclusion is the standard doxological phrase of verse 8, ''Yahweh's חסד abides forever.'' So חסד forms an envelope from verse 2 to verse 8. But the specificity of חסד is asserted in verse 7. The speaker remembers trouble, i.e., restriction, confinement, stress. And that burdensome historical circumstance is what Yahweh acts on:

> You did preserve,
> You did stretch out your hand,
> Your right hand delivered.[16]

Heaven and earth are now on notice because of quite concrete experience. A new regime is underway that no longer permits lowly people to be trampled. Because Yahweh makes the move, everything else will have to change. In the last line, the ''work of your hands'' is none other than the lowly who owe their whole life to and depend completely on this one who intervenes in unheard of and unexpected ways.

Psalm 34

The shaping of new life requires discipline and fidelity to principle. In this song of thanksgiving, the moment of rescue is remembered. But the speaker cannot refrain from instruction that counsels others in how to consolidate and sustain the new orientation, so this psalm has strong features of wisdom instruction. That the psalm has such deliberate intentionality is also evident in its acrostic construction, which suggests it is not an emotional outburst of gratitude but a quite disciplined statement for new world building.

1. The thanksgiving of verses 1-7 contains the regular features: a summons to grand, sweeping praise and reference to the specificity of Yahweh which evokes the praise. The resolve to praise is broadly hymnic; the specific reference is of a personal liberation. In verse 2 the speaker summons "the afflicted" (אנוים). In verse 4 he alludes to "fears" and in verse 6 he is "poor." All of these together refer to a desperate person who is socially marginal for whom Yahweh has intervened. Indeed, the intervention is massive, miraculous, and irresistible (v. 7). The verbs applied to Yahweh are "answer" (ענה), deliver (נצל, v. 4), hear, save (ישע, v. 6), deliver (חלץ, v. 7). The superscription explicitly links this psalm to David's rescue from Abimelech (1 Sam. 21:10-15). We may take that reference as one important case that helps dramatize the generalization the text affirms. What is clear is that the rescue is concrete and historical and resists every spiritualizing. This prayer is for those who find themselves resourceless against the powers of this age, and then are remarkably released for new life.

2. Verses 8-14, especially 11-14, are a wisdom instruction about how to live in the new world for which God has released the speaker. While verses 8-10 are not so clearly sapiential, some marks of wisdom are clear. These include the אשרי saying of verse 8, the summons to fear in verse 9, and the use of the metaphor in verse 10. The wisdom instruction is quite unambiguous in verses 11-14 with the summons of a wisdom teacher (v. 11; cf. Prov. 3:21; 4:1,20), reflecting on how to have and enjoy life and good (cf. "good" also in v. 8), a warning about false speech in verse 13 (cf. Prov. 12:19; 17:20), and an imperative very much like Prov. 3:7, which Gerstenberger sees as the "motto" for the wisdom of Proverbs.[17] Its location here affirms that release to new life and new orientation is not just "freedom from." It is also "freedom for." The newly oriented Israel must engage in society building, to develop forms of behavior which sustain the gift of new social possibility. Perhaps the teacher knows that if such things are not done intentionally, very soon the recently poor and afflicted will be back in the old context of hopelessness. So we have a nice juxtaposition of *liberation* (vv. 1-7) and *world building* (vv. 8-14).

3. The final portion of the poem (vv. 15-22) is a reflection on *righteousness*. The word צדק occurs three times in the Hebrew text (vv. 15, 19, 21),

and a fourth time in apparent translation in the Greek text in verse 17. The term is used in very different ways, but in any case it is used to tie our two themes together. On the one hand, the righteous are given well-being by God (vv. 1-7). That is, they are special objects of God's intervention and know themselves to be *recipients*. That is why they are thankful. On the other hand, the righteous are responsible for reshaping life (vv. 8-14). They know themselves to be summoned to *take initiative* in reordering social existence.

In Psalm 34 the emphasis is upon receiving. The righteous are those to whom Yahweh attends in peculiar ways:

> The eyes of Yahweh are upon the *righteous* (v. 15).
> The Lord hears the cry of the *righteous* (v. 17).
> Many are the afflictions of the *righteous* (v. 19).

It is precisely the righteous whom the Lord sees (v. 15), hears (v. 17), is near (v. 18), and delivers (vv. 19-20). The use of "the righteous" requires a "class reading" of the text. The righteous may or may not be the good, but they are surely the socially marginal, who no longer expect the dominant society to succor them, and so they look to Yahweh as the alternative source of help. Thus the cry of the righteous is an act of delegitimating the primary structures that have reduced people to helplessness. In verse 21 the righteous are not hated because they are marginal or because they are good, but because they look to Yahweh. They have discovered something remarkable and subversive about Yahweh.[18] Yahweh's peculiar inclinations are with the brokenhearted and the ones with crushed spirit. That is, Yahweh's solidarity is not with the ones who go from success to success, but the ones denied success.

Therefore verses 11-14, the summons to a faithful life, are not a call for "law and order" or conventional morality. They are rather a call to the revolutionary "good" that is antithetical to the "evildoers" (v. 16) who now order society. The climax of verse 21 is an argument that the resisters of the righteous will turn out guilty, even though they appear to be the ones who dispense justice.[19] There is a higher court, and in that appeal process, they will not do well.

Thanksgiving Songs of the Community

Since Gunkel it is conventional to regard songs of thanksgiving as belonging to the personal sphere. The counterpart in the public domain is the hymn. In general, this is a sound division. However, we may identify a few public songs that are hymnic, but are songs of thanksgiving insofar as they speak about a specific answer to a specific cry concerning a specific trouble.[20] Classification is not precise, but they are, in any case, songs of new orientation, because they celebrate an act of God's power that has moved Israel's life out of a time of disorientation.

Psalm 65

After verse 5b, this psalm is a standard hymn. But in verses 1-5a, there are more marks of thanksgiving.

1. Verses 1-4 are an act of praise. In the beginning the psalm is distinguished by the fact that the first three lines reiterate "to thee, to thee, to thee," which is perhaps a polemical use, implying not to Baal, not to any other god. This unit is in an envelope, beginning with "Zion" and ending with "temple," so it is obviously sung in the Jerusalem liturgy. The center of this unit is in verses 2b-3, concerning a single matter. The problem is *sins* or *transgressions*. The resolution which is celebrated is "You have covered (forgiven) them." The term rendered "forgive" (כפר) is a priestly term, not meaning "pardon" in a juridical sense, but a priestly act of covering over the guilt to rob it of its power. So we have a public celebration of God's forgiveness.

Let us not miss the dramatic claim. The whole people (together with the king, presumably) concedes its guilt and celebrates its forgiveness. Such a scene is nearly unthinkable in our public life. Of course, our society is not a theocracy. Religious pluralism makes it problematic, but the main problem is not pluralism, for we have sufficient resources in common religion for that.[21] The problem is that public imagination is so filled with pride, self-serving complacency, and moral numbness that we could hardly imagine an act of public repentance or acknowledgment of forgiveness, for to ask for and receive forgiveness is to be vulnerable.[22] If we were to use this psalm, we might reflect on the dimensions of guilt which vex public life, e.g., colonialism, exploitative economics, or misuse of the ecosystem of creation. Our public life is not lacking material for such a liturgical act.

When the British government contemplated a "service of thanksgiving" in St. Paul's Cathedral in London after the Falkland Islands excursion, many citizens wrote letters to the *London Times*. Some wanted to celebrate victory; others wanted to give thanks for an end to hostility. One letter recalled that in 1944 Archbishop Temple wanted to begin the service for the "victory" of World War II with the words, "Our spirits are troubled." Psalm 65 reflects a public imagination capable of a troubled spirit, not so full of self, but able to reflect on its life in light of the majesty of God, a community forgiven and therefore ready to begin afresh.

2. The pivot of the psalm is in verse 5. The thanks is for Yahweh's mighty intervention in powerful ways that have given victory and liberation. And this action of Yahweh is in response to the cries of Israel, "Thou dost answer." Israel knows that such intervention is not automatic in the course of history. The

outcome of the conversation is always open in the exchange of "cry and answer." The psalm is the speech of a liberated people. We are not told what the disorientation was; perhaps it was drought or war. But what emerges now is a people prepared to get on with its public business, because Yahweh has acted.

3. The remainder of the psalm (vv. 5b-13) is a hymnic form that articulates God's powerful work in the arena of creation. This is the God who establishes, who stills, who makes, who visits, who enriches, who provides, who waters, who crowns. In verses 12-13, the rhetorical pattern is changed, so that the elements of creation—pastures, hills, meadows, valleys—are now the subject and not the object. But the changed rhetorical pattern does not alter the key claim: Yahweh's staggering generosity and power cause creation to "bring forth." This is indeed creation theology which gives thanks for the ordering and blessing of all of life.[23] It is this which leads scholars to relate the psalm to the blessings of the harvest. The God of this psalm not only intervenes in the historical processes of oppression, but also governs the reliability of creation, which gives life.

Two observations: First, it appears that there is something of a mismatch between the subject of verses 1-5a and the doxology that follows. But the restoration of creation is perhaps taken as a sign and measure of God's forgiveness and God's readiness to begin again.

Second, it is worth thinking about the claims of such a rhetorical effort. Have we come to such a profane understanding of reality, such a reduction of creation to commodity, that we are incapable of speaking in this way?[24] The problem is not that we are scientific and believe in secondary causes, but that we are autonomous and believe in no cause beyond self. Such a doxology as this serves to keep life securely in the context of creation-imagination and prevents the reduction of life around us to commodity. This community begins again with wonder at the beginning again of the creation process. The loss of wonder, the inability to sing songs of praise about the reliability of life, is both a measure and a cause of our profanation of life.

Psalm 66

It is uncertain whether we may speak of a category of "communal thanksgiving," for the tendency is either to have the communal thanksgiving evolve into an individual song of thanksgiving (as in Psalm 66: 13-20), or to become a general hymn of praise without reference to the particulars that belong to thanksgiving. Nonetheless, these psalms do suggest that on occasion the whole community had complained, the whole community had been saved, and therefore the whole community had given thanks.

1. Verses 1-3 are a quite general summons to praise, dominated by the standard imperatives: "shout, sing, give glory, say." And these are answered

in verse 4 with the description of what they did: "bow down, sing, sing." What is commanded in verses 1-3a is reported as completed in verse 4. The summons is addressed to "all the earth" in both verses 1 and 4. That is, this is a public act, and because the summons is public, the deliverance and the thanks are also a communal agenda. The nations are not summoned to observe a private transformation. This inversion is here for all to see.

That the other nations are called to praise this God means that we are in a contest to determine whose god is really God. Out of that contest, victory is proclaimed, presumably for the one God who is able to transform life. The proclamation, i.e., the verdict reached on the basis of the evidence, leads to the enthronement of the winning God, even though that specific formula is not used here.[25] The argument is made in polemical, doxological form that the God of Israel is the real God and is to be worshiped by the other gods as well. Nowhere in this psalm is the victorious God identified as Yahweh. The reason, I believe, is not that this is an *Elohist* tradition, but that the psalm wishes to use generic language to include other peoples in the worship of this God. The evidence of God's power is so compelling that the nonbelieving nations must concede the point. The new orientation leads the other nations to grant the main claim of Israel. The unspoken counterpart is that the gods of the nations are either subordinate or are dismissed as no gods at all.

The verdict in the mouth of the nations is in v. 3. It is the nations who voice the inevitable conclusion that the enemies of this God are helpless. The first section of this psalm is thus quite generalized.

2. The thanksgiving motif is more explicit in verses 5-7. It is remarkable that in naming a specific act of power and rescue, Israel reverts yet again and characteristically to the Exodus (cf. Psalm 114). That event comes immediately to Israel's mind and mouth. It is the paradigmatic liberation event to which all other subsequent events point. Israel's primal memory is of liberation, and it is liberation precisely from the gods of the other nations, paradigmatically the gods of Egypt. Thus when the nations concede this point, they are conceding the delegitimation of their own gods. The point is a theological one about which god is the real God. But the point is also a sociopolitical one; it is the triumph of the *power of liberation* over the *power of control*. The theological point of *which god* is tied closely to the *social possibility* willed by the various gods.

3. After a repeated summons to praise in verse 8, we finally arrive at the specific occasion of thanksgiving in verses 9-12. The community recalls its time of difficulty, its season of disorientation. Even this is credited to God's sovereign action. That is, in this psalm, even the disorientation is seen to be the working of God: "you tested us, you tried us, you brought us into the net, you laid affliction on our loins, you let men ride over our heads, (and as a result) we

went through fire and water'' (cf. Isa. 43:2). The psalmist does not think for
one moment that the trouble is an accident that falls outside God's power or
concern. Nor does it occur to the poet that this is grounds for rejection of Yahweh. Nor is it suggested that this is punishment. This psalm is incredibly submissive about the point of trouble, but in the context of the psalm, this acknowledgment of the trouble is only preparation for the real point. The psalm is
not really interested in questions about how we came to be in trouble. The accent is on the release and restoration which is worked by this same God.

The trouble is stated in verses 10-12a. But the trouble is surrounded by the
key positive affirmation of verses 9 and 12b:

> You kept us in the land of the living...
> Yet you brought us to a place of well-being.[26]

Both statements are difficult. The ''land of the living'' is not a very conclusive
metaphor, and things are not clarified in verse 12 by the difficult word רויה.
But the two phrases together suggest a safe place of well-being. The remembered complaint is surrounded and overcome by these actions of Yahweh's
power which rescued. The decisive verb is ''rescue'' (ישׁע), again an exodus
allusion. Thus the current deliverance is a replication of that model deliverance, as the community is once again set free. The mighty will of Yahweh will
not stop until freedom and justice are wrought. No amount of imperial control
and scheming can finally deter this God. The paradigm of exodus permits Israel to see clearly what is happening in its own life, before its very eyes. Because
it is the same God, the exodus recurs again and again, in new circumstances.

4. The remainder of the psalm (vv. 13-20) is much more an individual
song of thanksgiving. The individual keeps a vow and comes to the altar with a
sacrifice of thanksgiving (vv. 13-15). Then the deliverance is recounted, under
the standard structure of *cry* (קרא, v. 17), *hear* (שׁמע, v. 19). That is how Israel's life of faith operates. Israel addresses Yahweh in need. Yahweh responds to transform the situation of need. The final blessing (perhaps parallel
to v. 9) is then a return deep into the memory. The formula, ''He has not...
removed his steadfast love,'' looks very much like the dynastic promise to David in 2 Sam. 7:15. The promise holds. The people is not abandoned.[27]

It is neither necessary nor permissible to split Psalm 66 into separate communal and individual units. The second half shows a member of the community fully participating in and appropriating the communal deliverance as his
very own. The function of the psalm is to solidify the new ordering of well-
being that permits life and that comes exactly from God's powerful praise and
action. Israel's life is not now at the mercy of other hostile powers, for God's
חסד overrides the threat. It follows that as the community experiences this,
trusting persons in the community take it as a very personal assurance in their

own life. This psalm shows the move from communal affirmation to individual appreciation, which is what we always do in biblical faith.

Psalm 124

This psalm of thanksgiving is highly disciplined and intentional in its articulation. It gives thanks for a communal deliverance, though again we are not told anything beyond quite general metaphors.

1. Verses 1-5 are a wonderful symmetrical statement that twice names Yahweh with the opening participle, "if it had not been" used as a subjunctive. Thus, "If it had not been the Lord...if it had not been the Lord." And the contrast is set by the following three statements of "then," which lay out the dire results if Yahweh had not been involved. The psalm presents such a negative scenario only to dismiss it because, in fact, Yahweh was present and on our side. Thus the negative is only a ploy to celebrate how it is with Yahweh's commitment. The thanks that follows is in celebration that Yahweh was and is "on our side," and therefore the possible bad things did not happen. They could have, but it is Yahweh's tenacious commitment to Israel that precludes the destructive work of the enemy. The key evangelical assertion is that Yahweh is *for us*, with us, on our side, belongs to us—utterly committed.

The threats are presented in varied imagery, but they mostly refer to the power of the evil chaotic waters. Even the opening verb, "swallow," in verse 3 probably refers to being swallowed up by the evil waters. The waters are Israel's best way of speaking about a general, massive, and seemingly irresistible threat. They are the "presumptuous waters," the waters that know no limit and respect no boundary. But as we have seen in Psalm 114 with reference to the exodus and in Psalm 29 with reference to standard myths about the flood, Yahweh's sovereignty puts the waters back in bounds and robs them of their force.[28]

2. Verses 6-7 use a quite different image. The invitation to praise is grounded in the double use of "escape," only this time the imagery is of snares, which suggests that Israel is the hunted and will be devoured. But again, Yahweh has not permitted it.

3. The conclusion in verse 8 sounds like a serene verdict that is based on the preceding particulars. The course of the theological affirmation is interesting. It ends with a strong affirmation of Yahweh's powerful sovereignty over all he has made, heaven and earth, waters and snares. Nothing is in doubt at this point in the psalm. But the same discussion begins at a very different point in verse 1 with the passionate, partisan claim that Yahweh is for Israel. The Psalm thus moves from *partisan claim* to *universal affirmation*. In our pattern of presentation, the psalm reflects a move from the anxiety of *disorientation* to the stability and confidence of the *new orientation*. The psalm is a move from

an anxious specificity to a confident generalization. Israel's new life, free from threat, is utterly focused on this God who will never hand us over.

The Once and Future King

These are the songs of new orientation par excellence. They give public liturgical articulation to the "new kingship" of Yahweh, which has just now been established. It is likely that the enthronement songs are one version of *victory songs* that celebrate Yahweh's victory over Israel's enemies. In these psalms kingship is granted to Yahweh on the basis of the victory just won. Perhaps the primary example of the victory song in the Old Testament is the song of Miriam in Exodus 15, which is reckoned as a very early liturgical statement of the exodus. It traces the triumph of Yahweh in detail and likewise the defeat of Pharaoh and the Egyptian gods. It is not our purpose to study that song in detail, but we may note the following features:

1. Even though the psalm is historically specific, it makes appeal to and use of the mythic vocabulary and patterns of presentation which belong to the Near Eastern genre of victory song.[29] The victory song is a strange mixture of the peculiarly historical experience of Israel and the common mode of expression from the Near East.

2. The substance of the song is essentially narrative. It tells the story of the move of Israel by the power of Yahweh from slavery in Egypt to settlement in the land. Israel's celebrative hymnody is first of all a testimony to what has happened.

3. The conclusion of verse 18 is a formula of enthronement, a conclusion to the narrative, a verdict upon the historical process just reviewed. This verdict could stand alone in a liturgical formula without the preliminary narrative, because the verdict is finally what counts. One might notice the free-standing formulas of Christian worship, the Doxology and the Gloria Patri, which are in fact victory claims that announce the triumphant authority of Yahweh and deny the authority of other gods.

The victory-enthronement songs in the Psalter are probably derived in one way or another either from the exodus recital or from the Zion recital in which the exodus is retold in more mythic language. We begin with one example each from the exodus and the Zion traditions.

Psalm 114

Psalm 114 is a hymn that stays very close to the narrative experience of the exodus. It is evident that the specific liberating event is here presented as having cosmic proportion.

1. In a quick move, verses 1-2 comprehend the entire sojourn history of

Israel from the exodus (Egypt—"people of strange language") to a land settlement ("sanctuary"—surely a reference to Jerusalem—"dominion"). The long tale told in the Hexateuch is summarized. That is possible because the entire memory has vitality in the community. It is sufficient to make allusion without spelling out in detail.

2. The middle part of the psalm (vv. 3-6) is a carefully constructed piece in two parts. First there is a narrative description (vv. 3-4) and then a closely correlated taunt song (vv. 5-6), based upon the description. Clearly the actual liberation memory has now been "processed" for liturgical purposes. Now the memory asserts that all creation is mobilized for the liberation.[30] Any part of creation that is not responsive to this freedom for Israel is an enemy of the liberating God and is under assault. Four elements are named: sea, Jordan River, mountains, hills. They are personified as the key actors in the drama of liberation; they become exceedingly agitated. It is possible that the water (sea, river) is represented as an enemy of Yahweh, though there is not a hint of that interpretation in the exodus narrative. Thus when the waters recede, they are understood to withdraw in terror before Yahweh's show of power. The two other elements, mountains and hills, could be understood as either rejoicing or responding in terror. Either way, what is claimed is that the exodus event is so momentous that even the fixtures of the cosmos are unfixed. The exodus event and tradition announce in heaven and earth that there will be no more imperial business as usual.

The tellers of this tale enjoy mightily the disruptive power of Yahweh. They are so sure that they tease and taunt. They wonder why the sea is such a coward and why the river is unable to stay in its place. Thus the contrast is between Yahweh, whom the nations thought marginal, and the elements of creation, which seem so sturdy. Now the humble God is exalted, and the exalted elements are humiliated. It is no contest. The exodus is now sung as a cosmic inversion. What happened with that slave band is no mere tribal event, but an event that concerns all of creation.

3. Given this understanding of reality, the conclusion of verses 7-8 is unavoidable. The whole earth is summoned to be frightened. The pivotal word in the psalm is *dance*, (חול) twist and turn, in pain and anguish, because the whole known world is now under assault. The address is to "earth" (ארץ) which imagines itself stable and serene. But now it is all in jeopardy. The agent of the jeopardy is אדון, the real, sovereign Lord. The exodus name, *Yahweh*, is not used. It is enough to name the decisive name of sovereignty, for the terrorized nations understand exactly what is being said. The conclusion of the poem (v. 8) is an additional doxological point linking this God to the miracle of water in the wilderness (cf. Exod. 17:6; Num. 20:11; and derivatively Isa. 41:17). The last line recalls the exodus language of verse 1. It shows in yet an-

other way that Yahweh accepts nothing as it is, but always changes everything. Nothing is secure when the God of liberation begins to make his move. The chaotic orientation of Egyptian slavery is ended. The Lord of freedom works a new orientation.

Psalm 114 is an invitation for each new generation to participate in this world-transforming memory, to be identified with the tradition and given life by it. It is in a narrative way, an enthronement psalm, though that special language is not used. The psalm intends to enhance Yahweh at the expense of all other gods (e.g., sea, river). In terms of social function, we may suggest that the psalm means to contrast Yahweh, the agent of freedom, with every structure, agent, and power of the status quo. The psalm makes available a radical reading of reality for those who want to join in. No part of the world is in fact as it appears, for all of it must face the decisive sovereignty of God, whose will is for transformation.

Psalm 29

This psalm, more clearly than Psalm 114, is an enthronement psalm. It utilizes a very different set of metaphors. Here there is nothing to connect the poem to the saving recital of Israel's creed. Indeed, it is the scholarly consensus that this is an older Canaanite psalm, taken over by Israel, wherein only the name of the deity has been changed. Thus it reflects Canaanite mythology and rhetorical structures. This may therefore be one of the oldest of the psalms, showing Israel most directly related to the religious articulations of its cultural context.

1. The summons to worship (vv. 1-2) is addressed to the "sons of God" (RSV, "heavenly beings"). The imagery here is a meeting of the heavenly court of the gods and their messengers. Enthronement language is characteristically global, even cosmic, and finds its most expansive metaphors available to a scene offered us in a liturgy among the gods.[31] We (and Israel) are not participants, but spectators in the action of the poetry. But we see the "real worship" in which our human worship may derivatively participate and replicate. The gods are summoned to assign honor, glory, and sovereignty to this God, as distinct from the other gods who cannot make such a powerful claim. By an act of worship, they are invited to cast their vote for the true God.

2. That this is a song of new orientation is evident in verses 3-9a, which present the chaos (cosmic disorientation) in which this God has been at work to conquer. It may be that the narrative characterizes a great rainstorm that sweeps off the Mediterranean Sea (v. 3) through Lebanon (vv. 5-6) and on to the southern desert (vv. 7-8). But the phrase "many waters" (v. 3) suggests that the images are more than historical, though they may also have some his-

torical, geographical connection. That phrase and perhaps the general picture
may be a reference to the global waters of chaos as in Gen. 1:2.

While the hymnic statement describes the fearful threat against created order, it also testifies that it is Yahweh who is powerfully at work to subdue the
storm and overcome the disorder. So it is the powerful *voice* of Yahweh,
named repeatedly, which moves decisively and forcefully to undo the old order
and to tame the forces of chaos. There is nothing here of faithfulness or justice;
it is raw untamed power. Yahweh is shown to be more powerful than all that resists Yahweh. Yahweh is so powerful that he can twist mighty trees (v. 9).

3. The other gods watch this decisive action, and they render their verdict
(vv. 9b-10). The other gods watch the display of power. They applaud, they
vote, they salute. They assign sovereign authority to this one and to none other,
as they cry out, "Glory!" That is what they were summoned to do in verses
1-2, but they do not do so until they have the evidence of power from verses
3-9a. This cry of recognition has a function not unlike the Doxology or the doxological formula at the conclusion of the Lord's Prayer. It leads to enthronement (v. 10). This God is now stably and comfortably seated on top of the
mighty waters. He has subdued the waters, which are no longer a threat (cf.
Mark 4:35-41). The real king tames chaos. His throne, established atop the
flood, shows that the conquest is real and expresses utter contempt for the de-
feated waters.

4. When chaos is overwhelmed and driven from the field, a blessing is appropriately given from the newly established throne by the newly recognized
king (v. 11). It is the promise of שלום, precisely the opposite of the chaos that
seemed to be more powerful. This declaration of שלום is as decisive and
world-changing as the word *peace* in the familiar benediction of Num.
6:22-26. The movement from *glory* (vv. 1-2, 10) to *peace* (v. 11) is not unlike
the angel song at Bethlehem (Luke 2:14). The establishment of the new king
brings with it new well-being to the world. The action of the psalm is to sing
into place the new order that overcomes chaos. Psalm 29 makes no appeal to
the exodus or to Israel's particular memory. It is a psalm that speaks about order in a way that overrules all anxiety about life, and the very act of singing the
song is itself a practice of that new order.

These two psalms together (Israel's faith memory in Psalm 114; Israel's
common inheritance among the nations in Psalm 29) provide the basis for new
life and for hope in the governance of God. The new life is based in the new
kingship of Yahweh, wrought either over the historical enemies of Egypt or
over the chaotic threats present in creation. As a liturgical piece, Psalm 29 is a
concrete enactment of kingship. The new order requires the honoring of God,
but it also requires the capacity and power to reorder life. That is cause for singing, on earth, as in heaven.

Psalm 96

This psalm is something like an extrapolation from Psalm 29. It closely parallels it and seems to be derived from it. Psalm 96 both *enacts the new governance* and then *characterizes the shape of the new governance*. Under our rubric, this psalm not only asserts a new orientation, but tells what it is like.

1. Verses 1-6 are a summons to praise. This is a standard form of praise consisting of two parts:

a) An imperative *summons*, given here six times: "sing, sing, sing, bless, tell, declare."
b) The *reason for praise* in verses 4-5, which tells positively of God's presence and negatively of the routing of the idols. The reasons given for praise are recited as the very form of praise.[32]

This psalm is a celebration that the future now belongs to this God, not to the feeble idols, who are in fact agents of chaos. The praise that articulates this good news of enthronement is "a new song." A new song must be sung for a new orientation. In the ancient world a new orientation was typified by a new reign, introduced by inauguration or coronation. Likely a genuinely new song was commissioned for such a grand, public event. This is a new God who has not been known in this way for these people until now, so there must be new music to match.

2. The vocatives of verses 7-9 are closely reminiscent of 29:1-2. Much of the language is the same. The crucial difference is that the vocative now addresses "families of the peoples" and not "sons of God." The worship initiated here and the new social reality begun here happen on earth, not in heaven. We are now not spectators of heavenly worship (as in Psalm 29) but now participants called to receive the gift of newness.

3. The key assertion of this psalm is in verse 10: "Yahweh reigns." Its precise meaning is disputed among scholars.[33] It could be taken to refer to an ongoing reality of the God who already reigns. But if we take this formula as a proclamation at coronation, to say "Yahweh reigns" means that he has just now become king. That is, the liturgical enactment is not just a recollection, but it is a making so, just as at Easter we understand the resurrection to be "today," and we understand ourselves to have been present. Now such a formula as "were you there?" is not chronological affirmation but liturgical experience. And that is how this psalm formula might best be taken. This psalm marks the beginning of a new reign. Liturgy is not play acting, but it is the evocation of an alternative reality that comes into play in the very moment of the liturgy. So this moment is when God's rule is visible and effective.

4. The remainder of Psalm 96 tells what the new regime is like (vv.

10b-13). The result of the newly won kingship of Yahweh brings a reliable, equitable order to creation. The newness is in the international arena, "among the
nations." There will be equity (v. 10). There will be, as a result, cosmic rejoicing, among the "heavens, earth, sea, field, trees." The elements of creation
will join in celebration, just as the "sons of God" shouted "Glory!" in 29:10,
just as we join in Christmas as "heaven and nature sing" at the birth of the
King. So creation celebrates, acknowledges the sovereignty of this one, and
salutes the new ruler and prepares to obey.

In Psalm 114 there was terror and dread. Now from the same parties of
creation, there is glad celebration and reception. This exuberant language suggests three dimensions of celebration. First, this can be regarded as poetic hyperbole, the delight of Israel writ as large as possible. Second, the psalm may
want to talk about the celebration of the other gods who yield to Yahweh, but
this has now reduced the other gods to the elements of creation. Third, it could
be a recognition that the whole created order—not just Israel and the other
nations—has been terribly skewed and scarred by injustice. Injustice and inequity constitute a cosmic problem. Such injustice for "sea, field, trees" may be
in the form of ecological abuse and exploitation. No wonder they sing and rejoice; that is now ended, with the coming of the just king.

The ground for the new celebration is a new orientation worked by this
new king who comes triumphantly into situations of injustice and makes them
right. The word "judge" (שׁפט) is used twice here, along with "judge" (דין)
in verse 10. Those two words are not to be taken negatively, as we incline to
do, both juridically and theologically, as in "the judgment of God." Rather the
terms refer to God's action of intervention to look after the rightful claims of
the weak ones who have no power to make their own claim or look after themselves (cf. Isa. 1:16-17; Ps. 82:2-4,8; 72:1-4). So "judgment" means the establishment of a new power structure and a new value center, one characterized
by right and reliability, overcoming the fickle, arbitrary, capricious, exploitative social order.

Psalm 96 thus focuses on (a) the moment of inversion through enthronement when something new begins, and (b) the long-term implementation of
that rule for a new ordering of life. Put in conventional theological terms, the
enthronement is the new *justification* of the world; the hoped-for new life is the
practice of *sanctification* of the world. The psalm is not only about the event
(which most psalm scholarship seems to assume), but is also about the long-
term process which has been begun here. Such a psalm is always an act of profound hope, for such a realm has clearly not been established simply by the use
of the psalm. But liturgical use of the psalm is more than hope. It is making the
future momentarily present now through word, gesture, practice. This psalm
celebrates in face of the old order still present to us, an order of injustice and

faithlessness. But that old order is an order which in fact has no serious claim to make. This liturgy is the beginning of the dismantling of that order.[34]

The other explicit songs of enthronement (Psalms 47, 93, 97, 98, 99) can be dealt with in more summary fashion because they articulate the same themes we have seen in Psalm 96.

Psalm 93

This psalm begins with the formula of enthronement, "Yahweh reigns." Then verse 1b describes the royal procession of the new king who comes in victory to claim his realm. Though brief, it is a majestic picture. Verse 1c states the resulting well-being of the world. It has seemed precarious, but now is solid and reliable. In verses 3-4, the power of Yahweh is contrasted with the power of the chaotic waters. Everyone knows that the flood waters of chaos are overwhelming and irresistible. Note in verse 4 the phrase "many waters" which we have seen in 29:3. But Yahweh is clearly more powerful than all the threats of chaos. And so in verse 5, the well-established king issues a decree for the new order. Here no substance to the decree is given. In Ps. 29:11, the new decree is *shalom*. In 96:10b-13 right, faithfulness, and equity are decreed. Through the assertion of Yahweh the psalm discloses the transformation of created life. Israel never lingers on mythic form without moving to earthly issues of equity.

Psalm 97

This psalm also begins with the royal formula, "Yahweh reigns," and characterizes the glad response of earth and coastlands. The new king-god is not simply there but *comes* in a triumphant procession (vv. 2-5).[35] And that process is a mixture of celebration and dreadful awe. The new king-god is sure to triumph. Verses 3-4 sound like a thunderstorm as we have seen in Ps. 29:3-10a. Verse 5 shows the trembling of the mountains. But along with *massive power*, the actual *substance of governance* is characterized by "righteousness and justice" (v. 2), "righteousness" and "glory" (v. 6). This is not only sheer force. It is also an introduction of human value into the life of the world. The new orientation will be one in which even the weak have rights not trampled on by the strong. The power of the new king is not noteworthy unless social transformation is the purpose of the power. That kingship serves earth is a seed of incarnational faith.

The establishment of this governance is good news and bad news. It is good news to trampled Judah (v. 8). The chosen of Yahweh have been helpless and yearn for an intruder who will give life. It is bad news for all those who organize life around idols—exploitative symbols—which can reduce *people* to *things* (commodities), even as the true *God* is traded off for a controllable *ob-*

ject. To understand the yearning of the people in this psalm, we must understand that the *trade-off of gods* is matched by a *reduction of people.* The matter
of idols is not a matter of statues and figurines. It is a matter of changing symbols and values. As the true God is diminished, so the value of human persons
is diminished in commensurate fashion.[36] The smashing of idols is not a narrow religious agenda, but has to do with creating free space for the practice of
humanness.

In verses 10-12 the celebration of Israel is given concrete covenantal definition (which was absent in Psalm 93). The programmatic statement of verse
10 indicates the criterion by which all will be judged. "Hate evil" is derived
from the covenantal love of "good," of justice, of Yahweh (cf. Amos. 5:15).
The "saints" of verse 10 are the covenant keepers, and life is cast in terms of
righteousness and wickedness. Thus the raw power of the new king is mediated
in terms of the torah commitments of Israel. God's rule requires obedience.
The real God is not morally indifferent, but permits a new public life of humane caring. New orientation is a life of disciplined response to God's will for
justice.

Psalm 97 thus has a movement similar to that of Psalm 29:

sheer power ─────────────────►covenantal ethics
Psalm 29: glory (vv. 1-2)──────►peace (v. 11)
Psalm 97: the new king (v. 1)──── ► righteousness, vindication (vv.
                                                                                     10-12).

The climactic element is a contrast of the wicked and the righteous. In the
normal course of public life, the unresponsive wicked control things. But the
kingship of Yahweh causes an inversion. The wicked are exposed for what
they are. They are denied their preeminence. Conversely, the righteous, the
ones who keep covenant and do Yahweh's will, are given life and power. The
genre of the psalm seems to focus on the celebration of divine power. That is
what enthronement is all about. But the Israelite handling of that genre insists
that such power is always in the service of torah values. The newly enthroned
king-god is welcomed precisely by the marginalized poor who may now expect
a better life.[37] It is for this reason that the psalm moves from "joy" ("rejoice") (v. 1) to "joy" (vv. 11-12). They are the ones who have something
about which to rejoice.

Psalm 98

The same themes are present here as in the other enthronement psalms.

1. The "new song" is introduced again (v. 1), with the reasons given in
verses 1-3, introduced by כִּי. The recital of reasons is less cosmic and more

fixed on the memory of Israel. The "marvelous things" need not be, but are likely, the saving events of Israel's history (cf. v. 3). The vocabulary sounds as if it has such a reference. Three times in verses 1-3 the verb "save" or "deliver" (ישע) is used. This is matched by the terms "righteousness, steadfast love, faithfulness" (אמונה, חסד, צדקה), the central words of Israel's covenant tradition (cf. Jer. 9:24). "The earth" is here not the recipient of these actions, but a mightily impressed spectator. The basis for Yahweh's exaltation is found now in intervention on behalf of Israel. Notice how the genre has been largely transformed from Psalm 29 in which there is no reference to any Israelite agenda until the last verse. Now the cosmic assertion is firmly grounded in the life of Israel.

2. The middle section of Psalm 98 (vv. 4-6) is a massive summons to praise, with a series of imperatives. The invitation is to "all the earth," and the dominant metaphor is once again kingship. The establishment of Yahweh's rule causes a general rejoicing.

3. The invitation is continued in verses 7-8, with the subjects now familiar to us: "sea, world, floods, hills." Again the *summons* to praise is matched by the *reasons* that mark the new kingship. Yahweh will judge, which means he will establish a rule marked by righteousness and equity. The new kingship corresponds to the vocabulary of verses 2-3. The world will be fully turned in a new direction.

Psalm 99

This psalm sounds the same themes of new governance, but in a different form. In this psalm, the specifically Israelite traditions are more visible.

1. The hymn begins with the enthronement formula we have come to expect: "Yahweh reigns." The appropriate response is cosmic trembling, because this king shakes loose all old governance.

2. The celebration of Yahweh's kingship is articulated in verses 1b-5. Verse 1b is in fact a parallel to the opening line. But we treat it with what follows, because the reference to the cherubim links the new enthronement to the Jerusalem temple (cf. 1 Kings 8:7). This section of the psalm nicely interweaves the two basic traditions of Israel. On the one hand, there is *the Jerusalem tradition of presence*. This is carried in the reference to cherubim, to Zion, and to the "footstool."[38] This tradition affirms God's attentiveness to the Israelite establishment. On the other hand, there is *the Mosaic tradition of liberation*, which is expressed as "lover of justice," agent of "equity, justice, and righteousness" (צדקה, משפט, ישר), and by allusion to Jacob. This tradition asserts that where God comes, there is radical social transformation. The kingship of Yahweh combines the *assurance of presence* and the *abrasion of liberation*, and the tradition refuses to let us choose between these accents.

3. Verses 6-7 link Yahweh's kingship more decisively to the oldest torah tradition of Moses and Aaron, with reference to the wilderness sojourn and to the Sinai commandments. There is also reference to Samuel, because Samuel is remembered as the one who insisted on the kingship of Yahweh in order to resist all human kings, whom he regarded as pretenders and as threats to and diminishments of the kingship of Yahweh (cf. 1 Sam. 8:7; 12:15, 25). It is striking that this liturgical piece, no doubt sponsored by the Jerusalem dynasty, should invoke the name of this resister to the dynastic principle. The basic verbs here of "call" and "answer" (cf. Isa. 65:24) articulate what is most important and characteristic in Israel, since the initial cry of Exod. 2:23-25. It is Israel's most normal business to *cry*, and it is Yahweh's most faithful preoccupation to *answer*. The center of this faith is God's attentive responsiveness to this community in need.

4. The last element of the psalm (vv. 8-9) states the two-sidedness of this awesome kingship: God *forgives*, and God *punishes*. Both sides affirm that this God is a free person who is never captive. It is not known in advance how God will be present in forgiveness and punishment. The juxtaposition of these two themes is reminiscent of the foundational creedal statement of Exod. 34:6-7, which posits God as both the one who saves and the one who judges.[39] But the last statement of Mosaic juxtaposition is resolved in verse 9 with one more summons to worship. This is a call to the temple, for God's overriding characteristic is holiness. It is the temple that provides the means and opportunity for a meeting with the holy one.[40] This psalm rather remarkably draws together the key elements of Israel's faith tradition. God's enthronement makes *holy presence* accessible and makes *righteous will* more urgent. Neither emphasis can be minimized without distorting who this ruling one is.

Psalm 47

This psalm is also an enthronement psalm, though its texture is somewhat different from the others commonly grouped with it. Specifically the formula of enthronement (v. 8) differs from the parallels, for it lacks the specific name Yahweh and has instead the more general statement, "God reigns." However, specific reference to Yahweh and to the people of Yahweh elsewhere in the psalm makes that linguistic difference only an incidental one.

1. Verses 1-4 are structured like a covenantal hymn in two parts. First in verse 1, there is a summons to praise with two imperatives. The summons, as in the other psalms of this group, is to all peoples. Second, in verses 2-4, introduced by the preposition כִּי we are given reasons for the praise that is urged. The twofold reason given is characteristically a juxtaposition of two themes in Israel's faith. One reason for praise of God is his *universal sovereignty over all peoples*. The other reason is *God's peculiar selection of Israel* as his special fo-

cus of love, with the gift of special land. God's sovereign rule encompasses both the general governance of the nations and the special commitment to Israel. The two are always in tension, never resolved.

2. In verse 5, we have a special enthronement formula, probably enacted liturgically. "Gone up" means to ascend to the throne (cf. Ps. 29:10).[41]

3. Verses 6-7 are another nicely structured hymn with the two parts of imperative summons (with the fourfold verb "sing"), and the basis in verse 7 with a declaration of kingship.

4. In the concluding lines of verses 8-9, we still retain the juxtaposition of nations and Israel, providential rule and election love. After the royal decree of verse 8a, the psalm refers to the governance of the nations and to the people of Abraham. However, a translation like the RSV, "...peoples gather as the people of the God of Abraham," claims too much. The text is in fact more elliptical, for it lacks the connective "as" and reads simply,

> princes of the peoples are gathered,
> people of the God of Abraham.

I suggest that while the psalm wishes to affirm both, it leaves open and is reluctant to specify the relationship between the two. A closer resolution of that juxtaposition is found in Isa. 19:23-25, where the nations do indeed become the beloved peoples of Yahweh. But that text affirms more than is here. One conclusion is that the text intends to keep that relation open and unresolved. The ultimate vision of Jerusalem is for all peoples to become peoples of Yahweh (Isa. 2:2-4). But that need not mean members of Israel's covenant. In New Testament proclamation, this kind of statement might suggest that all peoples are to be brought under the sovereignty of this God, but not all by the way of Jesus. There are other sheep, valued sheep, not of this fold (cf. John 10:16).

Summary

The enthronement psalms, taken liturgically, eschatologically, politically, are an affirmation that all peoples—Israel and the nations—as well as the whole created order, are accountable to God's governance. That is an enormous claim in a world bent on autonomy, threatened by normlessness. This rich metaphor of God's kingship may be considered theologically under at least five themes.

1. There is no doubt that the festal theme of Yahweh's enthronement draws heavily, if not decisively, on the *royal liturgy and ideology of the ancient Near East*.[42] Thus the Israelite version of this common claim is that Yahweh is not simply an Israelite God, but the God to whom all the nations are subject. Such a cosmic and universal claim precludes the reduction of Yahweh to a

tribal, partisan, or sectarian God. As all nations are accountable, so all nations have a right to expect from this ruler a fair governance.

2. The theme of *kingship of God in Israel* also appeals to the old Moses-Sinai tradition.[43] While these psalms are predominantly Zion-oriented, they allude to and play upon this covenant tradition, which is older than the temple tradition. That tradition asserts that from the earliest moment Israel's faith is articulated in a political metaphor. That Yahweh is a royal power serves to destabilize every other royal power and to relativize every temptation to absolutize power. This kingship is a gift of freedom, for allegiance to this liberating God tells against every other political subservience (cf. Lev. 25:42).

3. Because these songs probably belong to the Jerusalem liturgy, the kingship of Yahweh has intimate symbolic, political, and ideological connections to the kingship of the Davidic dynasty.[44] On the one hand, it could be that Yahweh's kingship is simply that of the dynastic claim writ large.[45] There is no doubt this element operates, and it needs to be carefully analyzed. But at the same time, this connection suggests that the kingship is the authorization and requirement of the Davidic ideal. It is Yahweh's character that is decisive for the character of all political authority in Israel—judge, king, and priest.[46] That Yahweh is a "lover of justice" makes it unavoidable that Davidic kings who are agents of and regents for Yahweh must exercise just governance, especially for the marginal.[47] Thus from the justice of Yahweh (cf. e.g., Deut. 10:17-18), we move inevitably to the same expectation for David (Ps. 72:1-4). Yahweh's kingship is politically significant as a way of *analyzing* all human exercise of power. But it is not only *critique*; it is also *authorization* for the peculiar vision of political authority held in Israel.

4. Christians will want to project these psalms toward the New Testament, for Jesus' central proclamation (cf. Mark 1:14-15), exposited in many parables, concerns the kingdom and kingship of Yahweh.[48] The New Testament does not proclaim the kingdom of Jesus, but the kingdom *of God*. That sweeping symbol comes to concrete expression not in a grand liturgical or political act, but in specific, powerful acts of compassion which transform (cf. Luke 7:22, which is an enactment of the commission of Luke 4:18-19). Jesus' ministry is a living out of the liturgical assertion of these psalms.

5. Our prayer life is a continued insistence on this metaphor. So Christians pray daily that God's kingdom come on earth (cf. Matt. 6:10). Thus the liturgical act of these psalms of coronation is a sign and expectation. Obviously, we are still short of implementation of the sign. So the liturgical decree of God's rule invites hope. And the hope of these psalms is important, for without this powerful transformative symbol, the pitiful regimes of the present age claim to be, and seem, absolute and eternal.[49] Thus without this disruptive metaphor, oppressive regimes seem to be eternally guaranteed. It is not different on the

American scene with our absolutizing of military capitalism. But we live in hope, because this metaphor keeps all present power arrangements provisional. They are all kept under scrutiny and judgment by this one who will finally govern.

Thanksgiving Generalized to Confidence

The songs of thanksgiving that we have already considered are poems concerning the immediate resolution of life into a new orientation after trouble. This new orientation comes as a surprising gift of God. Those songs review the lament and the troublesome situation of disorientation. Then they narrate the resolution and give thanks for it. They are marked by immediacy and concreteness.

The songs of confidence that we now consider are also songs about the new orientation.[50] But they are not so immediate, for they are more distanced from the crisis and reflective. And they are not so concrete, for they have generalized from the specific situation of deliverance and now can begin to speak generically of a relationship with Yahweh that is utterly trustworthy in the face of every threat. Presumably that deep conviction has grown out of a specific experience, else how would one know to trust? These psalms are some of the best known and best loved, for they offer a faith and a life that has come to a joyous trusting resolution. The speaker of these poems cannot imagine a situation that would cause doubt or trouble enough to jeopardize the trust. The relationship has been tested severely, and Yahweh has shown himself to be profoundly reliable and powerful. That is to be celebrated.[51]

Psalm 27

This psalm is difficult to categorize under any rubric, for it seems to contain two different and unrelated elements. Verses 1-6 are indeed an expression of confidence, but verses 7-14 sound more like a complaint. Thus to treat the whole as "confidence" is uncertain. I do so, however, under the impression that this motif is overriding, even in the lament. Confidence wins out over trouble.

1. Verse 1 in two parallel statements lays down the premise of the entire psalm. Then follow, in parallel, two rhetorical questions. The speaker invites an inventory of all the agents of threat and fear that might be named. But the insistence of the opening line is that nothing we may think of is severe enough to shake confidence in Yahweh who is light, salvation, and stronghold. The assertion is vigorously put as the first two lines begin with the naming of the sure one: Yahweh![52]

2. Verses 2-6 are a specific exposition of the claims made in verse 1. Verses 2-3 are a review of concrete threats in the form of slanderers, enemies, invading army, and war. Note the absence of specificity. But specificity is not important. For any concreteness of threat that may be brought to the images is overcome. For the psalmist, Yahweh prevails against every threat. Verse 4 is the remarkable affirmation this poet has made of life. The resolution is not unlike Ps. 73:25-26, in which the speaker craves only the protection and fellowship of Yahweh. So here, this speaker has been able to sort out what is at issue. He is not divided in loyalty or fragmented in priority. His one yearning is that the presence of Yahweh, known decisively in the temple, should be available. The temple presence is the reorienting factor (as it was in Ps. 73:17). Perhaps this speaker resembles the speaker in Ecclesiastes. Both of them have tried everything—work, pleasure, money—and none satisfy. But they draw different conclusions. The teacher in Ecclesiastes ended in cynicism. The speaker in Psalm 27 concludes that the one yearning of the human person is for Presence, after all that the world offers is tried and found wanting.

Temple presence makes all other concerns in life quite secondary. It is only Yahweh who makes this one utterly safe (vv. 5-6)[53] and this leads to praise and sacrifice. A great deal of scholarly speculation concerns the temple setting and the nature of the offering, the situation of rescue. Apart from hypotheses, however, we are given no specifics. But that does not matter. What counts is the kind of unshakable conviction expressed as "confident" (בטח) in v. 3, in which the speaker knows about the alternatives but reckons none as finally serious. Life is completely staked on the reliability of God.

3. Verses 7-12 are a prayer of need. The confidence of verses 1-6 of course does not eliminate trouble from life, and this deep faith does not cause the speaker to deny reality or to remain mute about it. But verses 1-6 surely provide a trustful, buoyant context in which trouble is handled and understood differently.

The lament is marked by eight imperatives in a 3/2/3 pattern:

hear, be gracious, answer (v. 7);
turn not, cast me not off (v. 9);
teach, lead, give me not up (vv. 11-12).

The speaker looks to Yahweh to keep him safe and free from destruction. These petitionary imperatives are interspersed with a number of motivations:

I seek your face (i.e., I am counting on you) (v. 8);
God has been helper and resource in the past (vv. 9-10);
Enemies are at hand (v. 12).

As in other laments, the motivations are intended to move God to answer the lament faithfully.

4. The last two lines (vv. 13-14) are a return to deep trust. This statement is governed by "I believe" (אמן): "I have utter confidence." The metaphor of the "land of the living" may be generally taken as a reference to the good life. Or with von Rad, it might refer to admission to cultic practices, so much sought after in verses 4, 8.[54] It certainly need not be taken as allusion to life after death. The psalm concludes with four insistent imperatives of confidence. The earlier imperatives had been addressed to God to get God to do his share in the relationship. Now the imperatives are addressed to the cohorts of the speaker, to get them to trust the relationship. So he says, "Wait, be strong, take courage, wait." But the rendering "wait" is misleading, for it means "hope" (קוה). Thus it is a voice in the disorientation that is fully confident of new life to be given. Finally, there is an utterance of God's name as crucial as the double use at the beginning. The complaint is real, but it is powerfully contained in the trust before and after. This psalmist has past experiences of God's care that prevent excessive anxiety in the present. The governing verbs seem to be "trust" (בטח) in verse 3, and "believe" (אמן) in verse 13. This speaker knows that God's alternative to the present is reliable and will endure until fruition.

Psalm 23

It is almost pretentious to comment on this psalm. The grip it has on biblical spirituality is deep and genuine. It is such a simple statement that it can bear its own witness without comment. It is, of course, a psalm of confidence. It recounts in detail, by means of rich metaphors, a life lived in trustful receptivity of God's gifts. The psalm may be divided into three parts. In verses 1-2 and verse 6, Yahweh is spoken of in the third person. In verses 3-5, Yahweh is directly addressed as "thou." Therefore, it seems likely that the middle section is more immediate and more intense to the faith experience of the speaker. It seems closer to the actual memories of deliverance, and the two images of *table* and *cup* seems to have some specificity. The opening (vv. 1-2) and ending (v. 6) around verses 3-5 are more reflective and general comments that may be based on this experience of direct address.

One is struck by the use of names and pronouns. The name of Yahweh is uttered only twice, abruptly at the beginning and at the end, so that the poem, like this trustful life, is lived fully in the presence of this name which sets the parameters for both life and speech. At the center of the psalm is the magisterial *thou*, which seems to govern the psalm. There are other pronominal suffixes, but this is the only strong independent pronoun referring to God. Too much should not be made of it, but I suggest the three uses provide a sketch for the faith and experience of the psalmist:

Yahweh → Thou → Yahweh
(v. 1)   (v. 4)   (v. 6)

The other, most interesting, grammatical element is the repeated and pervasive first person pronoun, which abounds everywhere in the psalm. In some other contexts (as in the lament of Psalm 77), the repeated reference to self sounds like an unhealthy obsession. But here that is not the case. Here the "I" statements are filled with gratitude, yielding, trust, and thanksgiving. The "I" here knows that in every case, life is fully cared for and resolved by this thou who responds to and anticipates every need.[55] Life with Yahweh is a life of well-being and satisfaction.

The phrase that immediately follows the initial utterance of the name of Yahweh is equally abrupt and decisive for the psalm: "I lack not" (חסר). Israel refuses to split things into spiritual and material. It affirms that Yahweh is the satisfaction of all wants and needs. Thus, as in Ps. 73:26, Yahweh is one's portion. That can be taken as a "spiritual" satisfaction, as though fellowship with God is the end of all needs. The psalm makes clear that Yahweh is the satisfaction of every kind of need, so that the affirmation never could mean only religious yearning. The images of cup and table guard against spiritualizing, for they concern real food and real drink.

The satisfaction of lacks can be appreciated in an Israelite context if the psalm is related to the meaning of Israel's memory.[56] In Exod. 16:18 it is precisely manna, the surprising bread of heaven, that is the resolution of hunger, so that no one lacks. And in Deut. 2:7 the entire wilderness tradition is seen as a story in which there were no lacks, because God's steadfastness and goodness (cf. Ps. 23:6) is found adequate in the face of every threat to life. This psalm can recall situations of threat, but the poet knows that the powerful solidarity of Yahweh more than overrides the threat. The whole memory of Israel presses the psalmist toward trust.

The most poignant part of the psalm appears to be in verse 4 with the direct "thou" of address. The structure of the language is reminiscent of the lament and salvation oracle. Thus I suggest that this formula stands at the end of the conversation between God and Israel that encompasses three patterns of psalmic speech:

lament	→ *salvation oracle*	→ *song of confidence*
I am afraid (cf. Ps. 56:3)	→ Do not fear	→ I will not fear
Why have you forsaken?	→ I am with you (Isa. 41:10)	→ You are with me (Ps. 23:4).

It is God's companionship that transforms every situation. It does not mean
there are no deathly valleys, no enemies. But they are not capable of hurt, and
so the powerful loyalty and solidarity of Yahweh *comfort*, precisely in situations of threat. As the assertion of ''comfort'' is exile-ending (cf. Isa. 40:1-2),
so here it is wilderness-ending. The end of forlornness is access to the temple,
where life is ordered anew. Yet it is not the *place* but the vitality of the *relationship* which transforms. The temple comes only as a consolidation of the relationship. For one whose life has been transformed by such solidarity, a life of
worshipful praise is a crown for time to come, a safe place in which to live for
now. Psalm 23 knows that evil is present in the world, but it is not feared. Confidence in God is the source of new orientation.

Psalm 91[57]

This remarkable psalm speaks with great specificity, and yet with a kind
of porousness, so that the language is enormously open to each one's particular
experience. Its tone is somewhat instructional, as though reassuring someone
else who is unsure. Yet the assurance is not didactic, but confessional. It is a
personal testimony of someone whose own experience makes the assurance of
faith convincing and authentic.

1. The psalm from verse 1 to verse 13 is an extended assurance, but there
seems to be a rhetorical pause after verse 8. So we may take verses 1-8 as a first
rhetorical unit. The first two verses are a statement of confidence, ending with
the word ''trust'' (בטח). These verses combine the *intimacy of personal faith*
(note the word ''my refuge, my fortress, my God'') with a *metaphor of the majestic transcendence of God* (''Most High, the Almighty'').[58] And that of
course is the claim of the psalm: that the awesome power and presence of Yahweh is made available to and is committed to this traveler who must go in dangerous places. The psalm interweaves two different kinds of images. The first
one is about *a safe place,* as though one has found a place to hide from the
threats.

Verses 3-6, however, are not about a safe place, but a *safe journey* when
one is exposed. The images read like the dangers of *Pilgrim's Progress,* in
which one is constantly beset with threats. These threats are not spiritual
seductions, but actual threats to physical life—although the metaphors can be
turned in both of these directions. The psalm notes all the threats and dangers:
''through many a toil and snare I have already come.'' Yet in each case Yahweh is more than adequate, always here with what is needed *to snatch* from the
trap of evil, *to cover* and hide from assault under his wings (cf. Luke 13:34), *to
defend* with arms if necessary. The traveler must proceed on roads where there
is no civil order and no police protection, where one is at the mercy of the
forces of darkness. But the traveler is unscathed midst the threats of day and

night, darkness and noon. The metaphor of dangerous journey is remote from us with our guarded highways and our well-ordered society, but this is a journey taken in the midst of social chaos, where one has no guarantee of safe conduct. Yet God is an escort who makes safe passage possible.

As a result (vv. 7-8), all those who attack are done in. This escort is powerful and attentive and will let no intruder cause harm.

2. The same metaphors are sounded in verses 9-13, with some reiteration. Now for the third time, God is said to be "refuge" (vv. 2, 4). The text is somewhat unclear, but only here is there a direct and independent pronoun, "thou." This is an intense acknowledgment of trust. In this line, the image of refuge is in parallel to "habitation," in the sense of a safe "den," the same word as in 90:1. Thus in verses 11-13, we are again on the journey, and now protection is vouchsafed by a host of bodyguards (angels) who are armed and who fend off every threat, including sharp stones on the path, and snakes and lions that lie in wait. This is indeed royal treatment.

The poem praises safe *place* (vv. 1-4, 9-10) and safe *journey* (vv. 5-6, 11-13). Either way, in place or on path, one is safe, because Yahweh is an attentive protector adequate to every challenge. Without this escort, one is surely doomed to trouble and death. One is still exposed, but no harm can come, because the speaker is not alone.

3. In verses 14-16 we have something of a surprise—for this psalm or any other. This is the direct speech of Yahweh in the form of a decree of assurance, which seems to respond to the trust of verses 1-13. It is the great faith of the speaker that evokes this response of assurance. Yahweh responds because the speaker has yearned passionately for Yahweh. Yahweh is faithful and responsive to those who rely on him.

Yahweh's responsiveness is an overriding commitment: "I will deliver, I will protect, I will answer, I will be with him, I will rescue, [I will] honor him, I will satisfy, [I will] show." The promise articulated in the human assurance (vv. 1-3) is now verified in divine speech (vv. 14-16). Perhaps the most striking formula for this profound commitment is in verse 15: "When he calls to me, I will answer him."[59] The initiative of trust and petition belongs with the poet. But Yahweh is resolved to answer and is very sure. Because of that, this psalm has reckoned with real life threats, looking them straight in the face. But none will prevail against this God. The language is the language of martial protection. But the verb חשק is the language of intimacy that lies underneath the externals of power and protection. It concerns cleaving and yearning and desiring. It is that which binds Yahweh to this psalmist. The songs of confidence are words of trusting people. In this psalm the last word belongs to Yahweh, and the last word is caring protection. It is the ground for confidence that the last word is not spoken *by* us, but *to* us (cf. John 6:68).

Hymns of Praise

"Hymns of praise" would seem to be a very general classification. Indeed, there is a tendency to treat the term as a synonym for the Psalms. But in fact, it has a more precise reference. It characterizes a public (as distinct from personal or intimate) song that is sung with abandonment in praise to God for the character of God's person or the nature of God's creating and liberating actions. I am not sure whether, in the pattern of orientation—disorientation—new orientation which we have pursued, these psalms should all be placed at the very end of the process as surprising, glad statements of a new ordering of life, or whether they should be treated as the very deepest and established statement of the old orientation that is firm, settled, and nonnegotiable.

I place them here because the extravagant form of celebration does not seem jaded or fatigued with old orientation. It still seems bright, focused, and engaged, reflecting some sense of wonder and marvel at the gift of life recently given. On the other hand, some of the hymns are much more "descriptive" than "declarative." They have lost all specificity and seem only to affirm a well-ordered world. They not only have left behind the concreteness of the thanksgiving song, but perhaps also the vitality and enthusiasm of the new orientation. So it is the speech of newness on its way to being old, tired, established, and immovable. We recall Westermann's distinction of descriptive and declarative,[60] and recognize that the descriptive hymns tend to be of the old orientation. More importantly is Goldingay's observation that specific *use* might lead to the location of the hymn at one point or the other.[61] But the *usage*, not the *content*, may determine its specific function in the community.

As a rule of thumb, we may assume that the more decisively declarative, the more the hymn speaks of new orientation; conversely, the descriptive hymn celebrates old orientation. We may also assume that the more the hymn focuses on historical liberation, the more likely it is about new orientation. Conversely, the more it focuses on creation, the more it is likely to attest to a long-established, enduring order, i.e., old orientation. We are in any case near to the closing of the circle by which the "new, new song" becomes an "old, old story."[62]

Theologically the hymn is a liturgical and unrestrained yielding of self and community to God. It is a disinterested, uncalculating ceding of life over to its pioneer and perfecter (Heb. 12:2). It is an act of self-abandonment that embodies the first answer of the Westminister Catechism: "The chief end of man is to glorify God and enjoy him forever." The hymn is the way in which the faith community does its glorifying and enjoying in that specific destiny, as a foretaste of what is promised.

Psalm 117

This psalm is well known, because it is the briefest of them all. It is also a good place to begin hymnic analysis, because it offers one clear model in two parts.[63] The first element is characteristically *a summons to praise*. In this psalm it is "praise" and "extol" (v. 1). The second element, introduced by the preposition "for" (כִּי), gives the *reason or basis* for the praise enjoined. In this psalm it is the attribution to God of *steadfastness* and *faithfulness*. These are the reasons for the summons to praise and why it should be done.

Two things should be noticed. First, the address is comprehensive. This exaltation of Yahweh is intended to include all peoples. This may seem inordinately pretentious as a ritual activity. Such rhetoric in the temple reenforces the claims of the temple (and the dynasty). But it also keeps alive a vision of all peoples gathered in one act of worship. Second, the ground of praise lacks all specificity. We are not told the basis of trust in Yahweh's "steadfast love" and "faithfulness." This is indeed a summing up of the whole faith tradition of Israel in the most general terms. The other hymns are exegesis of this tersely expressed claim. That is, this Psalm articulates in brief all that is to come in the other, fuller expressions.

Psalm 135

This psalm is a complex statement. We deal with it next because it stays very close to the actual historical memory of Israel. Indeed, it is sometimes treated with Psalm 136, which is a detailed and exacting recital of Israel's history.

1. Verses 1-3 are an extended summons to praise. Already in the summons, verse 3 hints at the ground of praise; Yahweh is "good" and "gracious."

2. But the more fundamental ground is introduced by the double כִּי in verses 4 and 5. Those two motivational claims express the range of the bases. Verse 4 is tightly related to the historical experience of Israel and is picked up again in verses 8-14. On the other hand, verse 5 is a claim for Yahweh *vis-à-vis* the other gods, so it has a scope well beyond Israel. This theme is extended positively in verses 6-7, which speak about the creative power of Yahweh. And in verses 15-18 it is pursued negatively; Yahweh is contrasted with the gods of the nations, who are declared impotent and powerless. These two motifs together are an exquisite summary of what Israel says in hymns. The *historical claim* bears witness to Yahweh's steadfast compassion. The claim of Yahweh testifies to Yahweh's cosmic sovereignty and majestic power. Yahweh's creative power is contrasted with the powerlessness of idols. *Steadfastness* (shown

in Israel) and *power* (shown among the nations) are the bases for praise and celebration of the good order God has given, in which we now live.[64]

Psalm 103

This is perhaps the best-known and best-loved of all the hymns. The themes are characteristic of the hymn.

1. Verses 1-2 are a summons to praise. The formula, "Bless the Lord, O my soul," is so familiar to us that we do not notice how odd it is. It is the self summoning the self to praise, i.e., the self reminding self of the fact that all of life must be finally referred to God's goodness. This hymn begins with the worshiper talking to himself. The term rendered "benefits" might be translated as "payoffs." It refers to the rewards and punishments this God reliably gives.

2. The basis for praise is the marvelous series of participles in verses 3-6, which summarize God's characteristic action. Though lacking in specificity, this list shows a memory of God overcoming every kind of disorientation. The verbs tell the tale: "forgives, heals, redeems, crowns, satisfies." We should notice that in verse 6, we have what seems to be a last element in the list which is often left outside the recital: "works." This last verb is a reminder to us that Israel always keeps the goal of justice visible. Most interesting is the reference to "steadfast love and mercy" (v. 4), characteristically salvific language.

3. Verses 7-8 include two rather surprising elements. Verse 7 contains a specific reference to the liberating, disclosing events around Moses. They are curious here, cited perhaps because it is the Moses events which fully embody the recital above in a concrete way. It is as though, when Israel thinks of such things as listed in verses 3-5, Moses inevitably comes to mind. Second, verse 8 contains a creedal recital, derived from the Mosaic statement of Exod. 34:6-7, which marks God with attributes of fidelity and specifically reiterates the words of verse 4. This characterization is parallel to the one we have seen in Ps. 145:8-9 at the beginning of our study.

4. Verses 9-14 have a rather interesting Hebrew pattern. Two lines begin with a negative. Then there are two lines (vv. 11-14) which begin with the particle כִּי as a basis for the argument, and two lines in between use the letter כְּ to introduce a contrast. The point of the entire section is to announce that Yahweh's way of working and standard of judgment is not like any we expect. We may expect enduring anger, but we do not receive it. The term that is rendered "requite" in verse 10 is גמל, the same word as "benefit" in verse 2. So now we see that the "payoffs" of Yahweh are not exacting, but stunningly generous. In verse 11, this unit speaks of "steadfast love," now for the third time, and shows it to be the basis for God's goodness. The result is that Yahweh shatters all expectations and does not treat us as we might anticipate. God utilizes

the generosity and concern of a caring father. The ground for newness is not in needy Israel, but in the will of the loving father.

5. Verses 15-18 complete the contrast. We are surprised because we expect God to judge according to calculating human standards, but these are not God's ways (cf. Hos. 11:8-9). Yahweh is utterly unlike humankind, which is transitory and unreliable. Apart from all of those norms, Yahweh is marked by steadfast love and righteousness, so long as the partner keeps covenant. Notice that this is the fourth use of "steadfast love" (v. 17). This provides a sketch of the remarkable God that Yahweh is. This God powerfully transforms things (vv. 3-5), operates from generosity, not calculation (vv. 9-14), and is free of all conventions.

6. It is no wonder that the concluding summons to praise is expansive (vv. 19-22). The psalm began by calling the self. But now it is all creation, earth-creatures and heavenly angels, who are needed adequately to assert who this unutterable God is. Notice the psalm is not specific. Its concern is not specific memory but that the person of Yahweh should be rendered adequately and faithfully. The key to this discernment of Yahweh is "steadfast love."

Psalm 113

This psalm exhibits the characteristic features of the genre. It is a celebration of Yahweh and holds in wondrous tension the *push to a cosmic claim* and *the specificity of liberation memory*.

1. Verses 1-4 issue a sweeping summons to praise that focuses on *the name* (vv. 1-3). This is the song of those who delight to sound the name "Yahweh," because the name itself is freighted with all the memories, claims, and gifts that are necessary to a joyous life. The summons is used in verse 2 for all *time*; in verses 3-4 it is issued for all *places*. The poem has a vision of all creation in all times and all space gathered as a single entity around the throne. Our conventional use of such a vision is an eschatological one, a hopeful vision of creation resolved and gathered around the throne. Here it is a cultic enactment or anticipation of such a hope.

2. Verses 5-6 offer a vision of the majestically enthroned deity who presides over all. This governance is in no way heavy or oppressive, but it is a governance that summons all nations and creatures to new obedience. The worship of the Jerusalem temple must have regularly enacted such a claim, and indeed, if we listen to our own liturgies, we make the same claims. It must have been such an affirmation and enactment in the temple that evoked the vision of Isaiah who saw "the real king" (Isa. 6:1ff.). Implicit in this sweeping claim is a dismissal of the gods and an expectation that the other nations will finally abandon their "no-gods" for this true God. There is no suggestion that the nations must become Israelite, but such texts as Isa. 2:2-4 and Micah 4:1-4a do seem to

assume that all nations finally come to Jerusalem. This heavenly vision is to be embodied in a concrete liturgical act.

3. The distinctiveness of Yahweh ("like whom there is no other") is not based on grand cosmic claims, for that by itself has no substance. And so lying behind such liturgy as a kind of "reality check" is the concrete memory of Israel (vv. 7-9), which recites and recalls the *transformative interventions* central to the faith memory of Israel. This part of the psalm echoes the song of Hannah (1 Sam. 2:1-10, especially vv. 7-8). That song in all its concreteness sounds like a celebration of a helpless, powerless peasant community that regards Yahweh as its only friend and ally against powerful, exploitative enemies—Egyptian, Canaanite, Philistine, or whatever. The references in verses 7-8 of Psalm 113 are not simply to specific individuals; this is a "class action suit" arguing that Yahweh's central business is the enhancement of the powerless against the powerful. The supreme example of this inversion is the birth given to the barren (v. 9).

Hannah herself in the accompanying narrative is a case in point (1 Sam. 1:2). Every Israelite who sang this song would immediately pass in review the history of barrenness that has become well-being and fruitfulness. The song alludes to all the "mothers of barrenness" in this history: Sarah (Gen. 11:30), Rebekah (Gen. 25:21), and Rachel (Gen. 29:31). Now it is surprising that in a great festal day in Jerusalem the congregation should name the names of these oddly transformed women, but that is the nature of Israel's faith. Out of these *concrete* pasts come the grand generalizations of the hymn. Thus the hymn offers the "scandal of particularity." The nations are summoned to worship precisely on the basis of this nonnegotiable remembering. The one who sits enthroned in splendor is known to be peculiarly allied with the broken-hearted, who cannot help themselves (Isa. 57:15). Any invitation to a "theology of glory" is not permitted to silence the power in pain that belongs to a theology of the cross. While Israel's hymnody sometimes overrides that specificity, it does not do so in this psalm. The doxology belongs first in the mouths of the barren made fruitful (cf. Isa. 54:1-4), the poor still hopeful. Such praise requires the nations to notice all of life in a new way, from the bottom up, clear to the throne.

Psalm 146

In what is probably a characteristic hymnic structure for Israel, this psalm follows the same general course as Psalm 113.

1. The summons to praise in verses 1-2 is extravagant, with a fourfold statement, two imperatives, and two first-person assertions. The summons is

referred to the self (as in Psalm 103), unlike the expansive address of Psalm 117.

2. The middle section of the psalm (vv. 3-7) offers a contrast. It asks where one should lodge one's trust. In the enthronement psalms we have seen the rule of Yahweh contrasted with the idols. Here the same contrast is made, only now the negative counterpart is human agents rather than idols. But the substance of the contrast is the same: the others are powerless to save.

The negative assertion (vv. 3-4) is not unlike that of 103:15-16. Humankind is transitory and will die, and in situations of real need is unreliable (cf. Isa. 2:22). Lost in translation is the play on "man" (אדם) and "earth" (אדמה). The positive contrast is Yahweh (vv. 5-7), again echoing the positive assertion of 103:17-18. These verses are in the form of a wisdom saying about the fortunate. The substance of the Yahwistic claim is characteristically twofold. First, there is a cosmic claim about Yahweh as creator, faithful to his creation. But then in verse 7, the praise moves, as Israel normally does, to the specific Israelite goal of *justice*. Behind the universal claim is the historical memory of justice, which is what finally makes Yahweh reliable. The juxtaposition of cosmic and liberation claims is like the doxological statement of Deut. 10:17-18, which makes the same move. These voices in the new orientation remember quite explicitly the moment of rescue from the disorientation.

3. The remainder of the psalm (vv. 7b-9) extrapolates from verse 7a and appeals to Israel's memory. In hymnic fashion, specificity is lacking, and the recital is in a series of participles like Ps. 103:3-6, with parallels to Ps. 145:13-20.[65] The recital concerns inversion of hopeless situations, with particular reference to the sojourner, widow, and orphan, examples in Israel of the socially marginal and powerless. Running through that statement of generous advocacy is the quite different theme of righteous and wicked (vv. 8-9), those who do and do not adhere to Yahweh's covenant. It is striking how the temple rhetoric of kingship finally must appeal to the specific acts of justice and righteousness that are the core of Israel's faith.[66] These categories of righteous and wicked do retreat a bit from the unqualified generosity of the other accompanying theme.

4. The concluding formula of verse 10 returns to the more cosmic claim and roots the matter securely in Zion. It is this "Zion connection" with justice and righteousness that subsequently roots the Amos tradition of justice and righteousness in Zion, from whence comes justice (cf. Amos 1:2).

Psalm 147

In the remainder of the psalms we will consider, we will see a tendency to move increasingly away from the concreteness of Israel's faith to more general, universalizing themes. (Psalm 149 is an odd and surprising exception to this tendency.) Of the two structural elements, *summons* and *basis*, we will see that the basis grows less and less, until the summons becomes almost the entire hymnic expression. When that happens, we have come full circle to the psalms of (old) orientation, for now Israel celebrates an order, but seems no longer to recall its foundations in specific acts of compassion and justice.

The disappearance of a concrete basis is an interesting rhetorical development. But it is also a telling sociological and theological matter, for it takes the present order "out of history." When Israel cannot any longer remember the specific acts that created this situation, there is inevitably an inclination to absolutize the order and to imagine that it has always been so.[67] Thus the specific bases not only provide a ground for certitude and gratitude, but also for criticism. When the praise of the summons is uncriticized by the basis, we can be sure things are being absolutized beyond criticism, which is in any case the temptation of temple hymnody.

That process of loss of the specific begins to be evident in Psalm 147, but we will see it much more in 148, 100, and 150 (with 149 resisting that tendency).

1. Verses 1-6 could well be a psalm by themselves, for they include the three elements we have seen elsewhere:

a) A summons to praise, followed in verse 1b with a כי of a basis.

b) The first basis is in verses 2-3, 6, which sing of Israel's liberation tradition. Verse 3 refers to acts of social compassion; verse 6 alludes to the powerless who are victimized, and verse 2 alludes to something like the end of exile. This need not refer to a particular exile, but understands exile-ending as Yahweh's characteristic action.

c) Verses 4-5 recite Yahweh's great power known in Israel. Never are the traditions of *creation* and the memory of *liberation* seen as mutually exclusive. Both bear witness to the same God. The juxtaposition of motifs suggests that these psalms never stand alone or without a context. So we must hear and understand them in the midst of Israel's full worship, which included a variety of other motifs.

2. A second hymnic unit in verses 7-11 reiterates similar elements. After the call to praise, the basis begins in verses 8, though without the usual preposition. The basis mainly concerns creative power, but the last word is חסד which probably still alludes to the liberation tradition of Moses.

3. A third rhetorical unit in verses 12-20 touches the same elements. After the summons, the basis begins in verse 13 with the preposition. In the participial form we are given a recital of God's benevolent creative acts, which make the abundance of creation possible. The only mention of the Israelite historical tradition in this unit is verses 19-20. It is an odd juxtaposition, but it does show Israel's persistent reference to distinctive election status.

Each of the three sections could stand alone. We may note a continued weakening of "the Israelite historical connection" in the interest of a more sweeping cosmic claim. In the third unit the creation elements have largely carried the day. Perhaps other elements in the context would correct this, but that weakening seems visible here.

Psalm 148

In this psalm the linguistic pattern is completely preoccupied with the summons. The repeated and extended summons constitutes the act of praise, varied only by the difference of vocative, which sweeps the entire created world. Indeed, if one focuses on those addressed, one has an inventory of God's creation. All of these creatures are now called to answer back to the one who gave life.[68] It is a bold touch to classify the great elements of creation simply as part of the worshiping congregation, including the heavenly bodies, the great animals, the elements of weather, and in verses 11-12, the human creature as well.

The basis of praise is expressed only in verses 5b-6 and 13b-14, but it is everywhere assumed. The basis offered does not do other than the summons, for in this case, both basis and summons attest to Yahweh's majestic and incomparable power. The idea of God's graciousness may be implied, as always in creation speech, but in the rhetorical pattern, it is power and not graciousness which overwhelms the assembled creation.

The last verse makes the standard Israelite connection almost a footnote (as in Ps. 147:19-20). Rhetorically this is presented as being equal in importance to the other acts of creation, but structurally appears almost as an addendum to the psalm.

Psalm 100

This psalm offers a summons to praise which seems to be an invitation to enter the temple (v. 1). Because of the reference to his "face" (פנה) (presence), we are prepared for the reference in verse 2 to the peculiar identity of Israel as God's people (cf. Ps. 95:7). Even in the Jerusalem temple the election tradition is still recalled. The temple holds together universal and particular religious claims. The summons in verse 4 is followed by a characterization of the one to be worshiped as good, loyal, and faithful. These attributes emerge out of Israel's faith experience, but now we are dealing only in summaries.

Psalm 149

This psalm bears all of the conventional marks of a psalm, yet its development is unusual and offers a surprising emphasis.

1. Verses 1-4 are a standard summons (vv. 1-3), with a basis introduced

by כִּי in verse 4. That is the first rhetorical unit. But the summons already puts us on notice. This song to be sung is a ''new song,'' thus an enthronement motif. We may expect something more concrete and urgent in such a formula. But it is to be sung, unlike some of the enthronement hymns, which have global invitations, in ''the assembly of the faithful,'' i.e., in the Israelite covenant community. The language seems to allude to an early, premonarchical concept of Israel, though that is not an argument for dating the psalm. Instead, it is an indication of the social model that the psalm has in mind, whatever its date. The concept of the congregation of the faithful (cf. Mic. 2:5; Ps. 1:5) refers to an intimate, intense, and intentional covenant community that has not been dissipated by more inclusive concerns. The psalm thus is likely to reflect a more self-conscious and militant agenda not interested in broad-based accommodation. It is more likely to be a psalm that stands closer to the gift of new orientation and does not take things so much for granted. In verse 4 it is affirmed that the basis for praise is victory (יְשׁוּעָה—salvation, liberation). This psalm is sharper than the more generalizing ones among which it is placed.

2. The second half of the psalm (vv. 5-9) has a series of optatives that function as summons. But where we might expect a basis, as in the usual pattern, this psalm issues a call to action on the basis of praise. It is action that is powered by and grows out of the act of praise. The action that is urged is warlike action that concerns vengeance, chastisement, binding in chains, execution of judgment. I do not know what to make of this, for it is quite unexpected in the hymns. It is a statement of sobering historical realism. Praise of God is not flight from historical reality. In its songs Israel does not escape from either historical responsibility or historical temptation. One cannot tell whether this is responsibility (to fend off oppressors) or temptation (to gather imperial power). Either way, it is clear that Israel's praise of Yahweh keeps one foot in and one eye firmly on historical reality. There is no liturgical or spiritual escape from the hardness of history. The liberation questions will not be siphoned off in song.

This psalm could be defensively concerned to maintain an old orientation. It might be a reflection of having arrived at a place where the gift of orientation is no longer a surprise to be enjoyed, but is now a possession to be defended. In this psalm there is no more talk about God's free healing power for the powerless. This psalm may sound like the voice of the powerful acting to consolidate and expand. On the other hand, if this is a little community arrayed against some empire, then the action urged is to be understood differently. I find this psalm very difficult to interpret, precisely because the proposed action could have very different intentions.

If the present arrangement of the collection of Psalms is intentional as Westermann has urged,[69] and if Psalm 1 and 150 are deliberately placed to show that torah *obedience* leads to *praise*, then this psalm has as its partner Psalm 2. The second psalm of the collection may match the next to the last. This would make an appropriate connection, because Psalm 2 concerns the anointing of a king in defiance of the nations, and Psalm 149 also urges some resistant behavior. Both psalms may lie very close to the royal temptation to absolutize power.

Psalm 150

The conclusion of the Psalter is this extravagant summons to praise, which seeks to mobilize all creation with a spontaneous and unreserved act of adoration, praise, gratitude, and awe. There are no ''bases'' given; no reason needs to be given.

As a poem for the conclusion of the collection, this psalm is a good match for Psalm 1. We have suggested that Psalm 1 is a formal and intentional introduction to the Psalter. It asserts in a decisive way that life under torah is the precondition of all these psalms. In relation to that, Psalm 150 states the outcome of such a life under torah. Torah-keeping does arrive at obedience, yet obedience is not the goal of torah-keeping. Finally, such a life arrives at *unencumbered praise*. As Israel (and the world) is obedient to torah, it becomes free for praise, which is its proper vocation, destiny, and purpose. In this light the expectation of the Old Testament is not finally *obedience*, but *adoration*. The Psalter intends to lead and nurture people to such a freedom that finds its proper life in happy communion that knows no restraint of convention or propriety. That is the hope for Israel and for all creation.

5

A Retrospect: Spirituality and Theodicy

There can be no doubt that the Psalms are an important resource for spirituality and have been so for countless generations. That is indeed why we continue to study them. These words have mediated to persons and communities the presence of God. The format for our presentations of the Psalms has assumed that authentic spirituality, i.e., genuine communion with God, is never removed from the seasons, turns, and crises of life. So the modes of God's presence (and absence) and the quality of communion are very different in times of orientation and disorientation. What one says in conversation with God is deeply shaped by one's circumstance of orientation and disorientation. Relationship with God is not immune to the surprises and costs of our daily life.

However, spirituality by itself is an inadequate basis for reading the Psalms. For the most part, to place Psalms in the domain of spirituality is a Christian approach, indeed, even an approach of a part of the Christian tradition. A very selected reading of the Psalms has been necessary to keep the Psalms within the confines of conventional spirituality. Taken by itself, the conventional perspective of spirituality does not fully take into account the decisively Jewish character of the Psalms.[1] Throughout this study I have been aware of the startling assertion of Jose Miranda: "It can surely be said that the Psalter presents a struggle of the just against the unjust."[2] To be sure, Miranda's judgment is also a partial perspective and does not include everything to be found in the Psalter. But it does point to something important that may draw us into the categories of Jewish faith. The struggle of the oppressed against the unjust, when cast theologically, is the issue of *theodicy*. These con-

168

cluding comments explore the ways in which the notion of *spirituality* is treated in the Psalms in relation to the issue of *theodicy*. I do not want to schematize excessively, but I suggest that theodicy is a characteristically Jewish concern that may correct or discipline a Christian restriction of the Psalms to privatistic, romantic spirituality. That is, *communion with God* cannot be celebrated without attention to the *nature of the community*, both among human persons and with God. *Religious hungers* in Israel never preclude *justice questions*.[3] Indeed, it is through the question of *justice* that *communion* is mediated:

> So if you are offering your gift at the altar, and there remember that your brother has something against you, leave your gift there before the altar and go; first be reconciled to your brother, and then come and offer your gift (Matt. 5:23-24).

My use of the category of theodicy has three dimensions. If spirituality is a concern for *communion with God*, theodicy is a concern for a *fair deal*. The juxtaposition of these themes, spirituality and theodicy, is to bring together *communion* and a *fair deal*. Such a juxtaposition is remarkable, because we do not normally worry about a fair deal when treating communion with God. But the psalmists do. And any spirituality we think we find in the Psalms that does not raise serious questions about theodicy has misunderstood the nature of psalmic faith.

The conventional idea of theodicy concerns God in relation to evil.[4] If God is *powerful* and *good*, how can there be evil in the world?[5] If the question is posed in this way, religion can offer no adequate logical response. Logically one must compromise either God's power or God's love, either saying that evil exists because God is not powerful enough to overrule it, or because God is not loving enough to use God's power in this way. To compromise in either direction is religiously inadequate and offers no satisfying response.[6] Today the theological discussion seems to insist on holding on to God's love even at the risk of God's sovereign power.[7] What faith offers is a sense of trust that is prepared to submit.[8] That deep trust summons us to hard rethinking about the categories in which we do our reflection.

The characteristic way of handling theodicy in Old Testament scholarship,[9] and in the theological enterprise more generally, is to see that the question becomes acute in Israel in the 7th-6th centuries B.C.E., around the collapse of Jerusalem, temple, and dynasty.[10] This approach sees the crisis growing out of a historical circumstance and brought to expression in a rich literary development. The historical experience of Israel suggests that God punishes capriciously, that the suffering is inappropriate to the disobedience; therefore God's justice is questioned. Specifically, the old theories (Deuteronomic and sapiential) that good people prosper and evil people suffer are reexamined.[11]

Because the problem is so difficult, there is a rich array of literature that offers a series of imaginative probes around the question of God's justice, the best known of which is Job.

It cannot be denied that this is an important question. However, such an approach narrows the issue to a religious question about the character of God.[12] Though the question grows out of historical experience and finds literary expression, it is treated as a theological question without any serious attention to other payoff systems of reward and punishment that are practiced in political and economic ways. But serious theodicy is always linked to social arrangements of access and benefit.

We have already noted that genuine communion with God is never removed from the seasons, times, and crises of life. Or said another way, the question of theodicy is never a narrow religious question. It must be understood sociologically as a question about law, about the rule of law, about the reliability of the system of rewards and punishments.[13] Theodicy then concerns the character of God as practiced in the system of values in a social matrix.[14]

If we are to take seriously the question of theodicy in the Psalms, we must see that it cannot be reduced to or contained in a narrow question about God. Rather, theodicy is the rationale or legitimacy for the way in which society is ordered.[15] It is a statement or agreement or compromise about how a society defines good and evil, right and wrong, power and powerlessness. The practical effect is that theodicy is a theory of power about who makes decisions and who obeys them, who administers and controls good, who has access to them and on what terms. Or said another way, theodicy is an agreement about world-definition, about who gets to have a say, about who the authoritative interpreters are, and whose definitions and interpretations are "true" in this community.[16] Theodicy is about the legitimacy of one's view of the world. The legitimacy of a worldview as "true" concerns theological matters, but it also includes all the power questions of law, economics, and politics. Therefore, reflections on theodicy always spill over into the public dimensions of life.

Every theological settlement of the theodicy question is closely allied to a social scheme.[17] If it is a statement about God, it inevitably includes a statement about the "truth" of God's agents—the priests, kings, prophets, theologians. In the language of Robert Merton, *theodicy* concerns the legitimacy of a *nomos*, a rule of God about which there is assent and a general consensus.[18] So long as the consensus holds, and no one dissents from the arrangement, then there appears to be no question of theodicy. It is correct that there is no *crisis* in theodicy, but that is a *consensus* about theodicy all the same. Theodicy operates in times of equilibrium, as well as in times of crisis, but it is often hidden. We are agreed, and so we instruct our children, that this is the order to be honored and obeyed. We objectify and reify that order in a positivistic way,[19] so that there is no room outside the consensus from which to mount a criticism.[20] Obviously such an accepted theodicy is a form of social control and conformity.[21] There is no crisis, but there is a theodicy, conventionally legitimated by the rule of God.[22]

A *theodicy of consensus* is operative in every stable society. In our Western society, we have had a consensus of justice about how to organize marriage and the respective roles of men and women. Because there was consensus and the arrangement was properly legitimated, it was experienced as just. Now that a criticism has been mounted (through feminist voices), we begin to see that the arrangement was not always just, and so the conventional theodicy is in crisis. And it is easy to see how this becomes a God-question, because in conventional industrial society, the family arrangement was not only perceived as workable and just but as legitimate, blessed and approved by God as the right way to order social life. Now it is clear that if God continues to legitimate that social arrangement as the proper and only form of life, then God's justice is much in question. The shift from a *consensus about theodicy* to a *crisis in theodicy* can be identified in every liberation movement that questions the old settled arrangements.[23]

A crisis occurs in a societal scheme of theodicy when some members of the community (perhaps a class or social group) conclude that the agreed settlement is inequitable and not to be honored.[24] There may then be a harsh end to docility and the articulation of vigorous dissent. Because the challenged theodicy includes both a *doctrine of God* and a social *system of authority*, the challenge may take one or two forms:

1. It may be concluded that the entire arrangement, theological as well as social, is to be rejected, because the legitimating God is in collusion with the human exploiters, and the collusion is so deep and unjust that the whole system must be rejected. Seen in that radical way, the exodus-conquest tradition is a protest against an established Egyptian theodicy. Israel rejects not only Egyptian civil authority, but also the Egyptian gods. The Egyptian gods are seen to be so enmeshed with the unjust social system that it must all be rejected. And in rejecting the entire social system, Israel introduced a new social system (torah)[25] and a new God (cf. Josh. 24:14-15; Judg. 5:8). That is, Israel adopted an entirely different *scheme of theodicy*, erected a new *nomos* in the form of torah, and the entire movement was marked by egalitarianism.[26]

2. On the other hand, it may be concluded that the human system is corrupt and unfair, but the legitimating God is reliable. Then a distinction can be made, so that by appeal to and in the name of the still trusted God, the old system is rejected as unjust and disobedient to the will of God, who is just.[27] This could be the case in ancient Israel in the rejection of the old greedy judges and

the establishment of the monarchy as a new social system (1 Sam. 8:1-5), the northern rejection of the exploitative dynasty of the south (1 Kings 12:16), or the purging of the monarchy around the boy king (2 Kings 11:17-20). In each case, the justice of Yahweh is not questioned, but only the social systems which claim Yahweh's legitimacy. In each case, the human agent is rejected and the divine legitimator is retained.

In our day, there are also feminist theologians who radically criticize the social system, but who in the very name of God propose a new social system, i.e., a new functioning theodicy. In the Old Testament, both modes are present: sometimes appeal is made to Yahweh against the system; sometimes appeal is also made against God, as in Job.

From this social analysis of theodicy, the conclusions of Jon Gunnemann follow.[28] Social *revolution* of a serious and sustained kind is in fact an act of *theodicy*. The precondition of revolution is a theodicy that declares that some should be happy and others should be miserable because they lack access to the blessings. Revolution happens when that theodicy is perceived as unacceptably unjust. That is, every stable society assigns persons to places in life that are relatively powerful or powerless. That arrangement is necessary to maintain equilibrium; it feeds on a functionalist sociology. Serious revolution, as Gunnemann characterizes it, is not simply an effort to transfer goods and rights of special benefits from one group to another. It is rather a rejection of the ground rules, a challenge to the paradigm that makes this arrangement possible. It is an attempt to change the rules of access and distribution so that a more just and humane practice can be initiated. What appears as *order* to some will be experienced by others as *exploitation*. What appears as *subversion* on the part of the old regime may be perceived as *quest for justice* on the part of those who undertake the change. What the old regime regards as *sacred nomos* is seen by others to be *legitimated lawlessness*, but nonetheless lawlessness, *anomie*.[29] And so, drastic alternatives are required that change the rules of the game. That surely is what the exodus is about in Israel and every appeal that is subsequently made to that tradition.

Thus, our understanding of theodicy includes the following dimensions:

Theodicy is a *religious crisis* about the character of God.
Theodicy is a *social crisis* that doubts the social settlement of goods and
    power and assaults the legitimation of that settlement.
Theodicy is *revolutionary action* that seeks to displace the rules of the
    game.

Miranda's comment merits our attention because it affirms to us that psalmic spirituality is preoccupied with the question of theodicy, though the question may be put in any of these three dimensions. This conviction may help us understand and appreciate why it is that the Psalms frequently and pervasively speak about the "righteous" and the "wicked," about the *righteousness of God* and the trustworthy *rule of God*. What emerges from this dominant vocabulary is that Israel is not interested in spirituality or communion with God that tries to deny or obscure the important issue of theodicy. An unjust relation with God is no relation at all. A skewed communion is not a communion worth having. The Psalms crave for and mediate communion with God, but Israel insists that communion must be honest, open to criticism, and capable of transformation. These are the prayers of a people with a deep memory of liberation and a profound hope for a new kingdom. This people is not prepared to submit again to the yoke of injustice as they had done in Egypt (cf. Gal. 5:1). The Psalms suggest that Israel is nearly incapable of an address to God that does not confront the issue of justice and righteousness.

The issue may be handled in two ways, as we have suggested above. On the one hand, in a few texts *God, along with the social system*, seems to be rejected. In these harsh statements, the critique is made not only of "the enemy" but also of God who has been unjust or absent. In those extreme cases, the issue of theodicy is acute and painful, because in fact the psalmist has no other court of appeal and so must come back in appeal to the very one who has been accused.[30] In these cases, the prayer questions whether God is just, without even speaking of the social system God legitimates.

On the other hand, more often, appeal is made to God, *against the system*. In those cases God is assumed to be just and faithful, but it is "the enemy" who has perverted God's way and so must be judged. In that case, the appeal to God makes sense, for it is against one who has violated God's known will.[31]

The *vocabulary* of justice and righteousness, of wickedness and innocence, as well as the *forms* of accusation, lament, and thanksgiving, prepare us for a sustained reflection on the theme.

We have seen that the psalms of orientation tend to be consolidating, stability-enhancing, and inclined to urge conformity. These psalms reflect a theodicy that is accepted and celebrated without question. They reflect society "in a state of homeostatic equilibrium."[32] They mean to affirm the order, to generate new allegiance to the order, to give the order more power and authority, and to inculcate the young into it. This may be an act of good faith, but such a voice also benefits from the present arrangement.

Therefore, even if there is not a social crisis, the social arrangement is no less a theodicy. It means to affirm and insist that the *nomos* holds, and the way to life is to submit to this unquestioned order.[33]

In this religion God is indeed confessed as equitable and just. And for these people the present arrangement, blessed by God, does yield an abundant life. These psalms, as Mowinckel understood, not only celebrate *nomos*, but generate it.

When these psalms are used, that is their function. And so, a spirituality that focuses on these psalms is not likely to be disinterested. It celebrates the coherence of life and the justice of God because that is how they are experienced. This is life fully oriented, finding the current rules on earth and in heaven adequate. Such a spirituality intends to keep life fully oriented.

Gunnemann, quoting Johnson, uses our terminology. Such a theodicy may "define violence as action that deliberately or unintentionally disorientates the behavior of others."[34] Then revolution is treated as a "disease."[35]

From this perspective, we may observe three dimensions of disorientation that are commonly treated as pathological:

It is pathological to challenge the present order of economic and political power.
It is pathological to suggest that God may be unjust.
It is pathological to speak, as some of these psalms do, in a voice of disorientation.[36]

The psalms of disorientation occur and make sense to us when the consensus about theodicy has collapsed and there is a crisis in the ordering of life. We have explored a variety of directions in which these psalms may develop. The fact that they take many different postures is not difficult to understand. It is because in a season of disarray one does not know how best to move. Three strategies are evident, following the three foci that Westermann has discerned:

1. They are a *yearning for retaliation* against the unjust enemy who has made life so disoriented.

2. They are *assaults on Yahweh* as the legitimator of the theodicy, because on some occasions not only is the social system awry, but the God who legitimates the system seems also to have failed. Not only the *nomos*, but the *guarantor of nomos* is in question. This speech is incredibly bold, because the speaker has nowhere to address the speech except back to the same agent.

3. Occasionally the speech of disorientation has a yearning for a *return to the orientation* and is able to accept the fault, as in "the seven psalms."[37] But even in these, the righteousness of God is discerned as something other than it had been perceived. The righteousness of God becomes a point of appeal that lies outside the standard explanations.

In any case, this speech is revolutionary in that it violates the conventions of the fully ordered world. But Gunneman observes that such speeches of violence "may have a meaning that *does* orient the behavior of others, namely, the members of a revolutionary party, or of a marginal group, or of a social class; or it may represent the attempt on the part of such groups to bring into being a new system of meaning for the society as a whole. Revolutionary violence disorients only those who remain committed to the established order or those against whom the violence is directed.''[38]

I find Gunnemann most helpful, though I have to some extent changed the terms of his analysis. In the Psalms we do not have violent acts, but only violent speech. And the violent speech is often directed against Yahweh, who is perceived on occasion as the perpetrator of violence. What is important in this analysis is that the aim is to ''bring into being a new system of meaning for the society as a whole.''[39] But a new system of meaning will not come without abrasion, and that is what these psalms offer. A disruptive break with the *theodicy of consensus* is a prerequisite to a new *theodicy of justice*.

The psalms of new orientation celebrate a new settlement of the issue of theodicy. The crisis is past, and there is again a stable paradigm for social life. Revolutions do not so readily succeed, but in the life of the liturgy, one advances the hunch and hopes that this result will come. The liturgical event is a foretaste of the real settlement. So these psalms of new orientation speak about the new state of things when life is whole and well-ordered, when the system is just and God is known to be righteous and just. It is for that reason that the starting point for such psalms may be either the songs of personal thanksgiving or the enthronement psalms. In the former, one has had an intimate and undeniable *experience of new order*. In the latter, one gives public articulation to the *establishment of a new governance* that has moved decisively against the idols that are the agents of unjust order.[40] What is clear in these psalms is that this is not a return to the old theodicy. There is here no knuckling under to the old regime, the old God. There is rather a celebration of the coming of God, who now establishes a new rule. In the language of the sociologist, this is the establishment of a reliable *nomos*. In the parallel language of Israel, it is the governance or the torah that matters. And these psalms reveal a happy readiness to live according to the *nomos* that now replaces the old *nomos*, which had been so distorted that it was in fact a way of *anomie*.

With this analysis of theodicy, we may now return to the matter of the Psalms as resources for spirituality. The Psalms are resources for spirituality, but any psalmic spirituality that denies or avoids the parallel issue of theodicy misses the point. That is, the spirituality of the Psalms is shaped, defined, and characterized in specific historical, experiential categories and shuns universals. Such recognition does not require a fresh exegesis of each psalm, so much as hermeneutical insistence about the categories through which the psalms are to be understood. The Psalms have been central to a spirituality which is individualistic, otherworldly, or centers on a quest for meaning. But if I read it rightly, these Psalms characteristically subordinate ''meaning'' to ''justice.'' The Psalms regularly insist upon equity, power, and freedom enough to live one's life humanely. The Psalms may not be taken out of such a context of community concerns.

When we pray these Psalms, in community or in private, we are surrounded by a cloud of witnesses who count on our prayers. Those witnesses include first of all the Jews who have cried out against Pharaoh and other oppressors. But the cloud of witnesses includes all those who hope for justice and liberation. This does not detract from the conviction that God is powerful Spirit. It does not reduce the Psalms to political documents. It rather insists that our spirituality must answer to the God who is present where the questions of justice and order, transformation and equilibrium are paramount. We dare not be positivists about our spirituality, as though we live in a world in which all issues are settled. The spirituality of the Psalms assumes that the world is called to question in this conversation with God. That permits and requires that our conversation with God be vigorous, candid, and daring. God assumes different roles in these conversations. At times God is the guarantor of the old equilibrium. At other times God is a harbinger of the new justice to be established. At times also God is in the disorientation, being sovereign in ways that do not strike us as adequate. We might wish for a God removed from such a dynamic, for a spirituality not so inclined to conflict. But the Psalms reject such a way with God as false to our daily life, and false to the memories of this people, who know they do not belong to the Egyptian empire but who hope for a new equilibrium in a kingdom of justice and righteousness. On this the Psalter insists passionately, vigorously, with boldness.

Notes

Preface

1. Brevard S. Childs, "Some Reflections on the Search for a Biblical Theology," *Horizons in Biblical Theology* 4 (1982):1-12, has powerfully made the case that the believing community is an important and indispensable reference for doing biblical theology. He does not suggest this to the neglect or disregard of the academy, nor do I. On the use of the Psalms in a pastoral context, see the general statement of Stephen G. Meyer, "The Psalms and Personal Counseling," *Journal of Psychology and Theology* 2 (1974):26-30, and the more helpful statement of Erich Vellmer, "Psalmen in einen Krankenhaus," *Textgemass*, ed. A. H. J. Gunneweg and Otto Kaiser (Göttingen: Vandenhoeck & Ruprecht, 1979), pp. 156-68.
2. Peter Berger and Thomas Luckmann, *The Social Construction of Reality* (Garden City, N.Y.: Doubleday and Co., 1966).
3. Among the more important sociological efforts in Old Testament study are Robert R. Wilson, *Prophecy and Society in Ancient Israel* (Philadelphia: Fortress Press, 1980), and Paul Hanson, *The Dawn of Apocalyptic* (Philadelphia: Fortress Press, 1975). Norman Gottwald, *The Tribes of Yahweh* (Maryknoll, N.Y.: Orbis Books, 1979), has provided a major stimulus for such an approach.
4. Rhetorical analysis in scripture study was given major impetus by the programmatic statement of James Muilenburg, "Form Criticism and Beyond," *JBL* 88 (1969):1-18. Among the more important works from this perspective are those of Phyllis Trible, *God and the Rhetoric of Sexuality* (Philadelphia: Fortress Press, 1978), and David M. Gunn, *The Fate of King Saul* (Sheffield: University of Sheffield, 1980) and *The Story of King David* (Sheffield: University of Sheffield, 1978). Mention should be made also of the work of Robert Polzin, *Moses and the Deuteronomist* (New York: Seabury Press, 1980), though his methodology is somewhat different. His introductory chapter is an especially important statement about the shift in methods.
5. On the royal psalms, see Keith R. Crim, *The Royal Psalms* (Richmond: John Knox

Press, 1962), and Aubrey Johnson, *Sacral Kingship* (Cardiff: University of Wales Press, 1967).

6. The "songs of Zion" include Psalms 46, 48, 84, 87, 122.

7. The psalms of historical recital include 78, 105, 106, 135, 136. Von Rad, "The Problem of the Hexateuch," in *The Problem of the Hexateuch and Other Essays* (New York: McGraw-Hill, 1966), pp. 48-78, has helped put these psalms in perspective in relation to the developing tradition.

8. On the fresh perspective of these radical prophetic traditions, see von Rad, *Old Testament Theology*, vol. 2 (New York: Harper and Row, 1965), pp. 263-77.

9. Brevard S. Childs, *Introduction to the Old Testament as Scripture* (Philadelphia: Fortress Press, 1979), pp. 515-18.

10. Finally, one must face the theological claim of the text. This is a literature of radical faith. It insists that the God addressed here is not the self writ large, but is in fact a response to the reality of this God, who is known in this particular history of darkness and darkness transformed. On the reality of this faith, see Hans-Joachim Kraus, *Theologie der Psalmen* (Neukirchen-Vluyn: Neukirchener Verlag, 1979), especially chaps. 1 and 6.

11. Cf. John Updike, *Rabbit Is Rich* (New York: Knopf, 1981), pp. 243, for the quote in the frontispiece.

12. Michael Scrogin, "Symbol of the Valley of the Shadow," *The Christian Century*, January 5, 1983, p. 8.

13. Jose Miranda, *Communism in the Bible* (Maryknoll, N.Y.: Orbis Books, 1981), p. 44, has provided the other point of reference in the statement in the frontispiece.

14. Stanley Hauerwas, *A Community of Character* (Notre Dame: University of Notre Dame, 1981), with his play on *Watership Down*, has offered a very different perspective on "Rabbit." So I make a play on the term *rabbit* from Updike to Hauerwas. The difference between these two species of rabbit is regular participation in a transformative liturgy (storytelling) which disorientates and reorientates.

Chapter 1

1. Gerhard von Rad, *Old Testament Theology* (New York: Harper and Row, 1962), pp. 365-70.

2. I do not intend "precritical" in a pejorative way, nor do I suggest that such treatments are inferior. I mean to say only that they are treatments of the Psalms that have not made use of the scholarly categories derived from the work of Gunkel, Mowinckel, and Westermann. The authors included here indicate that such a precritical use does not preclude a perceptive and powerful hearing of the Psalms. Among such works are the following: Dietrich Bonhoeffer, *Psalms: the Prayer Book of the Bible* (Minneapolis: Augsburg Publishing House, 1970); Solomon B. Freihof, *The Book of Psalms* (Cincinnati: Union of American Congregations, 1938); Michael Gasnier, *The Psalms, School of Spirituality* (St. Louis: B. Herder, 1962); C. S. Lewis, *Reflections on the Psalms* (New York: Harcourt, Brace and Co., 1958); Rose Agnes MacCauley, *Twenty Psalms for the Twentieth Century* (Notre Dame, Ind.: Fides Publishers, 1971); Thomas Merton, *Bread in the Wilderness* (Collegeville, Minn.: The Liturgical Press, 1963); David Rosenberg, *Blues of the Sky* (New York: Harper and Row, 1976).

These writers—Jewish, Catholic, and Protestants—are deeply rooted in traditions of piety and liturgy. My discussion does not depreciate such an approach, but intends to show that critical analysis aids and does not detract from a faithful hearing. Conversely it is evident that much critical study lacks the power and vitality of the precritical hearing, which therefore must be taken into account.

3. See James S. Preus, "Old Testament *Promissio* and Luther's New Hermeneutic," *HTR* 60 (1967): 145-61, and more generally Heinrich Bornkamm, *Luther and the Old Testament* (Philadelphia: Fortress Press, 1969).

4. See Hans-Joachim Kraus, *Theologie der Psalmen* (Neukirchen-Vluyn: Neukirchener Verlag, 1979), p. 11.

5. Quoted from Calvin's preface to his *Commentary on the Psalms* by Ford L. Battles and Stanley Tagg, *The Piety of John Calvin* (Grand Rapids: Baker Book House, 1978), p. 27. Cf. S. H. Russell, "Calvin and the Messianic Interpretation of the Psalms," *SJT* 21 (1968):37-47.

6. On the history of critical scholarship, see A. R. Johnson, "The Psalms," in *The Old Testament and Modern Study*, ed. H. H. Rowley (Oxford: Clarendon Press, 1951), pp. 162-209; Ronald Clements, *One Hundred Years of Old Testament Interpretation*, chap. 5 (Philadelphia: Westminister Press, 1976); John H. Hayes, *An Introduction to Old Testament Study*, chap. 8 (Nashville: Abingdon Press, 1978); and J. H. Eaton, "The Psalms and Israelite Worship," in *Tradition and Interpretation*, ed. George W. Anderson (Oxford: Clarendon Press, 1979), pp. 238-73.

7. See Hermann Gunkel, *The Psalms* (Philadelphia: Fortress Press, 1967), his own introduction to his study of the Psalms and one of his few statements on the Psalms available in English.

8. See Erhard Gerstenberger, "Psalms," in *Old Testament Form Criticism*, ed. John H. Hayes (San Antonio: Trinity University Press, 1974), pp. 179-223.

9. Sigmund Mowinckel, *The Psalms in Israel's Worship* (Nashville: Abingdon Press, 1962). Unfortunately, his epoch-making study, *Psalmenstudien*, 6 vols. (1921-24), has never been translated. Eaton, *op. cit.*, has a special inclination for this approach.

10. A lucid statement parallel to that of Mowinckel is offered by A. R. Johnson, *Sacral Kingship in Ancient Israel* (Cardiff: University of Wales, 1955).

11. See the especially fine study of Psalms related to liturgy by Harvey H. Guthrie Jr., *Theology as Thanksgiving* (New York: Seabury Press, 1981).

12. Claus Westermann, *The Psalms, Structure, Content, and Message* (Minneapolis: Augsburg Publishing House, 1980); *Praise and Lament in the Psalms* (Atlanta: John Knox Press, 1981); and "The Role of the Lament in the Theology of the Old Testament," *Interpretation* 28 (1974):20-38.

13. See my preliminary statement of this model, "Psalms and the Life of Faith: A Suggested Typology of Function," *JSOT* 17 (1980):3-32. See the subsequent exchange with John Goldingay, "The Dynamic Cycle of Praise and Prayer," *JSOT* 20 (1981): 85-90, and my response, "Response to John Goldingay's 'The Dynamic Cycle of Praise and Prayer,' " *JSOT* 22 (1982):141-42.

14. By a very different route, Brevard S. Childs, "Reflections on Modern Study of Psalms," in *Magnalia Dei: The Mighty Acts of God*, ed. Frank Moore Cross, Werner Lemke, and Patrick D. Miller Jr. (Garden City, N.Y.: Doubleday & Co., 1976), p. 384, arrives at the conclusion that the finished form of the Psalms correlates with human experience: "David is pictured simply as a man, indeed chosen by God for the sake of Israel, but one who displays the strengths and weaknesses of

all men....The titles, far from tying these poems to the ancient past, serve to con-
temporize and individualize them for every generation of suffering and persecuted
Israel.''

15. It may be helpful to see the lament speech in relation to situations of distress as an
example of a ''limit speech'' commensurate with a ''limit experience.'' Cf. Paul
Ricoeur, ''Biblical Hermeneutics,'' *Semeia* 4 (1975):108-135.

16. See George Benson's experiential exploration of this theme, *Then Joy Breaks
Through* (New York: Seabury Press, 1972).

17. The discernment of the two moves is illuminated by Ricoeur's presentation of two
hermeneutical postures, a hermeneutic of suspicion and a hermeneutic of restoration. Cf. Ricoeur, *Conflict of Interpretation* (Evanston: Northwestern University
Press, 1974), and L. Dornisch, ''Symbolic Systems and the Interpretation of Scripture,'' *Semeia* 4 (1975):6-7.

18. See the personal exploration of this theme by Robert McAfee Brown, *Creative Dislocation* (Nashville: Abingdon Press, 1980).

19. On this narrative presentation marked by specificity, see Westermann, *The Psalms,
Structure, Content, and Message*, chap. 2, and Guthrie, *op. cit.* Note especially
chap. 1 of Guthrie, where this way of speech is contrasted with the myths of maintenance. On pp. 18-20 Guthrie offers an insightful analysis of the probable social
context of this speech form.

20. See the statement of Goldingay cited in n. 13 and my response on this schematiza-
tion. The scheme should not be read too tightly and certainly not cyclically. It is offered simply as a means of relating speech form to actual life experience. My purpose is to show that critical categories can greatly enhance a more existential reading of the Psalms.

21. Bernhard Anderson, *Out of the Depths* (Philadelphia: Westminster Press, 1983),
pp. 243-45, has provided a list of New Testament usages. These should be
consulted to see the ways in which the Psalms were understood and used with reference to the history of Jesus.

22. See especially Robert Jay Lifton, *The Broken Connection* (New York: Simon and
Schuster, 1979).

Chapter 2

1. Claus Westermann, *Praise and Lament in the Psalms* (Atlanta: John Knox Press,
1981), pp. 116-42.

2. Westermann, *Elements of Old Testament Theology* (Atlanta: John Knox Press,
1978), pp. 102-104, has a poignant articulation of this point. See more generally
Part III and the parallel statement in *What Does the Old Testament Say About
God?*, pt. 3 (Atlanta: John Knox Press, 1979).

3. On *nomos* and *anomie* see Peter Berger, *The Sacred Canopy* (Garden City, N.Y.:
Doubleday & Co., 1967), pp. 19-28 and passim, and Robert Merton, *Social Structure and Social Process*, chaps. 4-5 (Glencoe, Ill.: The Free Press, 1957). James L.
Crenshaw, *Forsaken by God* (Philadelphia: Fortress Press, 1984), has explored the
ways in which these elemental certitudes are experienced as being in jeopardy.

4. Berger makes the case well that the ''canopy'' must not only appear stable and reliable, but also equitable. It is striking and unexpected that his third chapter is on theodicy, reflecting the sense that the sacred canopy won't hold. See Jon P.

Gunnemann, *The Moral Meaning of Revolution*, chap. 2 (New Haven: Yale University Press, 1979), on the political and revolutionary dimensions of the issue of theodicy. Unfortunately, theodicy has been generally treated as a speculative or spiritual problem. Gunnemann shows that it really has to do with the rules of the game being called into question, the rules ordering social power and economic goods.

5. See Berger, pp. 41-42, on the power of religious legitimation. See Robert Jay Lifton, *The Broken Connection* (New York: Simon and Schuster, 1979), especially chaps. 1-4, on the capacity of religious symbolization to keep things connected when they appear to be chaotic and disconnected.

6. The creative function of liturgy to "make worlds" (which Berger calls "world construction") is what lies behind Mowinckel's New Year Enthronement Festival hypothesis. Unfortunately, the power of his insight has been lost in two directions. On the one hand, his hypothesis has fallen into the hands of historical critics who have asked the wrong questions and have missed the point. On the other hand, the devotees of "myth" as an intellectual category have largely turned out to be rationalists who have understood myth as a rational, structural concept without reference to the liturgical enterprise through which myth has any continuing power or credibility. As S. H. Hooke and his associates have understood, myth without ritual is an absurdity without the vitality of imagination, passion, or commitment. At this point the norms of critical scholarship have likely worked negatively in understanding the Psalms. On the deadening reduction of imagination to concept, see Paul Ricoeur, *The Philosophy of Paul Ricoeur*, ed. Charles E. Reagan and David Steward (Boston: Beacon Press, 1978), pp. 223-45.

7. On the world-forming power of narrative/liturgy, see John Dominic Crossan, *The Dark Interval* (Niles, Ill.: Argus Communications, 1975), and more formally, Anthony Thistleton, *The Two Horizons* (Grand Rapids: Eerdmans, 1980), especially pp. 335-356.

8. On "redescribing," see Paul Ricoeur, "Biblical Hermeneutics," *Semeia* 4 (1975): 31, 127, and passim.

9. See Harvey H. Guthrie Jr., *Theology as Thanksgiving* (New York: Seabury Press, 1981), pp. 18-19: "From the temple-palace complex at the highest place in the kingdom, the place nearest to heaven, the order and security ensured by the cosmic sovereign flowed out into the city within whose walls people were safe under the protection of the king, the vice-regent of the cosmic sovereign...order is the more diluted the farther one goes from the temple-palace of the cosmic sovereign or the human king."

10. This point has been especially well articulated by Gustav Wingren, *Creation and Law* (Philadelphia: Fortress Press, 1958), pp. 92-93 and passim. His analysis is focused on the German experience, but is also generally illuminating. For a very different kind of analysis, see George Mendenhall, "The Shady Side of Wisdom," in *A Light Unto My Path*, ed. Howard N. Bream, Ralph D. Heim, Carey A. Moore (Philadelphia: Temple University Press, 1974), pp. 319-34. Both Wingren and Mendenhall consider the trap in which creation faith becomes a "mere cultural authority symbol" (Mendenhall, p. 333).

11. Brevard S. Childs, *Introduction to the Old Testament as Scripture* (Philadelphia: Fortress Press, 1979), p. 518, concludes: "However one explains it, the final form of the Psalter is highly eschatology in nature." The scholarly debate has tended to divide, either following Gunkel in an eschatological interpretation, or Mowinckel

in a cultic reading. But what needs to be seen afresh is that good liturgical activity which evokes and receives God is the gift of a new world (new creation) and is always eschatological in the sense that it subverts the old world now being superseded by the new world generated in the liturgical process. The eschatological and cultic dimensions must be held together or both will be misunderstood.

12. On the function and intent of the acrostic structure, see Norman Gottwald, *Studies in the Book of Lamentations*, chap. 1 (Chicago: Alec R. Allenson, Inc., 1954).

13. Rainer Albertz, *Persönliche Frömmigkeit und offizielle Religion* (Stuttgart: Calwer Verlag, 1978), has stated well the polarity and tension between such personal intimate religion and the large claims of the public cult. For our theme of "songs of creation," see also his earlier study, *Weltschöpfung und Menschenschöpfung* (Stuttgart: Calwer Verlag, 1974).

14. On the voice of created order as a disclosure of God, see von Rad, *Wisdom in Israel*, chap. 9 (Nashville: Abingdon Press, 1972).

15. See Glendon E. Bryce, *A Legacy of Wisdom* (Lewisburg, Pa.: Bucknell University Press, 1979), chap. 6.

16. On the development of this theological characterization, see Phyllis Trible, *God and the Rhetoric of Sexuality* (Philadelphia: Fortress Press, 1978), chap. 1 and the works by Dentan and Freedman cited there.

17. Popular theology is more informed by scholastic or even Stoic notions of God that speak of self-sufficiency, omnipresence, omnipotence, omniscience, terms not appropriate to Israel's primal characterization of God. The interpretative issues in this notion of God "from above" become clear when one sees the ways in which the suffering availability of God is experienced and expressed by Third World believers. See *Living Theology in Asia*, ed. John C. Knight (Maryknoll, N.Y.: Orbis Books, 1981), especially the essays by Kim Yong-Bok and Takao Toshikazu.

18. See Erik Erikson, *Identity and the Life Cycle* (New York: International Universities Press, 1959), pp. 55-65 and passim.

19. See "all" in vv. 14 (2), 15, 16, 17 (2), 18 (2), 20 (2). See Brueggemann, *Genesis* (Atlanta: John Knox Press, 1982), pp. 328-29, where I have contrasted this use of "all" for God's generosity with the "all" of social control in the Egyptian empire under Joseph.

20. See Norman Gottwald, *The Tribes of Yahweh* (Maryknoll, N.Y.: Orbis Books, 1979), pp. 686-88, on the dialectic of this two-sided affirmation and the social function of such an ambivalence.

21. Mitchell Dahood, *Psalms*, vol. 3 (Garden City, N.Y.: Doubleday & Co., 1970), p. 335, characterizes Ps. 145 as a "litany of sacred names."

22. *The Heidelberg Catechism* (Philadelphia: United Church Press, 1962), answer 27.

23. John Calvin, *Commentary on the Book of Psalms* (Grand Rapids: Baker Book House, 1979), p. 149.

24. *Ibid.*, p. 170.

25. Though it should not be pressed, the correlation of these themes to the Lord's Prayer may be noted: *(a)* deliverance from danger: "Deliver us from evil"; *(b)* protection from dangerous situations: "Lead us not into temptation"; *(c)* the overriding name of God: "Hallowed be thy name," on which see Karl Barth, *Church Dogmatics*, vol. 4, 4 (Grand Rapids: Eerdmanns, 1981), pp. 47-260. Barth has based his exposition of the Christian life on response to God's name, modeled after the Lord's Prayer.

26. Not to see God as faithful and not to respond in trust is what von Rad, *op. cit.*, p. 65, means by "practical atheism" = "folly."

27. John Calvin, *Institutes of Christian Religion*, vol. 1, 6, 2 (Philadelphia: Westminister Press, 1960), p. 72, asserts, "All right knowledge of God is born of obedience." See Charles M. Wood, "The Knowledge Born of Obedience," *ATR* 61 (1979):331-40.

28. Ps. 104:23 is a noteworthy exception to this, but a slight one given the extent of the psalm. Even there, it is followed by vv. 27-30, asserting that all creatures are radically dependent on God's attentiveness.

29. It is not clear that Psalm 8 derives from Genesis 1. The influence could be in the other direction, suggesting that the narrative derives from the doxology. Clearly creation faith is primarily doxological in its articulation.

30. See Brevard S. Childs, *Biblical Theology in Crisis* (Philadelphia: Westminister Press, 1970), pp. 151-63.

31. Hosea 4:1-3 presents a characteristic view that violation of torah (v. 2) leads to the undoing of creation (v. 3).

32. It is widely recognized that the placement of Psalm 1 at the beginning is an introduction to the entire collection. Claus Westermann, *Praise and Lament in the Psalms* (Atlanta: John Knox Press, 1981), pp. 250-258, has studied the way in which the various collections of the Psalms have been arranged. He has observed that Psalm 150 is a concluding doxology for the present book of Psalms (p. 256). But he has not suggested a relationship between Psalm 1 and Psalm 150. It seems possible that the present shape of the collection is designed to announce that a life grounded in obedience, leads precisely to doxology. Basil de Pinto, "The Torah and the Psalms," *JBL* 86 (1967):154-174, has shown that "torah spirituality" is pervasive in the Psalter.

33. Peter Berger, *The Sacred Canopy* (Garden City, N.Y.: Doubleday & Co., 1967), p. 22, writes of the legitimacy of *nomos* as permitting "the individual to have an ultimate sense of rightness, both cognitively and normatively...." The torah functions so in these psalms.

34. Berger, *ibid.*, p. 22, says *nomos* is a "shield against terror." What torah does for human community, God's creation decree has done for creation. Cf. Jer. 5:22. Cf. Berger, p. 26, on opposition to "chaos."

35. On the problem of transmitting this sense of *nomos* to the next generation, see Berger, *op. cit.*, p. 15. Michael Fishbane, *Text and Texture* (New York: Schocken, 1979), pp. 81-82, has an eloquent comment on Deut. 6:20-25 related to our theme: "Deuteronomy 6:20-25 discloses a tension between two generations' memories, sets of experiences and commitments. It questions the ability of fathers to transmit their laws and faith to their sons, who see these as alien and do not feel the same responsibility concerning them. ...That the fathers would want a continuity through their sons of their special relationship with God is understandable. But what was subjective and immediate to them is seen as objective and mediate to their sons. These latter have not experienced the experiences of the fathers, nor have they subjectivized and internalized them. One, in fact, suspects that Moses felt this intergenerational tension most poignantly. ...The teaching of the fathers in Deuteronomy 6:20-25 is an attempt to involve their sons in the covenant community of the future, and undoubtedly reflects the sociological reality of the settlement in Canaan. The attempt by fathers to transform their uninvolved sons from '*distempo-*

raries' to '*contemporaries*,' i.e., time-life sharers, is an issue of supreme and recurrent significance in the Bible.''

36. John Calvin, *Commentary on the Book of Psalms*, vol. 4 (Grand Rapids: Baker Book House, 1979), p. 400, n.1, comments, ''It is by far the longest, the most artificial and most diversified; yet in proportion to its length, it contains the fewest ideas of any in the book.''

37. Cf. Deut. 4:7-8 in which ''a God so near'' and ''statutes and ordinances so righteous'' are set in a peculiar juxtaposition. Obviously they are intimately related to each other. But it is equally clear that they are not synonymous. Israel knows that the commandments do not comprehend all there is of God.

38. It is worth noting that the capacity of torah to ''restore life'' (Ps. 19:7) is a close parallel to the very gift of God (Ps. 23:3); i.e., torah bestows the gift of life, as does Yahweh.

39. See the recent and helpful clarification of this point by Rick D. Moore, ''The Integrity of Job,'' *CBQ* 45 (1983):17-31.

40. On ''Yahweh as portion,'' see Gerhard von Rad, '''Righteousness' and 'Life' in the Cultic Language of the Psalms,'' in *The Problem of the Hexateuch and Other Essays* (New York: McGraw Hill, 1966), pp. 260-66, and Walter Zimmerli, *Old Testament Theology in Outline* (Atlanta: John Knox Press, 1978), pp. 93-99.

41. On entry into the sanctuary as the gate of life, see von Rad, ibid., pp. 243-66.

42. On the wisdom psalms, see Roland Murphy, ''A Consideration of the Classification 'Wisdom Psalms,' '' *SVT* 9 (1962):156-67, and Sigmund Mowinckel, ''Psalms and Wisdom,'' *SVT* 3 (1955):205-24. It is clear that I am not here interested in that entire set of psalms, for I have no interest in such a general grouping. Here I deal only with those wisdom psalms that reflect a well-oriented life of faith. Many of the wisdom psalms reflect the question of theodicy when that orientation has been unhappily violated. Wisdom psalms that seem to relate to elemental life situations include Psalms 127 and 128.

43. Philip J. Nel, *The Structure and Ethos of the Wisdom Admonition* (Berlin: Walter de Gruyter, 1982), has made the case that the motivation clause is a part of the completed form of the admonition. For a general summary of wisdom forms, many of which are present in this psalm, see chap. 2.

44. On order as the key agenda of wisdom instruction, see von Rad, *Wisdom in Israel*, chap. 5 (Nashville: Abingdon Press, 1972), and the fine popular summary of Roland Murphy, *Wisdom Literature and Psalms* (Nashville: Abingdon Press, 1983), pp. 25-42.

45. On the orientation of wisdom to a propertied class, see Brian W. Kovacs, ''Is there a Class-Ethic in Proverbs?'' in *Essays in Old Testament Ethics*, ed. James L. Crenshaw and John T. Willis (New York: KTAV, 1974), pp. 173-89; Robert Gordis, *Prophets, Prophets and Sages*, chap. 6 (Bloomington: Indiana University Press, 1971); and George Mendenhall, ''The Shady Side of Wisdom: The Date and Purpose of Genesis 3,'' in *A Light Unto my Path*, ed. Howard N. Bream, Ralph D. Heim, Carey A. Moore (Philadelphia: Temple University Press, 1974), pp. 319-334.

46. It makes a great deal of difference whether אֶרֶץ is rendered as ''earth'' or as ''land.'' As soon as it is rendered ''land,'' political power questions enter into consideration.

47. On ''the meek,'' see George W. Coats, ''Humility and Honor: A Moses Legend in Numbers 12,'' in *Art and Meaning: Rhetoric in Biblical Literature*, ed. David J. A.

Clines, David M. Gunn, and Alan J. Hauser (Sheffield: University of Sheffield, 1982), pp. 97-107.

48. See Gerhard von Rad, *Wisdom in Israel* (New York: Abingdon Press, 1972), pp. 65, 83.

49. In his *Institutes of Christian Religion* (Philadelphia: Westminister Press, 1960), pp. 35-37, John Calvin writes: "Without knowledge of self, there is no knowledge of God...Without knowledge of God there is no knowledge of self." In a sense somewhat different from that of Calvin, this psalm holds together the possibility of a human life of righteousness and the righteousness of God. The different sense is that this psalm believes such a life is possible, whereas Calvin explores the same realities with reference to a needed savior.

50. On this passage, see George Fohrer, "The Righteous Man in Job 31," in *Essays in Old Testament Ethics*, ed. James L. Crenshaw and John T. Willis (New York: KTAV, 1974), pp. 1-22, and especially the study by Galling cited in n. 11.

51. Claus Westermann, *Elements of Old Testament Theology*, chap. 3 (Atlanta: John Knox Press, 1978). See the characterization of such family and personal religion by Rainer Albertz, *Persönliche Frömmigkeit und offizielle Religion* (Stuttgart: Calwer Verlag, 1978), esp. pp.77-96.

52. These facts of experience where God is discerned but not visible have been variously presented by Peter Berger, *A Rumor of Angels* (Garden City, N.Y.: Doubleday & Company, 1969), pp. 52-75, who names experience of order, play, hope, damnation, and humor, and by Langdon Gilkey, *Naming the Whirlwind* (New York: Seabury Press, 1969), pp. 305ff., who names contingency, meaninglessness, temporality, and freedom.

53. Calvin, *loc. cit.*, with his assumption of Davidic authorship, takes the psalm to refer to reconciliation after David had been "an enemy of the public good" and "mortal was the feud."

54. Westermann, *Elements*, p. 93, takes "good" in Genesis 1 as "beautiful." See his more extended comments in *Genesis 1-11* (Minneapolis: Augsburg Publishing House, 1984), pp. 165-167.

55. One can easily imagine that this is the yearning of the father in the parable of Luke 15:28-33. The father is not concerned only that his elder son relate to him, but that the sons relate to each other. The psalm also lends itself to an ecumenical vision for the church, which comes to fuller expression in John 17:11. Calvin makes the ecumenical point, but cannot resist one more assault on the Papists.

Chapter 3

1. On cultural optimism and its inadequacy in times of genuine dread, see Robert J. Lifton, *The Broken Connection: In Death and the Continuity of Life* (New York: Simon and Schuster, 1980). Lifton's analysis suggests that the optimism may be ideological, functioning only to cover over the power of despair.

2. On the biblical evidence concerning the immutability of God, see Terence Fretheim, *The Suffering of God* (Philadelphia: Fortress, 1984). Current efforts at process theology are designed to overcome the problem of immutability, but it is likely that Karl Barth, *Church Dogmatics*, vol. 2, 1,31 (Edinburgh: T.&T. Clark, 1957), pp. 490-522, has handled it more effectively. See the comments of James L. Mays, "Response to Janzen," *Semeia* 24 (1982):45-51, with reference to Barth.

3. See Martin E. Marty, *A Cry of Absence: Reflections for the Winter of the Heart* (New York: Harper and Row, 1982).

4. On this creative function of language with reference to "redescribing," see Paul Ricoeur, "Biblical Hermeneutics," *Semeia* 4 (1975):29ff., but especially 30-36. Sallie McFague, *Metaphorical Theology* (Philadelphia: Fortress Press, 1982), has embodied the program suggested by Ricoeur in a most remarkable and effective way.

5. On cultural ways of taming the terror and eliminating the darkness through the power and control of cultural forms, see Norbert Elias, *Power and Civility* (New York: Pantheon Books, 1982). See also the analysis of John Cuddihy, *The Ordeal of Civility* (New York: Basic Books, 1974), a study in the ways of social propriety that cover over or eliminate serious questions of social value.

6. There is no doubt that speech usage is an intense form of social control. The admonition to children, "Don't say that," is an attempt to stop the *expression* and hopefully to nullify the *experience*. No doubt the church's propensity to silence these psalms is such an exercise of social control by the censoring of speech. Note the ideological intention of silence in Mark 10:48.

7. On "limit experience" and "limit expression," see Ricoeur, *op. cit.*, pp. 108-145. Human experience is "redescribed" by the "eruption of the unheard" (p. 127).

8. McFague, *op. cit.*, pp. 177-192, has offered a most suggestive exposition of the metaphor of God as "friend."

9. See my discussion, "The Formfulness of Grief," *Interpretation* 31 (1977): 263-275.

10. On the power of the form, note the telling narrative comment of John Updike, *Rabbit Is Rich*, p. 73. In commenting on the wedding of his son Nelson, Harry is quite cynical. But he listens to the priest use the standard formulae of the Episcopal rite. He says, "Laugh at ministers all you want to, they have the words we need to hear, the ones the dead have spoken." Those words from "the dead" preserve the forms in times of chaos.

11. Hermann Gunkel, *Einleitung in die Psalmen* (Göttingen: Vandenhoeck & Ruprecht, 1933). See his brief summary in translation, *The Psalms* (Philadelphia: Fortress Press, 1967). See a summary of Gunkel's decisive contribution by Aubrey Johnson, "The Psalms," in *The Old Testament and Modern Study* (Oxford: Clarendon Press, 1951), pp. 162-81, and the more specific analysis by Erhard Gerstenberger, "The Psalms," in *Old Testament Form Criticism*, ed. John H. Hayes (San Antonio: Trinity University Press, 1974), pp. 198-205.

12. Claus Westermann, *Praise and Lament in the Psalms* (Atlanta: John Knox Press, 1981), especially p. 64. See his basic study, "Struktur und Geschichte der Klage Alten Testament," *ZAW* 66 (1954): 44-80, now reprinted in *Forschung am Alten Testament* (Munich: Chr. Kaiser Verlag, 1964), pp. 266-305.

13. Westermann, *Praise and Lament*, p. 33 and *passim*.

14. Rainer Albertz, *Persönliche Frömmigkeit und offizielle Religion* (Stuttgart: Calwer Verlag, 1978), pp. 24-37.

15. Karl Barth, *Church Dogmatics*, vol. 3, 4, 53 (1961), pp. 91-102, emphasized that serious prayer is marked by petition as it is marked by nothing else. The *asking* of Israel and the generous *response* of Yahweh characterize and define this relationship of need and care.

16. Perhaps the most intimidating motivation is that the dead cannot praise (as in Ps. 88:11) and the warning to God that the death of the speaker will diminish the praise of God. See the summary of this motif by Westermann, *Praise and Lament*, pp. 155-61. In a technical sense, this is regressive speech. As the perceived danger grows more acute, all propriety and civility are abandoned and the speech reaches the extremes of desperation.

17. See Westermann, *Praise and Lament*, pp.77-93.

18. Gerstenberger, *Der bittende Mensch* (Neukirchen-Vluyn: Neukirchener Verlag, 1980), has suggested that while the usage is not attached to the temple, it is a kind of liturgical work done in the clan or family, perhaps by the elders. It is liturgical in the sense that it is symbolic and routinized, but largely devoid of the official sanctions that usually accompany liturgy. In ''Der klagende Mensch,'' in *Probleme biblischen Theologie*, ed. Hans Walter Wolff (Munich: Chr. Kaiser Verlag, 1971), p. 69, he uses this formula: ''...kultisch gebundene und doch vom Heiligtum unabhängige....''

19. This is indeed the making of a new world through the ''social construction of reality.'' It is the argument of McFague that this is the purpose of metaphor. On the social function and social possibility of such work, see Peter L. Berger, *A Rumor of Angels* (Garden City, N.Y.: Doubleday, 1969) pp. 54, 63, on the role of the parent: ''To become a parent is to take on the role of world-builder and world-protector.'' The Psalms function in such a way.

20. Joachim Begrich, ''Das priesterliche Heilsorakel,'' *ZAW* 52 (1934):81-92, now reprinted in *Gasammelte Studien zum Alten Testament* (Munich: Chr. Kaiser Verlag, 1964), pp. 217-31. See the critical analysis of the hypothesis by Thomas M. Raitt, *A Theology of Exile* (Philadelphia: Fortress Press, 1977), esp. chap. 6. See also Edgar W. Conrad, ''Second Isaiah and the Priestly Oracle of Salvation,'' *ZAW* 93 (1981), 234-46.

21. Among the psalms frequently included in the grouping are 3, 4, 5, 7, 10, 17, 22, 25, 26, 28, 31, 39, 42, 43, 54, 55, 56, 57, 59, 61, 64, 69, 70, 71, 77, 120, 140, 141, 142. In addition, psalms treated as a special group of ''seven penitential psalms'' (6, 32, 38, 51, 102, 130, 143) may also be regarded as individual laments.

22. We may observe the strange configuration of theological assumptions here. On the one hand, it is conventional to refer everything to God, to assume that if something is wrong, it has to do with our part of relationship with God. But on the other hand, there is the assumption, quite unconventional to us, that what is wrong in relation to God may be God's fault and not the fault of the speaker. Thus at the same time, the relationship is taken with great seriousness, and the relationship is open to a harsh conversation between two partners, both of whom are at risk. Westermann, *Praise and Lament*, pp. 259-280, makes the point that these psalms are statements of protest, not submission.

23. On the creative, evocative power of rhetorical questions, see Gerald Janzen, ''Metaphor and Reality in Hosea 11,'' *Semeia* 24 (1982):7-44.

24. On the formula of God's distinctiveness, see C. J. Labuschagne, *The Incomparability of Yahweh in the Old Testament* (Leiden: Brill, 1966). On the uneasiness of Israel with these formulations in subsequent theological reflection, see Robert Polzin, *Moses and the Deuteronomist* (New York: Seabury Press, 1980), pp. 35-46.

25. We have seen this cluster of words in our exposition of Psalm 145.
26. On this theological theme, see my article, " 'Impossibility' and Epistemology in the Faith Tradition of Abraham and Sarah (Gen. 18:1-15)," *ZAW* 94 (1982): 615-34.
27. The formula, "Thou alone art God," is parallel to the affirmation made twice in Hezekiah's prayer in 2 Kings 19:15,19.
28. On the power of the creedal memory to invert situations of darkness, see my discussion, "Psalm 77—The 'Turn' from Self to God," *Journal for Preachers* 6 (1983):8-14.
29. Gerstenberger, "Der klagende Mensch," *Probleme biblischer Theologie*, 64-72, makes the point decisively that the laments in Israel are not acts of despair but of hopelessness. So on p. 72, "Alle Klage Israels hofft auf einen Durchbruch." In his article, "Jeremiah's Complaints: Observations on Jer. 15:10-21," *JBL* 82 (1963):405, n. 50, he has made a hopeful distinction in that regard between *Klagen*, which are acts of resignation, and *Anklagen*, which are acts of hopeful insistence. In that regard see his reference to Westermann in "Der klagende Mensch," n. 33.
30. On the "core" of the faith, see Walter Harrelson, "Life, Faith and the Emergence of Tradition," in *Tradition and Theology in the Old Testament*, ed. Douglas A. Knight (Philadelphia: Fortress Press, 1977), pp. 11-30. See his succinct statement on p. 20.
31. On such a move "from below," see Gen. 18:16-33. See my comments in *Genesis* (Atlanta: John Knox Press, 1982), pp. 162-76.
32. On the recurring tendency to triangling, see Murray Bowen, *Family Therapy in Clinical Practice* (New York: J. Aronson, 1978).
33. I have not included a discussion of Psalm 22 in this section, even though it is a primary example of the genre, because I assumed that sufficient discussion of that psalm is available elsewhere. See the excellent literary analysis of John S. Kselmann, " 'Why have You Abandoned Me?' A Rhetorical Study of Psalm 22," *JSOT* Supp. 19 (Sheffield: University of Sheffield, 1982), pp. 172-198, and the theological analysis of John Reumann, "Psalm 22 at the Cross," *Interpretation* 28 (1974):39-58.
34. On the primacy of the individual as the unit of self-perception, see Philip Rieff, *The Triumph of the Therapeutic: Uses of Faith After Freud* (New York: Harper and Row, 1966), and Philip Slater, *The Pursuit of Loneliness American Culture at the Breaking Point* (Boston: Beacon Press, 1970). This propensity to individualism is not simply a selfish choice made by persons, but the governing ideology that forms the "world" in which we function.
35. See Alasdair MacIntyre, *After Virtue: A Study in Moral Theory* (Notre Dame: University of Notre Dame Press, 1982). In an address to the Association of Theological Schools in Pittsburgh, June 21, 1982, Robert Bellah explored the implications of MacIntyre's thesis for faith and ministry.
36. Robert Lifton is not especially concerned with prayer, but his comments about the "symbol gap" are especially pertinent. I understand him to mean that we have no adequate symbols by which to speak about our public experience. As a result everything is forfeited to individualistic perception. Cf. Lifton, *Living and Dying* (New York: Praeger, 1975). Lifton's later work appears even less sanguine about the power of effective religious symbol.
37. The "oracles against the nations" in Amos 1–2 make clear that the public agenda

not only concerned "natural" disaster, but related with equal authority to the public practice of cruelty and inhumanity. Our own attempts to speak about current situations of cruelty and inhumanity are often self-serving and ideologically useful. But such ideological references have no credibility because they are not disinterested. They are only occasions for spouting ideology.

38. Samuel Terrien, "The Omphalos Myth and Hebrew Religion," *VT* 20 (1970): 215-38, has well exposited the social function of the temple as a "center." As Terrien knows well, the more radical traditions of Israel are highly suspicious of such a center, for it is never without ideological pretension.

39. The phrase is from James A. Sanders, *God Has a Story Too* (Philadelphia: Fortress Press, 1979), p. 20. On the same point, see his more programmatic essay, "Hermeneutics," *IBD* Supp. (Nashville: Abingdon, 1976), pp. 402-407.

40. The threat to the known world in our time is of course linked to the nuclear threat. Lifton has rightly argued that the massiveness and comprehensiveness of this threat is without parallel. Nonetheless, the rhetorical and existential articulations around the fall of Jerusalem must have equaled in intensity the jeopardy of the "known world." It may be excessive modernizing to make our threat without parallel, though "objectively" that is surely correct.

41. Among the psalms that articulate this concern in this form, see 12, 44, 58, 60, 80, 83, 85, 94, 123, 126.

42. The individual lament is liturgically resolved by a song of thanksgiving. The communal lament has no such obvious liturgical response, but it is clear that the enthronement psalms are such a resolution, for they celebrate a new communal orientation.

43. On the meaning of the temple as a symbolic center, see Terrien, *The Elusive Presence* (New York: Harper and Row, 1978). It is important to hold together its symbolic function as a statement about coherence and its political function as a legitimation of the political status quo. The problem of course is that it is nearly impossible to separate the two functions.

44. The reference is to William Butler Yeats, "The Second Coming."

45. Sociologically, the Psalms concern the loss of *nomos* and the social experience of anomie, on which see Peter Berger, *The Sacred Canopy,* chap. 3, and Robert Merton, *Social Theory and Social Structure,* chaps. 4-5 (Glencoe, Ill.: Free Press, 1957).

46. That is why in the Holiness Code, the temple is elaborately guarded against impurity. See Mary Douglas, *Purity and Danger: An Analysis of the Concepts of Pollution and Taboo* (London: Routledge and Kegan, 1978).

47. On the temple as ambivalent, see Carol L. Meyers, "Jachin and Boaz in Religious and Political Perspective," *CBQ* 45 (1983):167-78.

48. On the modern experience of such homelessness, see Peter Berger, *The Homeless Mind* (New York: Random House, 1973). My exposition assumes that such "homelessness" is articulated in these psalms.

49. Cf. Meir Weiss, "Die Methode der 'Total-Interpretation,' " *SVT* 22 (1972): 88-112.

50. Westermann, "Struktur und Geschichte," pp. 273-75.

51. For the dynamic intention of these psalms see Gerstenberger, cited in n. 28. For the transformative intention of the psalm and the power of inversion, see Norman K. Gottwald, *Studies in the Book of Lamentations* (Chicago: Allenson, 1954), on the theme of "reversal" and "reversal of reversal."

52. Yahweh must be "put in remembrance" (cf. Isa. 62:6). See Ralph Klein, "The Message of P," in *Die Botschaft und die Boten*, ed. Jörg Jeremias and Lothar Perlitt (Neukirchen-Vluyn: Neukirchener Verlag, 1981), pp. 57-66. Such language suggests the range of speech and the two-way communication that is proper to the Psalms.

53. The metaphor of "chaos" in creation faith has been useful for articulating "exile" in historical narrative. Functionally the terms of "chaos" and "exile" refer to the same realities. Notice the use in Isa. 54:9ff.

54. I have no doubt that it is the jeopardy of religious arrangements that evokes the uncritical enthusiasm for those arrangements which equates the holiness of God with every ideology cherished. The current identification of God's holiness with "righteous America" is an ironic and pitiful confusion of God and temple that can be analyzed only as idolatry.

55. That is the title of the book by Gabriel Vahanian, *Wait Without Idols* (New York: Braziller, 1964). It is unfortunate that his book got lost in the shuffle of "Death of God" prattle, for he is seriously discussing this very theme.

56. George Mendenhall, *The Tenth Generation* (Baltimore: Johns Hopkins University Press, 1973), pp.73-77, notes that this overstated yearning for vengeance is peculiar in the Bible. Its use here is a measure of the depth of passion related to the loss of temple.

57. In the ancient world of Israel, the key factor in the experience of normlessness is the loss of the temple. The temple is the public expression of *nomos*.

58. The mood suggested is like the bright new day after the thunderstorm in Dvorak's *New World Symphony*. The contrast of rhetoric here is like the contrast of tempo in the musical presentation.

59. On the interplay, tension, and contrast between "thanks" and "praise," see the fine presentation of Harvey H. Guthrie Jr., *Theology as Thanksgiving* (New York: Seabury Press, 1981), especially chap. 1.

60. On this dimension of the Psalter, see Brueggemann, *Praying the Psalms*, chap. 4 (Winona, Minn.: St. Mary's Press, 1982).

61. This is especially evident in the interpretations of W. D. Davies, *The Gospel and the Land* (Berkeley: University of California Press, 1974), and *The Territorial Dimension of Judaism* (Berkeley: University of California Press, 1982). I have reservations about that view.

62. Viktor Frankl, *The Will to Meaning: Foundations and Applications of Logotherapy* (New York: World Publishing Co., 1969).

63. The language of Neh. 1:4 echoes the psalm, "Sat down and wept." One can argue that the same stylistic formulae govern both pieces of literature, or one can be amazed at the resilient power of the tradition. I think that it was precisely the power of this psalmic tradition of grief that gave power to the historical moves in the Nehemiah tradition. This is an important example of the ways in which primal language leads life.

64. Kornelis H. Miskotte, *When the Gods Are Silent* (New York: Harper and Row, 1967), has given eloquent expression to the contemporary experience of this same reality. Effective psalm interpretation must draw an analogy between that modern experience and the situation presented in the psalm.

65. On the distance and nearness of God in this text, see Werner E. Lemke, "The Near and Distant God," *JBL* 100 (1981):541-555.

66. See Martin Buber, *Eclipse of God* (New York: Harper, 1957). Buber's reply to Jung (pp. 171-76) concerns what is at stake is the modern reduction of God to self-experiences. The Psalms bear witness to real absence. On the absence of God as a serious psalmic theme, see Barth, *Church Dogmatics* vol. 1, 2 (1956), pp. 28-30.

67. It is definitional to this faith that God must continue to be addressed in God's absence, against the inclination of modernity. This tenacity belongs to both Jewish and Christian piety, though it is at present much better articulated in Jewish probes. The Holocaust stands as the primal fact of God's absence. Elie Wiesel has observed that it is not possible for a serious Jew not to believe in God, but it is possible to "believe against God." That is surely what is happening in this psalm. Such a faith, in light of the cross and in light of the Holocaust, makes the rejection of God because of God's absence seem trite.

68. See the peculiar use made of this psalm by William Styron, *Sophie's Choice* (New York: Random House, 1979), p. 506: "Dat is some fine Psalm."

69. See the poignant statement in Job 30:26. On the other hand, the same inversion is used to very different effect in Amos 5:18-20. The one usage concerns a false response to faithfulness. The other concerns a false reading of one's true situation.

70. Mitchell Dahood, *Psalms*, vol. 3 (Garden City, N.Y.: Doubleday, 1970), p. 97, directly renders the terms in parallel, "Evil One, Satan." This is against the common tradition, and reflect Dahood's inclination to reread the text as reflective of a vigorous and vital polytheism.

71. The term *guilty* in v. 7 and the term *wicked* in v. 6 both render רָשָׁע. The juridical flavor of the whole is to be pressed without speculation about the reference of the term *satan*.

72. See the similar self-curse of Job 31:10.

73. The one characterized here is nearly antithetical to the portrait of Job in Job 31. George Fohrer, "The Righteous Man in Job 31," in *Essays in Old Testament Ethics*, ed. James L. Crenshaw and John T. Willis (New York: KTAV, 1974), pp. 2-22, suggests that Job 31 offers a picture of the model righteous man. Ps. 109 may offer the precise antithesis: the model wicked man who warrants the curses which have been visited on Job. Such an antithesis suggests that this psalm needs to be read in close company with the poem of Job.

74. P. D. Miller Jr., *Sin and Judgment in the Prophets* (Chico, Calif.: Scholars Press, 1982), has shown that the prophets assume a closed system relating offense and punishment. That closed system of reward and punishment is precisely what is urged in this psalm.

75. While the pictures drawn here and in Job 31 are contrasted, both statements are acts of hope. Neither assumes that things must stay the way they are. Both affirm an undiminished conviction of moral coherence as a context for righteousness as human conduct.

76. See my comments in *Praying the Psalms*, chap. 5. Any reading of the Psalms that does not see these presentations of vengeance as acts of profound faith likely is romantic and missing the main point. The point is that *the reality of God* is deeply engaged with *the negativity of life*. Much spirituality takes great care to separate *God* and *negativities*, but the Psalms do not flinch.

77. For such a political, juridical reading of the vengeance of Yahweh, see Mendenhall, *The Tenth Generation*, chap. 5.

78. On covenant as definitional, see Brueggemann, "Covenant as Human Vocation," *Interpretation* 33 (1979):115-29.

79. Too much attention has been given to the historical identity of the "enemy." The Psalms will have their proper vitality if "enemy" is taken as a metaphor that can be turned in many directions. I suggest that "enemy" be handled with the kind of imaginative freedom that David J. A. Clines, *I, He, We and They: A Literary Approach to Isaiah 53* (Sheffield: University of Sheffield, 1976), assigns to pronouns in his text. The specificity of the term is quickly established by the user of the psalm, if that is done with any serious passion at all. When there is in fact an enemy in one's picture, one has no need to ask about specificity.

80. Among the prophetic elements, the *lawsuit* of indignation slides over into a *lament* of grief and pathos, especially in Jeremiah. The two forms need to be held in deliberate tension.

81. On the cataclysmic aspect of the theophany, see the two standard studies by Kenneth J. Kuntz, *The Self-Revelation of God* (Philadelphia: Westminister Press, 1967), and Jörg Jeremias, *Theophanie: die Geschichte einer alttestamentlichen Gattung* (Neukirchen-Vluyn: Neukirchener Verlag, 1965).

82. Alan Paton, *Knocking on the Door* (New York: Scribner's, 1975; Cape Town: David Philip, 1975), pp. 89-90, has given choice expression to the inequality of God to which this psalm attests: "Do not pronounce judgment on the infinity nor suppose God to be like a bad Prime Minister.../Do not address your mind to criticism of the Creator, do not pretend to know his categories.../He is not greater than Plato or Lincoln, nor superior to Shakespeare and Beethoven./He is their God, their powers and their gifts proceed from him."

83. On these Psalms in the context of covenant judgment and covenant renewal, see Gerhard von Rad, *The Problems of the Hexateuch and Other Essays* (New York: McGraw-Hill, 1966), pp. 22-26.

84. Thus the psalm holds together the trivialization of God and the violation of the neighbor. Transgression of the two "great commandments" inevitably occurs together, disrespect for God and disregard of neighbor. Notice that the same wicked one may be identified in Ps. 109:6, who imagines both that God can be disregarded and neighbor can be exploited. This linkage is undoubted and uncompromising, and comes to a classic expression in 1 John 4:20.

85. This reduction of God to human categories and human expectations is sharply countered in Hos. 11:9. In that poem, the writer assumes until v. 8 that God would operate according to an exhaustive scheme of human retribution. But God's decision to break out of that scheme is presented in v. 9 as God's decision to be unlike human persons. The *otherness* of God is the ground of God's *freedom* but also the ground of God's *love*.

86. Guthrie, *op. cit.*, has seen that thanksgiving is a response to the inversion of life. On the form-critical aspects of the thank formulae, see James M. Robinson, "The Historicality of Biblical Language," in *The Old Testament and Christian Faith*, ed. Bernhard W. Anderson (New York: Harper and Row, 1963), pp. 130-150. The "historicality" of the language of thanksgiving is of great importance for the intent of these psalms.

87. Paul Ricoeur, "Naming God," *USQR* 34 (1979):219, shrewdly observes that "Listening excludes founding oneself." In *The Conflict of Interpretations* (Evanston: Northwestern University Press, 1974), p. 451, notice his play on "hören/zugehören," "listen/belong to."

88. Variations on that theme dominate the commentaries both of Artur Weiser, *The Psalms* (Philadelphia: Westminister Press, 1962), and Hans Joachim Kraus,

Psalmen (Neukirchen-Vluyn: Neukirchener Verlag, 1961), and see the proposal of von Rad, cited in n. 82.

89. See his general thesis, "The Problem of the Hexateuch." That particular casting of the issue is now sharply criticized by scholars. However, chap. 13 in Norman K. Gottwald, *The Tribes of Yahweh* (Maryknoll, N.Y.: Orbis Books, 1979), advances a more attractive presentation of the same basic argument. Gottwald draws the psalmic material closer to the realities of social life.

90. Gottwald, *Tribes*, pp. 102-103, suggests a way to distinguish the narrative recital and the proclamation of law without separating the traditions, as von Rad had done. His attention to the realistic social context seems to me to avoid some of the problems of von Rad.

91. On "feeding" as crucial to the tradition, see Ps. 78:19.

92. Walter Beyerlin, "Gattung und Herkunft des Rahmens im Richterbuch," in *Tradition und Situation*, ed. E. Wurthwein and Otto Kaiser (Göttingen: Vandenhoeck and Ruprecht, 1963), pp. 1-29.

93. On the "anti-Exodus," see William L. Moran, "The End of Unholy War and the Anti-Exodus," *Biblica* 44 (1963):333-42. Moran shows how the Exodus memory can be turned against Israel when Israel is no longer responsive to the torah demands of Yahweh.

94. The dismantling of Israel because of disobedience should not be read as a religious fact devoid of social context. This threat needs to be read in a context of social reality. Idolatry has to do with oppressive social reality. When Yahweh abandons Israel to the idols, it is at the same time a comment on the power of the dominant ideology, which is likely to oppress.

95. See Norman Snaith, *The Seven Psalms* (London: Epworth Press, 1964), especially the introductory chapter. The seven psalms are 6, 32, 38, 51, 102, 130, 143.

96. Luther's exegesis of these psalms was offered in 1517. See the revised version from 1525, "The Seven Penitential Psalms," *Luther's Works*, vol. 14, ed. Jaroslav Pelikan (St. Louis: Concordia, 1958), pp.140-205.

97. The power of unforgiven guilt is well traced by Dostoevski, *Crime and Punishment* (New York: Random House, 1950).

98. On the capacity of a power agent to "reckon," see von Rad, " 'Righteousness' and 'Life' in the Cultic Language of the Psalms," in *The Problems of the Hexateuch and Other Essays*, pp. 243-253.

99. See the same vocabulary in Hos. 2:19-20, which in parallel fashion is concerned for a renewed covenantal relationship.

100. The argument here is like that of Karl Menninger in *Whatever Became of Sin?* (New York: Hawthorn Books, 1973). However, an evangelical reading of the text would suggest that that is the wrong question. The right question is, "Whatever became of God?" As Barth, *Church Dogmatics*, vol. 4, 1, 60 (1956) has seen, it is the *reality of God* which introduces the *notion of sin*. Where God has been trivialized, sin will surely be trivialized in the same way. Barth's argument is put in Christological terms, but the point is the same for Israel in the Psalms.

101. See Barth, *Church Dogmatics*, pp. 387-391, on the priority of God's righteousness as a necessary precondition of sin. His argument is cast in juridical categories, precisely the language of the Psalms.

102. This follows the standard reading of שׁבע for שׁמע.

103. On the elemental reality of "uncleanness" as underlying any notion of guilt, see Paul Ricoeur, *Symbolism of Evil* (New York: Harper, 1967). It is likely that the

profundity of this text has been missed because we so easily render the issue of de-filement into matters of moral guilt, which is not the point of the Psalm.

104. Cf. Ps. 24:4. The point of cleanness is to have access to the holy place, and there-fore to share in the monopoly of social power which is administered by the priests. One must "qualify" in order to participate.

105. Brevard Childs, "Psalm Titles and Midrashic Exegesis," *JSS* 16 (1971): 137-50, points out the value of the superscriptions for a canonical reading of the Psalms. By that, Childs does not take the superscriptions as historical data, but as clues about how the normative reading of the text has been conducted and understood.

106. Cf. the important article by Krister Stendahl, "The Apostle Paul and the Intro-spective Conscience of the West," *HTR* 56 (1963):199-215. The Psalms of an-cient Israel did not, any more than Paul, participate in such a notion of guilt.

107. See Sigmund Mowinckel, "Psalms and Wisdom," *SVT* 3 (1955):204-24; Roland Murphy, "A Consideration of the Classification 'Wisdom Psalms,' " *VTS* 9 (1963); and the summary of Erhard Gerstenberger, "Psalms," in *Old Testament Form Criticism*, ed. John H. Hayes (San Antonio: Trinity University Press, 1974), pp. 218-21.

108. This carefully wrought summons might be taken as an early critique of the educa-tional notion of "separate but equal."

109. The conventional translation, reflected for example in Kraus, takes the meaning to be the reverse, so that אדם is "simple folks" and איש is "lordly folk." How-ever, my sense is that אדם regularly means royal personage. Note the use of אדם subsequently in the poem.

110. This reading reflects a textual change from אח to אך to create correspondence with verse 15. The text as it stands has "brother." Dahood, *Psalms 1-50*, vol. 1 (Garden City, N.Y.: Doubleday, 1966), p. 298, retains the reading אח but rend-ers it as an interjection, "alas!"

111. Brevard Childs, *Isaiah and the Assyrian Crisis* (London: SCM Press, 1967), pp. 128-36, identifies this conclusion as a "summary appraisal form." See also James L. Crenshaw, "Wisdom," in *Old Testament Form Criticism*, pp. 260-61.

112. The verb in v. 12 is לון, which permits the ambiguity of "dwell." However, the parallel in v. 20 is בין, which requires a different rendering. The RSV renders both as "abide," which does not reflect the differences in the text.

113. See the textual question, n. 110.

114. That death works its inexorable power without reference to or intervention from God is consonant with the proposal of Klaus Koch, "Is There a Doctrine of Retri-bution in the Old Testament?," in *Theodicy in the Old Testament*, ed. James Crenshaw (Philadelphia: Fortress Press, 1983), pp. 57-87, that the Old Testament has a notion of deed and consequence which functions as an automatic process without reference to God. Thus, that death works its way need not be linked to the judgment of God in any direct way. Positively, Koch, *The Prophets* (Philadel-phia: Fortress Press, 1982), pp. 56-62, has articulated the same "force" in justice and righteousness.

115. This critical view of wealth is quite in contrast to the perspective of Psalm 112. In that psalm (v. 3) "riches and wealth" are parallel to righteousness. Obviously, that psalm reflects a very different "life world," one of the fully oriented which gives no hint of self-critical awareness.

116. The use of the word *trust* draws this matter close to Luther's exposition of the first commandment: "Whatever your heart clings to and relies on, that properly is your

God.'' The connection between trust in God and faithful economics or trust in an idol and exploitative economics is a learning still to be pursued in biblical theology, though Marx offers important suggestions on this linkage.

117. This psalm could provide entry into a study of the biblical data concerning wealth and poverty and the systematic realities behind them. Convenient access points for such study may be found in Martin Hengel, *Property and Riches in the Early Church* (Philadelphia: Fortress Press, 1974), and Ronald J. Sider, *Rich Christians in an Age of Hunger* (Downers Grove, Ill.: InterVarsity Press, 1978).

118. Here I make intentional use of the construct of Peter Berger, Brigitte Berger, and Hansfried Kellner, *The Homeless Mind* (New York: Random House, 1973). While they intend to deal with the problem of modernity, I suggest that the religious problem of homelessness is an old one, which this psalm intends to counter. Walter Harrelson, ''A Meditation on the Wrath of God: Psalm 90,'' in *Scripture in History and Theology*, ed. Arthur L. Merrill and Thomas W. Overholt (Pittsburgh: Pickwick Press, 1977), pp. 181-191, has discerned a deliberate ambiguity in the ''hiding place,'' but Harrelson also sees the psalm coming to a positive judgment.

119. Von Rad, ''Psalm 90,'' in *God at Work in Israel* (Nashville: Abingdon Press, 1980), pp. 210-23.

120. Harrelson treats these metaphors in terms of judgment. However, the metaphors in these verses seem to me to move in a different direction of finitude, for the vocabulary of wrath is withheld until subsequent verses.

121. Dahood retains the Hebrew text, but treats ''Israel'' as a vocative rather than an indirect object.

122. Ernst Würthwein, ''Erwägungen zu Psalm 73,'' in *Wort und Existenz* (Göttingen: Vandenhoeck und Ruprecht, 1970), p. 167, has most clearly indicated what is at stake. Says he, whoever changes the reading *(a)* makes out of an irrational electing gracious God, a rational retributive God; *(b)* makes out of the community of Israel with its history of unmerited miracle, individuals who gain good results out of their qualifications; *(c)* makes out of grace which believes, recompense which must be shown; and *(d)* makes out of a life ordering that lays claim to an unquestioned worth, a free will that expects a reward for a performance.

123. That of course is the assumption of Martin Buber, *Right and Wrong* (London: SCM Press, 1952), pp. 34-52.

124. The language of ''second naivete'' is especially that of Paul Ricoeur; cf. *Semeia* 4 (1975):7, 19.

125. Michael Fishbane, *Text and Texture* (New York: Schocken, 1979), pp. 79-83, has a perceptive statement of the abrasion between generations in accepting the faith story of the older generation.

126. It is interesting to note the metaphor of ''beasts'' here in relation to the same metaphor in Ps. 49:12, 20. There it refers to the cynical wealthy who will die dishonored and uncared for ''like a beast.'' Here it is a confession about the speaking self who recognizes he was as unresponsive as a beast.

127. Sallie McFague, *Metaphorical Theology* (Philadelphia: Fortress Press, 1982), pp. 177-92, has a most suggestive analysis of the metaphor of ''friend.''

128. The word טוב occurs at the beginning and end of the psalm (vv. 1, 28) and may best be translated with the metaphor of ''friendship.'' Cf. William L. Moran, ''A Note on the Treaty Terminology of the Sefire Stelas,'' *JNES* 22 (1963):173-76,

and the additional comparative material by McCarthy from Ebla [*Biblica* 60 (1979):247-53], and Egypt [*BASOR* 245 (1982):63-64].

129. On "portion," see von Rad, " 'Righteousness' and 'Life' in the Cultic Language of the Psalms," in *The Problem of the Hexateuch and Other Essays*, (New York: McGraw-Hill, 1966), pp. 259-66. In the notion "Yahweh is my portion," the need for *place* is again resolved in terms of a *relationship*, just as we have seen in Psalm 90. Notice von Rad, p. 257, on "bring near," the same verb as in our psalm, with specific reference to cultic participation.

130. That *autonomy* leads to perishing (אבד)is an insight very old in the tradition of Israel, on which see Deut. 8:11-20, with the same verb.

131. Buber, pp. 37-38.

132. Carroll Stuhlmueller, *Psalms*, vol. 2 (Wilmington, Delaware: Michael Glazier, 1983), p. 11, is inclined to a mystical discernment of the turn in the psalm.

Chapter 4

1. In a variety of works, and most recently in *The Broken Connection* (New York: Simon and Schuster, 1980), Robert J. Lifton has studied these phenomena in our society and has made current the diagnostic phrase, "psychic numbness."

2. See Peter L. Berger, *The Sacred Canopy* (Garden City, N.Y.: Doubleday, 1967). It is that "canopy" which gives credibility to the symbols through which experience is mediated. Lifton has suggested that we now have a "symbol gap." That is, we have no symbols credible and powerful enough to cope with the experiences available to us.

3. Claus Westermann, *Praise and Lament in the Psalms* (Atlanta: John Knox Press, 1981), and *The Psalms: Structure, Content, and Message* (Minneapolis: Augsburg, 1980). The structure of the full form is the move from *plea* to *praise* which comprehends much of Israel's spirituality.

4. See Brueggemann, "From Hurt to Joy, From Death to Life," *Interpretation* 28 (1974):3-19. Daniel Via, *Kerygma and Comedy* (Philadelphia: Fortress Press 1975), has explored the same structure in the faith of the New Testament. It is a helpful notion, as long as the "comedy" of this faith does not distract from the cruciality and centrality of suffering and death.

5. Westermann, *Praise and Lament*, pp. 25-35, has proposed this convergence of forms. It is correct to say that among form critics, Westermann's proposal has not met with general acceptance. But my judgment is that his argument is concerned with *function* as much as with a strict formal analysis.

6. See Brueggemann, " 'Impossibility' and Epistemology in the Faith Tradition of Abraham and Sarah (Gen. 18:1-15)," *ZAW* 94 (1982):615-634.

7. Westermann has made a distinction between "declarative psalms of praise" and "descriptive psalms of praise." The former stay closer to the concreteness of event and tend to narrative recital. They "tell what happened." Descriptive psalms are removed from the actual event and tend to generalize. Frank Crüsemann, *Studien zur Formgeschichte von Hymnus und Danklied in Israel* (Neukirchen-Vluyn: Neukirchener Verlag, 1969), has explored some of the form-critical marks of these genre. The problem is to try to make correlations between the *formal structure* of the psalm and its intended *social function*. Westermann's distinction is helpful in sorting out when the social function is one of *maintenance of equilibrium* and when it is *announcement of transformation*. This distinction has become decisive for

Westermann's understanding of Old Testament theology. See his fullest statement of it in *Elements of Old Testament Theology* (Atlanta: John Knox Press, 1978), especially pts. 2 and 3. Some of the same discernment is evident in Harvey H. Guthrie Jr., *Theology as Thanksgiving* (New York: Seabury, 1981).

8. John Goldingay, "The Dynamic Cycle of Praise and Prayer in the Psalms," *JSOT* 20 (1981):85-90, and see my response, "Response to John Goldingay's 'The Dynamic Cycle of Praise and Prayer,' " *JSOT* 22 (1982):141-42.

9. The problem of discontinuity and continuity in this matter is complex and difficult, because even the new statements after discontinuity tend to be articulated in the earlier forms. Peter R. Ackroyd, "Continuity and Discontinuity: Rehabilitation and Authentication," in *Tradition and Theology in the Old Testament*, ed. Douglas A. Knight (Philadelphia: Fortress Press, 1977), pp. 215-34, has discerned the ways in which the tradition always finds ways to push toward continuity. But in the same volume, see Walther Zimmerli, "Prophetic Proclamation and Reinterpretation," pp. 69-100, for an accent on the work of discontinuity. See my comments in *The Creative Word* (Philadelphia: Fortress Press, 1982) on the necessary dialectic of establishing consensus and shattering that consensus.

10. It is difficult to determine whether the Psalms speak of something genuinely new or as something always there but only newly perceived. Our conventional domesticated religion inclines to the view that things are not really new or changed, but are only newly perceived. I should think it possible to do a socio-economic analysis of this matter. My sense is that the better educated (which is a function of economics) and the better situated we are, the more we are likely to take the view that things do not really change but are only perceived differently. Conversely, the less fortunate we may be economically and the less intellectually sophisticated, the more we find it credible to entertain and affirm a genuine newness. In psalm study, the crucial work of Mowinckel suggests that in the cult something genuinely new was wrought. That is, the cult is not mere replication, but is a generative action. Jürgen Moltmann, *Theology of Hope*, chap. 2 (New York: Harper and Row, 1967), has well contrasted "*epiphany* religion and faith in terms of *promise*." The problem is an exceedingly complex one because we face the general problem of myth and history, the hermeneutical problem of the ancient intentionality, and the sociological problem of our own perceptual world. But I suggest that the phenomenological observations of Grönbeck and Mowinckel concerning ancient ritual practice and the claims of evangelical faith (as Moltmann presents them) come to a common point here. That point is that the new orientation is a genuine happening and not simply a change of perception. Sallie McFague, *Metaphorical Theology* (Philadelphia: Fortress Press, 1982), is helpful here in seeing that metaphor always asserts is/is not. That is how it is in the ritual.

11. In the grouping of individual songs of thanksgiving, the following psalms may be included: 9, 41, 107, 116. It is clear how closely related are the lament and thanksgiving songs, because both motifs may occur in the same psalm.

12. Westermann, *The Psalms, Structure, Content and Message*, chaps. 2 and 4. See also Guthrie, *op. cit.*, pp. 43-59, who shrewdly links the *credo* hypothesis of von Rad to the function of תּוֹדָה in the Psalms.

13. The language is necessarily metaphorical, because only such language can articulate such matters. Notice the repeated references made by Wayne A. Meeks, *The First Urban Christians: The Social World of the Apostle Paul* (New Haven: Yale University Press, 1983), pp. 93, 104, 138, 174, 1980, to the metaphorical power of

the resurrection. I understand this to be very different from the ways in which Dahood thinks he finds allusions to resurrection in the Psalms.

14. The תודה (thanksgiving) has the dual intent of *thanksgiving* and *confession* of faith. See Guthrie, chap. 1 and Westermann, *Praise of God*, especially pp. 17-35.

15. This last juxtaposition occurs, not between the two parts of the psalm, but within the second part of the psalm.

16. Here is an example of the way in which Exodus language is used to articulate a personal experience.

17. Erhard Gerstenberger, *Wesen und Herkunft des sogenannten 'apodiktischen Rechts' im Alten Testament* (Neukirchen-Vluyn: Neukirchener Verlag, 1965), p. 49.

18. Psalm 82 provides an early and perhaps normative statement of this affirmation. See Guthrie, *op. cit.*, pp. 34-43, and J. J. M. Roberts, "The Davidic Origin of the Zion Tradition," *JBL* 92 (1973):339-344, on the social function of this psalm.

19. Verse 22 lies outside the acrostic structure of the psalm and so must not be considered a part of the psalm.

20. Communal songs of thanksgiving may include Psalms 67, 92, 118.

21. On the positive side of civil religion informed by these traditions, see Robert Bellah and Phillip E. Hammond, *Varieties of Civil Religion* (San Francisco: Harper and Row, 1980), and on the commonality of faith see Will Herberg, *Protestant, Catholic, Jew* (Garden City, N.Y.: Doubleday, 1955).

22. Robert Lifton, *The Broken Connection*, has discerned the numbness among us. The theological issue is how guilt and forgiveness can be genuinely experienced and enacted in a community of numbness.

23. On creation theology as a significant alternative tradition, see Westermann, *Elements of Old Testament Theology*, pt. 3.

24. See the eloquent statement of Abraham Heschel, *Who Is Man?* (Stanford: Stanford University Press, 1965).

25. Second Isaiah makes special use of this liturgical tradition. He presents the liberation from Babylon as a contest between gods (cf. Isa. 41:1-5, 21-29) which Yahweh wins. Kraus has followed Gunkel in holding that the psalms of enthronement derive from Second Isaiah, but the scholarly consensus is against that view. It is cult that mediates that way of discerning life.

26. The term here rendered "well-being" is רויה which may mean "luxuriant, well-watered."

27. Otto Eissfeldt, "The Promises of Grace to David in Isaiah 55:1-5," in *Israel's Prophetic Heritage*, ed. Bernhard Anderson and Walter Harrelson (New York: Harper and Row, 1962), pp. 196-207, has seen that the promises of David are democratized and made available to the whole community. See also Jean M. Vincent, *Studien zur literarischen Eigenart und zur geistigen Heimat von Jesaja, Kap. 40-55* (Bern: Peter Lang, 1977), pp. 66-107.

28. Jer. 5:22 offers a graphic metaphor for Yahweh's governance of the chaotic waters.

29. See the discussions of Patrick D. Miller Jr., *The Divine Warrior in Early Israel* (Cambridge: Harvard University Press, 1973), pp. 166-175; Frank M. Cross, *Canaanite Myth and Hebrew Epic* (Cambridge: Harvard University Press, 1973), pp. 112-144; and James Muilenburg, "A Liturgy of the Triumphs of Yahweh," in *Studia Biblica et Semitica* (Wageningen: H. Veenman and Zonen, 1966), pp. 233-51.

30. The same claim is made in the song of Josh. 10:12-13.

31. On the council of the gods, see Patrick D. Miller, *Genesis 1–11* (Sheffield: University of Sheffield, 1978), pp. 9-26.
32. Psalm 117 offers a clear model for the hymn. Indeed Psalm 117 is almost a pure form waiting to be claimed for more substantive and specific content. See the useful summary on the hymn by R. N. Whybray, *The Second Isaiah* (Sheffield: JSOT Press, 1983), pp. 30-34.
33. See the summary references of Aubrey Johnson, "The Psalms," in *The Old Testament and Modern Study*, ed. H. H. Rowley (Oxford: Clarendon Press, 1951), p. 190, and John H. Hayes, *An Introduction to Old Testament Study* (Nashville: Abingdon Press, 1979), pp. 299-304.
34. Norman Gottwald, *The Tribes of Yahweh* (Maryknoll, N.Y.: Orbis Books, 1979), p. 408 and *passim*, follows Mendenhall in explicating the sociological process of "withdrawal." I do not believe Gottwald or Mendenhall has fully appreciated the fact that such social withdrawal begins in the liturgical process, where the pain is enacted and alternatives begin to be acted out. In seeing the old tradition as "modalities of the cultic structure" (chap. 13), Gottwald hints at the process but has not worked it out in any extended way. The Psalms, I suggest, are the materials through which the *liturgical processing* and the *sociological act* are joined together.
35. The contrast between the God "who abides" and the God "who comes," is crucial for Moltmann's theology of hope. See M. Douglas Meeks, *Origins of the Theology of Hope* (Philadelphia: Fortress Press, 1974), pp. 80-92.
36. The critique of idols is fundamental to the dignity and worth of human persons in the image of God. Von Rad, *Old Testament Theology*, vol. 1 (New York: Harper and Brothers, 1962), pp. 212-19, has hinted at this, but does not carry the critique of idols far enough toward our understanding of humanness. See the pertinent comments of Walter Harrelson, *The Ten Commandments and Human Rights* (Philadelphia: Fortress Press, 1980), pp. 61-73, where the modern issue of humanness is more explicit.
37. Luke 19:47-48 articulates just such a good news/bad news reading of Jesus.
38. See Ps. 132:7. But note that in Isa. 66:1 it is the whole earth and not the temple which is the "footstool." Obviously this is a metaphor that has more than one possible usage.
39. See Gottwald, *op. cit.*, pp. 686-87.
40. Isa. 6:1-8 shows a remarkable convergence of themes which concern us, namely, the temple, the kingship of Yahweh, and the holiness of Yahweh. Clearly the temple as the presentation of an alternative reality is understood as the place of creative possibility.
41. No doubt these psalms and the cultic metaphors related to them are the metaphorical basis of the New Testament narrative of the ascension of Jesus. That event in the faith and memory of the church is no doubt a political event.
42. The literature is extensive. Reference may usefully be made to the two books edited by S. H. Hooke, *Myth and Ritual* (London: Oxford University Press, 1933), and *Myth, Ritual and Kingship* (Oxford: Clarendon Press, 1958).
43. See especially Martin Buber, *Kingship of God* (New York: Harper and Row, 1967), and the general review of Otto Eissfeldt, "Jahwe als König," *ZAW* 46 (1928): 81-105. George Mendenhall, "The Hebrew Conquest of Palestine," *BAR* 3 (1970): 100-120, and *The Tenth Generation*, chaps. 1, 7, 8 (Baltimore: Johns Hopkins University Press, 1973), and Gottwald, *op. cit.*, have understood most

clearly what the metaphor of Yahweh's kingship means sociologically and politically.

44. We will not pursue the "royal psalms," but as Aubrey Johnson has shown in close parallel to Mowinckel, they are clearly related to the kingship of Yahweh. These psalms include 2, 18, 30, 21, 45, 72, 89, 101, 132, 144. The king is Yahweh's regent. Scholars hold a variety of opinions concerning the formal (ontological) relation of the king to God, e.g., divine, sacral, historical, etc. But the function of the king is no doubt to guard the order of life and to reestablish it when it is lost. The royal disorientation is surely acted out in the New Testament through the drama of the crucifixion of Jesus and the ensuing chaos (cf. Matt. 27:51-54).

45. Carol L. Meyers, "Jachin and Boaz in Religious and Political Perspective," *CBQ* 45 (1983):167-178, has recently shown how the claims of the dynasty are intimately linked to those of Yahweh.

46. It is central to Gottwald's argument that the *theological image* and the *political reality* are closely linked to each other. Various nuances may be given to the relationship between the two, on the question which of the two is a function of the other.

47. The key text for this argument is Psalm 82 which we will not discuss in detail. It is sufficient to note that this psalm is a mythological statement that has enormous, direct political spin-off.

48. Sallie McFague, *Metaphorical Theology* (Philadelphia: Fortress Press, 1982), pp. 48-54, and *passim*, has shown how the metaphor of "kingdom" is central to Jesus as presented in the New Testament.

49. Brevard S. Childs, *Introduction to the Old Testament as Scripture* (Philadelphia: Fortress Press, 1979), pp. 517-18, has concluded that the present shape of the Psalter is fundamentally eschatological.

50. Among the psalms which may be grouped here are 11, 62, 63, 121. The psalms we will discuss are *individual* songs of confidence. Communal songs of confidence (which we will not discuss in detail) are Psalms 115, 125, 129.

51. The religious operation of these psalms may well be correlated to "basic trust" as Erik Erikson has articulated it.

52. Rom. 8:31-39 surely is based on this kind of trusting piety.

53. The same simple yearning is evident in Ps. 42:1-3, where intimacy with God is craved, but nonetheless is presented in the categories of the temple. The modern distinction between personal intimacy and institutional presence is not apparent in the Psalms.

54. Cf. von Rad, " 'Righteousness' and 'Life' in the Cultic Language of the Psalms," in *The Problem of the Hexateuch and Other Essays* (New York: McGraw-Hill, 1966), pp. 243-66.

55. The profound trust expressed here is echoed in the first answer of the *Heidelberg Catechism*: "What is your only comfort, in life and in death? That I belong—body and soul, in life and in death—not to myself but to my faithful Savior, Jesus Christ, who at the cost of his own blood has fully paid for all my sins and has completely freed me from the dominion of the devil; that he protects me so well that without the will of my Father in heaven not a hair can fall from my head; indeed that everything must fit his purpose for my salvation. Therefore, by his Holy Spirit, he also assures me of eternal life, and makes me wholeheartedly willing and ready from now on to live for him."

56. See David Noel Freedman, "The Twenty-Third Psalm," in *Michigan Oriental*

Studies in Honor of George C. Cameron, ed. Louis L. Orlin (Ann Arbor: Department of Near Eastern Studies, University of Michigan, 1976), pp. 139-66.

57. Terence Fretheim has observed that this Psalm is indeed a statement of "theology of glory," and so may properly belong to psalms of *orientation*. And he may be correct. The matter bears witness to the fact that these categories cannot be pressed too tightly or clearly. The point supports Goldingay's suggestion that usage determines function.

58. On the tension between the two and their relationship, see Rainer Albertz, *Persönliche Frömmigkeit*.

59. See the same repeated formula in Psalm 107—a highly stylized statement of this formula.

60. Claus Westermann, *Praise and Lament in the Psalms* (Atlanta: John Knox Press, 1981), pp. 22-24. In *The Psalms: Structure, Content, and Message* (Minneapolis: Augsburg Publishing House, 1980) Westermann makes the distinction much more visible.

61. John Goldingay, "The Dynamic Cycle of Praise and Prayer in the Psalms," *JSOT* 20 (1981):85-90.

62. The phrases, "new, new song," and "old, old story," of course, come from the gospel song, "I Love to Tell the Story." The phrases are used in an eschatological expectation that the "old, old story" will be transformed and become the "new, new song." I suggest, however, that the process in practice can also be reversed so that the songs of joyous new orientation become jaded, defensive, and taken for granted as old orientation. Note Goldingay, 88, who speaks of a "spiral" process. I do not regard this ambiguity as a weakness for the construct I have proposed, but only a requirement that the hermeneutical question of social function should be posed carefully and intentionally.

63. The usual form-critical analysis concerns the three parts of introduction, body, and conclusion. But such an analysis, while it may be correct, is so formal and empty as to be almost useless.

64. This celebration of the goodness of the order which God has given is theologically important, as Paul Hanson, *Dynamic Transcendence* (Philadelphia: Fortress Press, 1978), has shown. Hanson terms this the "cosmic" pole of the polarity God sets us.

65. See the most careful analysis of the pattern of hymns by Frank Crüsemann, *Studien zur Formgeschichte von Hymnus und Danklied in Israel* (Neukirchen-Vluyn: Neukirchener Verlag, 1969).

66. On that core of faith which turns up in unexpected ways, see Walter Harrelson, "Life, Faith and the Emergence of Tradition," in *Tradition and Theology in the Old Testament*, ed. Douglas A. Knight (Philadelphia: Fortress Press, 1977), pp. 11-30.

67. On the possible uses of historical memory for purposes of criticism and absolutism, see Gary A. Herion, "The Social Organization of Tradition in Monarchic Judah" (unpublished dissertation, University of Michigan, 1982) and his summary statement, "The Role of Historical Narrative in Biblical Thought: The Tendencies Underlying Old Testament Historiography," *JSOT* 21 (1981): 25-57.

68. On "answer" as a proper posture for creation, see Hos. 2:21-22.

69. Westermann, *Praise and Lament in the Psalms*, pp. 250-58.

Chapter 5

1. See Brueggemann, *Praying the Psalms*, chap. 4 (Winona, Minn.: St. Mary's Press, 1982).
2. Jose Miranda, *Communism in the Bible* (Maryknoll, N.Y.: Orbis Books, 1982), p. 44. Miranda comments that our propensity is to reduce the categories of "unjust/wicked" to religious categories of "atheism," which leaves the issues of social power untouched.
3. On the justice issues, see Frederick Herzog, *Justice Church* (Maryknoll, N.Y.: Orbis Books, 1980).
4. On the usual treatments of theodicy, see J. L. Crenshaw, "Theodicy," in *IDB Supp.* (Nashville: Abingdon, 1976), pp. 895-96, and the anthology ed. James L. Crenshaw, *Theodicy in the Old Testament* (Philadelphia: Fortress Press, 1983). A variety of literary-theological responses to the issue of God's justice may be noted. James L. Crenshaw, *Studies in Ancient Israelite Wisdom* (New York: KTAV 1976), pp. 31-35, has argued that creation theology is designed to resolve the question of theodicy. See also his article, "The Problem of Theodicy in Sirach," *JBL* 94 (1975): 47-64, and his citation of H. H. Schmid. Paul D. Hanson, *The Dawn of Apocalyptic* (Philadelphia: Fortress Press, 1975), has argued that apocalyptic is a quest for the justice of God. I am not aware that Hanson uses the term *theodicy*, but that clearly is the import of his hypothesis. This sort of analysis keeps the issue of theodicy rather closely focused on literary and theological issues, though Hanson does pay some attention to the sociological issues. More philosophical discussions include those of David Griffin, *God, Power and Evil: A Process Theodicy* (Philadelphia: Westminister Press, 1976), and John Hick, *Evil and the Love of God* (New York: Harper and Row, 1966).
5. The issue has been succinctly put by Archibald McLeish in *J.B.: A Play in Verse* (Boston: Houghton Mifflin, 1957), p. 14, "If God is God He is not good, if God is good He is not God. ..."
6. See the more popular treatments of Harold Kushner, *When Bad Things Happen to Good People* (New York: Schocken Books, 1981), and Sibley Towner, *How God Deals with Evil* (Philadelphia: Westminister Press, 1976). I regard Towner's book a most helpful discussion, with much more power than that of Kushner. The popular reception of Kushner's book is in any case a measure of the urgency and pervasiveness of the issue of theodicy, though his way of stating a resolution is perhaps too easy and somewhat romantic.
7. In Christian theology, the theological issue is the reassertion of *patripassianism*—"the suffering of the father." On this see especially the important work of Jürgen Moltmann, *The Crucified God* (New York: Harper and Row, 1974), esp. chap. 6. It is striking, however, that the main cues for Moltmann come from Jews. Thus see his reference to Heschel, and most importantly to the work of Wiesel on the Holocaust. It is especially the Holocaust that has made the question of theodicy both unavoidable and insoluble. On theodicy and the Holocaust, see the analysis of the work of Wiesel by Robert McAfee Brown, *Elie Wiesel, Messenger to All Humanity* (Notre Dame: University of Notre Dame Press, 1983), and Ulrich Simon, *A Theology of Auschwitz* (London: Gollancz, 1967).
8. On the foundational power of trust which survives in the face of such injustice, notice that Erikson's dominant theory of personality development makes basic trust a foundational issue, after which may come a sense of justice. Cf. Erik Erikson,

"Identity and the Life Cycle," in *Psychological Issues*, ed. George S. Klein (New York: International Universities Press, 1959), pp. 52-65 and *passim*. It is important that the sequence comes in this way. Brown, *op. cit.*, p. 154, records Wiesel's rabbinic story of trust and justice: "Three rabbis—all erudite and pious men—decided one winter evening to indict God for allowing His children to be massacred. What the introduction does not say is even more awesome: after the trial at which God was found guilty as charged, one of the rabbis looked at the watch he had somehow been able to preserve in the kingdom of night, and said: 'Oy! It's time for prayers.' And the three rabbis—'all erudite and pious men'—bowed their heads and prayed."

9. See the representative collection of essays edited by James L. Crenshaw, cited in n. 4.

10. On this literature, see Peter Ackroyd, *Exile and Restoration* (Philadelphia: Westminister Press, 1968), and Ralph W. Klein, *Israel in Exile* (Philadelphia: Fortress Press, 1979).

11. On such a theory and its criticism in the text, see Robert Polzin, *Moses and the Deuteronomist* (New York: Seabury Press, 1980), pp. 66-67, 148-162, and *passim*, and Bertil Albrektson, *Studies in the Text and Theology of the Book of Lamentations* (Lund: Gleerup, 1963).

12. This inclination of scholarship is supported by regularly comparing the literature to Babylonian parallels. The result is that the issue of theodicy gets expressed as a theoretical, speculative question that concerns an intellectual elite. Such a way of probing the question among scholars likely illuminates two aspects of the sociology of our scholarship. First, an intellectual elite defines all of the interesting questions it can as intellectual questions, on which we can do a characteristically analytical job. Second, one may guess that the question is thus made devoid of serious experiential power, because the scholarly community benefits from the present theodicy settlement and does not want the issue to extend beyond a speculative analysis. That is, the question tends to be well-removed from any serious social experience. At most, the question of theodicy is recognized as a practical one in the presence of an absurd death. But the real crisis of theodicy as injustice is not dealt with, because our consensus on theodicy is not recognized, and if it is unrecognized, it cannot be critiqued.

13. Such a discernment requires a critical approach to law, which sees law as a compromise settlement of goods and power. But when theodicy is kept as an intellectual problem and not a problem about law, we may continue our positivism about the law.

14. On the working of God in the social matrix, see Patrick D. Miller, *Sin and Judgment in the Prophets* (Chico, Calif.: Scholars Press, 1982), pp. 138-39.

15. The most helpful discussions I know on this theme are by Robert Merton, *Social Theory and Social Structure*, chaps. 4, 5 (Glencoe, Ill.: The Free Press, 1957), and Peter L. Berger, *The Sacred Canopy*, chap. 3.

16. Wayne A. Meeks, *The First Urban Christians* (New Haven: Yale University Press, 1983), p. 122 (building on the work of John Schutz) says of Paul's authority: "Authority is 'the interpretation of power.' The person in authority focuses and directs the power of those who recognize his authority, not under force, but by their acknowledgement that his directives are 'right.' Authority is thus 'a quality of communication,' which entails the belief that the 'rightness' of the communication

could be demonstrated if need be." Everything depends on whose interpretation is taken as "true."

17. This is the point of Marx' programmatic statement, "The criticism of heaven is thus transformed into the criticism of earth, the criticism of religion into the criticism of law, and the criticism of theology into the criticism of politics," in Karl Marx, *The Early Texts*, ed. D. McLellan (Oxford, 1971), p. 115 f. My point about much of our scholarly treatment of theodicy is that the criticism has not been "transformed," but remains a criticism of heaven.

18. Cf. Robert Merton, *Social Theory and Social Structure*, chap. 4, on the function of norm. Merton, of course, does not cast his argument in relation to religious concerns. I refer here simply to his understanding of *nomos* as "norm."

19. Berger, *Sacred Canopy*, chaps. 1 and 2, acutely characterizes this process of nurture in a positivistic consensus. For a splendid case study of a manipulated consensus, see John Gaventa, *Power and Powerlessness* (Chicago: University of Illinois Press, 1980), on the worldview among the poor in Appalachia.

20. A hidden theodicy is contained in the claim, "The system is the solution." Of course, the claim pays no attention to those for whom the system is not the solution, and it credits no claim that falls outside the system. On the "system" as "machine," see E. M. Forster, "The Machine Stops," in *The Eternal Moment* (New York: Grosset & Dunlap, 1964), pp. 13-85.

21. In the Old Testament I suggest that the term תם, rendered "integrity," is a way of reference to such social control and conformity. See my article, "A Neglected Sapiential Word Pair," *ZAW* 89 (1977):234-58. It is instructive that it is to his "integrity" that Job holds, i.e., he argues he has not violated the consensus theodicy of his community.

22. "Natural law" becomes a device to "keep people in their place." Berger *op. cit.*, p. 24, cites the obvious example: "For example, the sexual program of a society is taken for granted not simply as a utilitarian or morally correct arrangement, but as an inevitable expression of 'human nature.' "

23. The problem is to find authoritative warrant to speak against the old settled arrangements, which by definition must be rejected as against the norms. Theological appeal is regularly made to the "guidance of the Holy Spirit." See my discussion, *The Creative Word*, chap. 3 (Philadelphia: Fortress Press, 1982), on the consensus-disrupting work of the prophets.

24. The "withdrawal" from the orthodox theodicy is foundational to Gottwald's understanding of Israel's origin; cf. *The Tribes of Yahweh* (Maryknoll, N.Y.: Orbis Books, 1979), p. 85 and *passim*.

25. The problem is to understand Israel's *torah* in the social formative function of *nomos*. Our theological distortion of this comes from the "Lutheran" construct of grace and law, which makes it difficult to understand torah. But if torah be understood in the world-shaping sense, we may understand how torah is Israel's "delight," for it is the main defense against chaos.

26. Gottwald has fully appreciated the articulation of an egalitarian world view. But his few references to theodicy suggest he has not seen that the withdrawal from Egypt and the construction of a torah society are to be understood as an exchange of theodicies. That is, original problem of theodicy in the Old Testament is not the righteousness of Yahweh but the departure from the Egyptian system.

27. In general, the prophets take this position. While they sharply criticize social structures, on the whole they continue to regard Yahweh as an uncontaminated agent of

justice. Jeremiah appears to be an exception, for he carries his critique clear to the throne.

28. Jon P. Gunnemann, *The Moral Meaning of Revolution*, chap. 2 (New Haven: Yale University Press, 1979).

29. On *anomie*, see Merton, *op. cit.*, chap. 5.

30. Samuel Terrien, *Job: Poet of Existence* (Indianapolis: Bobbs-Merrill, 1957), p. 151, has seen that in Job 9:33; 16:19; 19:25, the poet anticipates that there is an appeal to one other than God. But it is a hunch not pursued in any way.

31. The appeal to God against political practice is caught in the sign of protest in the window of an English home: "Down with the landlord, long live the Queen." That is, the Queen is taken as a transcendent reference and is not perceived as a part of the same social scheme of ownership as is the landlord. So Israel can make a distinction between Yahweh and the earthly perpetrators of injustice, though in some psalms, they are drawn very closely together.

32. Gunnemann, *op. cit.*, p. 10, quotes Chalmers Johnson, *Revolutionary Change* (Boston: Little, Brown, 1966), p. 12.

33. Thus the torah psalms are not a practice of legalism, but submission to a reliable order. The torah psalms help "create the canopy."

34. Gunnemann, *op. cit.*, p. 12.

35. On this metaphor of "pathology" for dissenting behavior, see Gunnemann, *op. cit.*, pp. 10-11. Notice how that is handled in the Soviet Union, but not, I suspect, very differently in any community fearfully concerned with maintenance. Society can govern by taboo, which makes the threatening ones disqualified. See Fernando Belo, *A Materialist Reading of Mark*, chap. 1 (Maryknoll, N.Y.: Orbis Books, 1981), on the power of impurity as a tool of social control and maintenance.

36. On "madness," see Hos. 9:7. See Brown, *op. cit.*, pp. 74-79, on the need for madness and the urging of a ministry that does not completely repudiate madness. The Psalms do represent a madness when judged by standards of civility.

37. See the section, "The Seven Psalms," in chap. 3 in this volume (Psalms 6, 32, 38, 51, 102, 130, 143).

38. Gunnemann, *op. cit.*, p. 12.

39. Ibid., p. 12.

40. On new government and the banishment of idols as agents of unjust order, the example of the coming of the missionaries to Hawaii is a remarkable example. The missionaries arrived just as the old religion had been rejected and the idols smashed. The smashing of the idols which created a religious void was not done out of religious passion, but as an act of liberation by the women, who were kept in social subjection by the idols. Idols permit false and oppressive modes of human relationships.

List of Psalms Treated